*A Businessman's Guide to the
Foreign Exchange Market*

A Businessman's Guide to the Foreign Exchange Market

Brian Kettell, M.Sc. (Econ.)

City of London Polytechnic

Chapter 10 contributed by
Daniel Hodson,
Unigate PLC

Lexington Books
D. C. Heath and Company
Lexington, Massachusetts
Toronto

First published in 1985 by
Graham & Trotman Ltd.
Sterling House
66 Wilton Road
London SW1V 1DE

First published in the USA
by Lexington Books, D.C. Heath & Co.,
125 Spring St., Lexington, MA 02173

© Chap. 10 D. Hodson, remaining Chaps. B. Kettell 1985
ISBN 0 669 11093 0

Typeset and printed in Great Britain

This book is dedicated, by Brian Kettell, to Lesley-Anne Robb.

ACKNOWLEDGEMENTS

The author welcomes the opportunity to acknowledge the generous assistance provided on selected chapters by:

Susan Steele, European Director, Philadelphia Stock Exchange, London.
Richard Heckinger, Chicago Mercantile Exchange.
Peter Walton, Senior Lecturer in Accounting, University of Newcastle-upon-Tyne.

Many of the ideas developed here were also discussed with Steve Bell, Chief Economist and Assistant Director, Morgan Grenfell, in our co-authored *Foreign Exchange Handbook* (Graham and Trotman, 1983).

The publishers are indebted to the following organisations for permission to reproduce previously published material:

The Financial Management Association and AC Shapiro and D P Rutenberg, Her Majesty's Stationery Office, The Institute of Chartered Accountants in England and Wales, The London International Financial Futures Exchange, OECD, Standard Chartered Bank, John Wiley & Sons Ltd.

Responsibility for any error remains with the author.

CONTENTS

Introduction

Recurrent crises in international finance have often captured the news headlines in recent years. A cursory glance at any financial newspaper yields a multitude of examples: 'The dollar jumped in New York in reaction to renewed fighting in Beirut and prospects of higher US interest rates' – *Wall Street Journal* February 7, 1984. 'Sterling fell yesterday following rumours that Nigeria might cut its oil price' – *Financial Times* February 9, 1984.

Neither the meaning nor the implication of these matters is understood clearly by even well-informed citizens. The baffled readers of news reports regard them as part of the 'mystique' of international finance known only to the highly specialised experts, and they usually slip over to the next story. Yet there is nothing mysterious or bewildering about these occurrences. They all reflect the periodic adjustment of the international financial system and have at their root the fact that each country must, over the long term, live within its means.

A country must balance its international financial accounts in much the same way as a family deals with its finances. In the short run, any deficit in a family budget can be financed by depletion of previously accumulated assets (spending from savings) or by accumulation of liabilities (buying on credit or obtaining a loan). But this process cannot go on forever. Sooner or later the family must adjust its behaviour: either lower its expenditure or raise its income. The inability to go on financing deficits forever acts as a constraint on the economic behaviour of the family. An analogous rule applies to a country in its relations with the rest of the world. In the short run, an external deficit can be financed by drawing down previously accumulated assets, such as gold, or by accumulating debts to other countries. In time, however, an adjustment process must set in to eliminate the deficit.

It is at this stage that foreign exchange rate adjustments occur either by the country devaluing its exchange rate or by allowing the free action of the market to achieve the same effect.

Foreign exchange rate changes are not a new development. Indeed, a study of foreign exchange reveals it is clothed with a colourful history. Cleopatra financed her life of luxury partly by devaluing the drachma. Nero financed the rebuilding of Rome after the great fire by debasing the denarius. The Papal Court of Avignon initiated the first known Forward Exchange transaction in the thirteenth century. The Duke of Northumberland forestalled the British Labour Party Chancellor of the Exchequer, Sir Stafford Cripps, when, in 1551 he officially denied there was to be a change in the parity of sterling and carried it out soon after. Napoleon followed closely the quotation of sterling as an indication of the progress of his blockade of England.

The post World War II period from 1945 to 1973 was a period of more or less fixed exchange rates when exchange rate movements did occur, but were relatively infrequent. However, in early 1973, co-ordinated efforts to peg exchange rates were abandoned, and a new era of international monetary relations began. Currently, countries are free to choose the degree of foreign exchange market intervention that best suits their overall economic objectives. Most of the major developed countries no longer rigidly support internationally agreed upon exchange rates. (Most members of the EEC maintain their currencies within a pre-arranged range *vis-à-vis* other EEC currencies but not *vis-à-vis* the US dollar.) Thus market forces play a greater role, and official intervention a lesser role, in the determination of exchange rates today than they did before 1973.

Whether consequence or coincidence, the move towards less government intervention in the foreign exchange market has been accompanied by more volatility in exchange rates. Both day-to-day fluctuations and longer-term swings of exchange rates since 1973 have been larger.

The implication of these exchange rate movements for corporate profit-ability are immense. A couple of examples will make this clear. Assume a UK company exports goods to Japan. The value of the consignment is 20 million yen and the contract is signed on January 1 1984 and payment is to be made on April 1. The exchange rate at the contract date is Y201.97 to the pound giving a sterling equivalent of £99,024.61. However by the time of payment the exchange rate has moved to Y225.35, a yen devaluation and a sterling revaluation. When the exporter converts his yen at this new rate, he now receives £88,750.83 giving him a loss of £10,274.16. This loss, amounting to 10.3%, will make significant inroads into his profits and could even convert a profitable deal into an unprofitable one.

Take another example. Assume a US company imports goods from West Germany. The contract is signed on January 1 1984 and payment is to be made on April 1. The value of the contract is DM 500,000 and the exchange rate at the time of signing is DM 1.8490 to the US dollar giving a contract value of $ US 270,416. At payment date the exchange rate is DM 1.9545 giving a dollar equivalence of $255,819. The US importer now has made a saving of $14,597, some 5.4% of the contract.

In both these examples the exchange rate could have had considerable effects on the profitability of the companies concerned. Exchange rate movements of these orders of magnitude are the norm not the exception.

With central banks, governments and academics all favouring flexible exchange rates, companies can no longer ignore the consequences for their future profitability.

Corporate foreign exchange exposures can be managed for profit. Few areas within the span of corporate decision-making offer so much return for the effort involved. This book shows you how.

Having first outlined the 'nitty-gritty' of the foreign exchange markets it goes on to illustrate how companies can minimise the risks and maximise the opportunities for their companies of this continued foreign exchange market turbulence.

Chapter 1
The Foreign Exchange Market

WHAT IS THE FOREIGN EXCHANGE MARKET?

The foreign exchange market is the organisational framework within which individuals, firms, banks and brokers buy and sell foreign currencies. The foreign exchange market for any one currency, e.g. the United States dollar, consists of all the locations such as London, New York, Zurich and Paris where the dollar is bought and sold for other currencies.

Where is the market to be found?

The answer is nowhere and everywhere! Nowhere, in the sense that there is no one site or building where it can be said that the market operates, like the Commodities markets or the Stock Exchange. Everywhere, in the sense that the market is world-wide and operates in most of the major financial centres around the world.

In fact, the markets (plural, for there are markets for different currencies and for different types of transactions) are to be found in the dealing rooms of the commercial banks around the world who communicate with each other by telephone and telex, and whose deals are later confirmed.

Individuals and companies normally do not buy and sell foreign currencies for their own sake, but do so in order to pay for something else, e.g. a product, a service, or a financial asset. In that sense, foreign exchange transactions are fundamentally a part of the payments mechanism and consequently it is to the commercial banks that individuals and companies have turned to convert foreign exchange into domestic currency and vice versa.

Commercial banks are the natural channel for this business, and many of them operate in the foreign exchange market not only on behalf of their customers, but also on their own account.

Foreign exchange markets tend to be located in national financial centres near the related financial markets. The more important exchange markets are found in London, New York, Paris, Frankfurt, Amsterdam, Milan, Zurich, Toronto, Brussels, Bahrain and Tokyo. Formerly, there were two main types

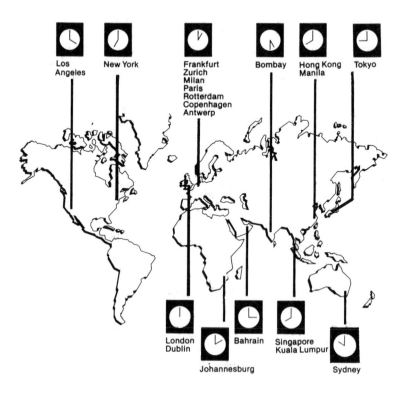

CLOSES   **LOS ANGELES**   OPENS
24.00 GMT/16.00 Local   15.30 GMT/07.30 Local
        CLOSES   **NEW YORK**   OPENS
        21.30 GMT/16.30 Local   12.30 GMT/07.30 Local
                CLOSES   **LONDON**   OPENS
                17.00 GMT/17.00 Local   08.00 GMT/08.00 Local
                    CLOSES   **FRANKFURT**   OPENS
                    16.00 GMT/17.00 Local   07.30 GMT/08.30 Local
                        CLOSES   **BAHRAIN**   OPENS
                        10.00 GMT/13.00 Local   04.30 GMT/07.30 Local
                        CLOSES   **SINGAPORE**   OPENS
                        10.00 GMT/17.30 Local   00.30 GMT/08.00 Local
                            CLOSES   **HONG KONG**   OPENS
                            09.30 GMT/17.30 Local   00.00 GMT/08.00 Local
                            CLOSES   **SYDNEY**   OPENS
                            07.00 GMT/17.00 Local   22.00 GMT/08.00 Local

Fig. 1.1 Standard Chartered Bank Group Dealing Centres

Source: Standard Chartered Bank.

of foreign exchange markets, the type adopted by the UK and the USA, and the European style, although this distinction is rapidly becoming blurred. The UK and US market is a market only in the abstract sense since it does not exist in one physical place like, for example, the Stock Exchange, but only in the sense that it is a communications system through which participants transact business. The communication system consists of a network of telephones and telexes that connect exchange markets all over the world. Thus the participants can remain in continuous contact with one another. Indeed, the communications system is so continuous that, despite time and space differences, there exists a single world market.

Banks in the Far East, including branches of major US and European institutions, begin trading in Hong Kong, Singapore and Tokyo at about the time most traders in San Francisco are going home for supper. As the Far East closes, trading in Middle Eastern financial centres has been going on for two hours, and the trading day in Europe is just beginning. The continuous overlap of foreign exchange trading in different centres is illustrated in Fig. 1.1. The foreign exchange market is a world-wide one, with leading banks represented in all the main trading centres through branches or affiliates. Because of the United Kingdom's geographical position, banks in London can deal with the Far East, Middle East and North America, as well as with the rest of Europe, in the course of the working day. This has resulted in London having a pre-eminent position in the market.

The New York foreign exchange market is extremely active when sharing a common time with Europe and has become more so with New York brokers now being permitted to effect trades between banks in New York and overseas, but it is perhaps a little thin at other times of the day. Because of the close geographical proximity of the United States and Canada, and because of the sizeable trade between the two countries, the largest markets for US dollars against Canadian dollars will be found in New York, Toronto, Detroit and Chicago. Since Canadian banks have significant operations in New York, there is active arbitrage in deposit interest rates between the two countries.

One implication of a 24 hour currency market is that exchange rates may change at any time. Senior bank traders must be light sleepers, ready to respond to a telephone call in the middle of the night alerting them to an unusually sharp exchange rate movement on another continent. Many banks permit limited dealing from home by senior traders, rather than from the dealing room of their banks, in order to contend with just such a circumstance.

Although the market is open for 24 hours, the dominance of London and New York means that, if dealing in large amounts, one is best advised to deal when either of those markets is open.

SIZE OF WORLD CURRENCY MARKETS

There are no authoritative figures as to the total volume of foreign exchange movements. The amount is probably between US$ 200–250 billion a day, or US$ 50–62.5 trillion a year. We know that real trade and investment flows amount to only US$ 1.8 trillion a year. Therefore we can assume that real flows account for under 2% of total foreign exchange activity.

The large volume of foreign exchange dealings relative to real, or trade and investment, transactions is rationalised by the need of banking institutions to lay off the risk over a wide area, thus giving depth and great competitivity to the market.

The core of foreign exchange operations is international trade and international investment. This accounts for about 2.3% of total foreign exchange activity, plus a further 2% from commodity dealing, hedging and money management. The main operators in this core market are commodity dealers, multinationals, the large oil companies and non-bank financial companies. The remainder of the market (some 95%) is inter-bank and is concerned with managing positions, arbitrage and speculative operations.

In billions of US dollars

Type of Transaction	March 1980 90 banks	April 1983 119 banks
Spot		
Direct with banks in US............................	62.4	93.8
Direct with banks abroad..........................	75.5	81.1
Through brokers.......................................	162.5	224.4
Subtotal..	300.4	399.2
Swaps		
Direct with banks in US............................	*	22.5
Direct with banks abroad..........................	*	51.7
Through brokers.......................................	*	130.2
Subtotal..	137.8	204.4
Outright Forwards		
Direct with banks in US............................	*	3.1
Direct with banks abroad..........................	*	3.7
Through brokers.......................................	*	4.6
Subtotal..	11.6	11.4
Total Transactions		
Direct with banks in US............................	*	119.4
Direct with banks abroad..........................	*	136.5
Through brokers.......................................	*	359.1
Grand Total	449.7	615.0

* Not available.

Source: Federal Reserve Bank of New York's Foreign Exchange Turnover Surveys (March 1980 and April 1983).

Because of rounding, figures may not add to totals.

Fig. 1.2 Foreign Exchange Turnover in the Inter-bank Market

THE FOREIGN EXCHANGE MARKET IN THE UNITED STATES

Foreign exchange market turnover in the United States totals $48 billion each business day, according to a sample survey conducted by the Federal Reserve Bank of New York. The survey included 119 banking institutions and 10 foreign exchange brokers throughout the United States and measured the gross volume (i.e. sales and purchases) of their transactions in foreign currencies during the month of April 1983. It showed that the daily volume of transactions handled by banks averaged $33.5 billion, and those handled by brokers averaged $14.1 billion.

The survey was the second one conducted recently. The most significant change from the previous survey conducted in March 1980 was the significant increase in the volume of transactions. Between 1977 and 1980 they multiplied nearly five fold from about $5 billion in April 1977. In March 1980 the total volume of foreign exchange transactions undertaken amounted to $669.3 billion; by 1983 the total volume rose to $998.4 billion, an increase of some 50% (See Figure 1.2)

Three factors are responsible for the massive increase in turnover in the US foreign exchange market since 1978. First, the United States has become increasingly internationalised. The share of United States exports and imports in gross national product has risen, forcing an increased awareness of the need to undertake foreign currency transactions rather than simply relying on the US dollar. Second, the dramatic sharpening of exchange rate fluctuations has created the potential for large exchange gains and losses, inducing changes in financial behaviour. Bank management and corporate executives have been forced to take a more positive attitude to foreign exchange rate movements. Third, three institutional innovations since 1978 have greatly increased the scope for more foreign exchange trading to take place:

(i) Foreign exchange trading banks, rather than doing business among themselves almost exclusively through the intermediation of United States foreign exchange brokers, began dealing directly with each other at home and using international brokers not domiciled in the United States when dealing abroad.

(ii) Foreign exchange brokers located in the United States began to broker internationally, accepting bids and offers from banks located abroad.

(iii) The advent of offshore banking within the United States. Offshore banking was made possible when the Federal Reserve Board in 1981 authorised banks to set up so-called International Banking Facilities (IBFs) exempt from certain US bank regulations which otherwise added to the cost of doing business in the US and gave the Euro markets a strong competitive edge.

These changes facilitated the expansion of foreign exchange trading by eliminating barriers to US participation in the market and by integrating the United States market more closely with markets overseas.

The 1983 survey also showed a dramatic rise in the Japanese yen's relative importance largely offset by declines in sterling and the Canadian dollar. Figure 1.3 shows that the Japanese yen became the second most actively traded currency, accounting for 22% of total turnover. Three years earlier the yen was fourth, with 10.2%. Trading in Deutschemarks remained the most active, accounting for 35.2% of all transactions, very close to March 1980's figure of 31.7%.

Fig. 1.3 Distribution of Foreign Exchange Turnover by Currency

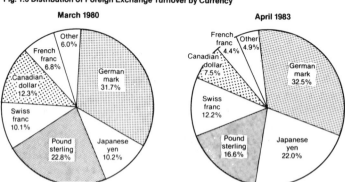

Because of rounding, figures do not add to 100 percent.
Source: Data based on Federal Bank of New York's Foreign Exchange Turnover Surveys (March 1980 and April 1983).

The 1983 survey also broke down the types of transactions (again see Fig. 1.3.) Some $443 billion (or 63%) of trading was done in the spot market. A great majority of these transactions (almost $400 bn.) represented inter-bank dealings. 33% of the deals were swaps, 4% were outright forwards.

WHY DOES THE FOREIGN MARKET EXIST?

Like all other markets, the foreign exchange market is in business to assist buyers to buy and sellers to sell. However, unlike other markets where money exchanges for goods or for services, in this one money exchanges for money! The motives for such exchanges arise, of course, from the needs of traders, investors and others who have currencies they wish to dispose of and/or seek currencies to acquire. To be more precise they can be categorised as:

   (i)   traders in goods and services, i.e. importers, exporters and multinational companies;
   (ii) investors;
   (iii) recipients and payers of dividends, interest, profits and royalties, gifts and loans;
   (iv) speculators;
   (v) arbitrageurs;
   (vi) central banks.

As we have seen, the foreign exchange markets are essentially concerned with the exchange of bank deposits and that banks are the principal participants. Banks act both on behalf of their customers and on their own behalf. The customers comprise:

(i)   central banks,
(ii) foreign banks,
(iii) governments,
(iv) companies,
(v)   individuals,

who for one reason or another wish to dispose of or acquire a bank deposit in a particular currency or currencies. However, as we have already discussed, of the total volume of daily business only a very small fraction is on behalf of customers wishing to finance their trading and capital flows. The vast bulk of all business is, in fact, done *between* the banks themselves. This is called inter-bank business and consists of banks contacting each other directly or through brokers to exchange currency deposits not just to meet their own customers' requirements but to maintain what they regard as adequate balances.

Although the term 'the foreign exchange market' is used, there are, in fact, three types of transactions undertaken. These are transactions in the spot, forward and deposit markets. In the spot market currencies are bought or sold for immediate delivery although in practice, settlement is made after two working days, e.g. Thursday's spot deals are for settlement on Monday, to allow for paperwork to be completed. Settlement must be made on the due day, neither earlier or later. In the forward market, currencies are bought or sold now for future delivery. The principal feature of this market is that payment is in the future although the exchange rate is agreed upon in the present.

Apart from the forward exchange market there are three other markets with a 'futuristic' element to them. These are the option date forward contracts, foreign exchange future contracts and currency options contracts. These will be discussed in turn both here and in Chapter 3.

In the deposit market currencies are borrowed or are lent and thus a bank will have to repay or will itself be repaid when the deposit matures (assuming it is not renewed). Deposit market trading can take place within a country with its own currency, e.g. the sterling inter-bank market in London or with banks in other countries in which case normally with 'eurocurrencies'. Eurocurrencies are currencies which are traded outside their country of origin.

QUOTATION AND INTERPRETATION OF SPOT EXCHANGE RATES

As the vast majority of traded currencies are maintained as bank deposits, the market is actually one of selling a deposit of one currency in exchange for a deposit of another currency. The price at which these deposits are exchanged is called 'the exchange rate'. Although an exchange rate is another term for 'price', it can be expressed in a manner not usual for other markets. For example, we can say that the price of £1 is $1.4950. However, we can reverse the equation to read the price of $1.4950 is £1.

Exchange rates can be quoted in two ways, what is known as the indirect method and the direct method. Under the indirect method currencies are expressed as so many units of foreign currency to one unit of domestic currency. Under the direct method (by far the most common) the domestic currency is expressed as equivalent to one unit of foreign currency (normally the United States dollar). Some examples will make this clear.

With one exception –sterling – it is the practice in London to quote the major currencies in terms of units of currency per US dollar – that is, the price of a dollar in terms of the other currency. The exception is sterling which is quoted the other way round, so a rate of 2.4000 represents the dollar price of a pound. Banks usually quote a two-way price in the market – that is, a rate at which they are ready to buy a currency, and a (dearer) rate at which they are prepared to sell. The difference represents a potential source of profit for the bank. For example, a bank quoting a sterling/dollar rate of 2.3995–2.4005 will be prepared to buy pounds at a rate of $2.3995 per £1 (the 'bid' rate) and to sell them at $2.4005 per £1 (the 'offer'). On the other hand, a bank which quotes 1.8015–1.8025 for the dollar against the deutschmark will be prepared to buy dollars at the rate of $1 per DM 1.8015 or to sell them at $1 per DM 1.8025.

It is the practice in the USA and most of Europe to use the direct method. The following are examples:

$$
\begin{aligned}
1\ \pounds &= \text{US \$ 2.2630} \\
1\ \text{DM} &= \text{US \$ 0.5782} \\
1\ \text{SFR} &= \text{US \$ 0.6230} \\
1\ \text{Can \$} &= \text{US \$ 0.8637} \\
1\ \text{FF} &= \text{US \$ 0.2467}
\end{aligned}
$$

On the other hand, if the national currency is taken as one unit and the equivalent is given in the foreign currencies it is 'indirect method' quotation. The practice in the UK and in Canada is to quote indirectly as follows:

$$
\begin{aligned}
\pounds 1 &= \text{US \$} & 2.2630 \\
\pounds 1 &= \text{DM} & 3.9225 \\
\pounds 1 &= \text{SFR} & 3.6450 \\
\pounds 1 &= \text{FF} & 9.1950 \\
\pounds 1 &= \text{LIT} & 1826.50
\end{aligned}
$$

However, whether the rate is quoted either in 'direct' or in 'indirect' method it is easy to find the other way of quotation as one is the reciprocal $(1/X)$ of the other. If the quotation is given in indirect method as £1 = US $ 2, the reciprocal of this is US $ 1 = £0.50 and is a direct quotation.

When asked for an exchange rate a dealer will give two rates, a rate at which he is willing to buy the currency and a rate at which he wants to sell the same currency. The general rule for any dealer is to buy the foreign currency high and sell the foreign currency low. But one should be cautious about which method of quotation is used.

When the direct method is used a dealer's rule is to buy the foreign currency low and sell the foreign currency high, thereby exchanging less of the national currency when buying and receiving more of the national currency when selling.

When the indirect method is used like the practice in the London dealing rooms, it is just the other way round: buy the foreign currency high and sell the foreign currency low. It may appear confusing, but the distinction between direct and indirect quotation creates this difference. Some examples for direct and indirect quotations are as follows:

Direct Method (In continental countries, for example in Germany)

Currency	Buying Rate	Selling Rate
US $	1.7050	1.7130
FF	2.3450	2.3510
SF	0.9195	0.9210

Indirect Method (In the UK)

Currency	Selling Rate	Buying Rate
US $	2.2345	2.2670
DM	3.8200	3.8840
FF	8.9950	9.0840

These rates will be good for large, round amounts. For very large amounts, or for smaller or odd amounts, a bank would normally quote a wider spread; and the range of amounts for which a quotation is good will vary to some extent with the currency concerned and market conditions. Generally, however, a quotation in sterling/dollar would be good for round amounts of £½ million and for between £½ million and £5 million, and a quotation in dollar/deutschmark would be good for round amounts of $½ million and for between $½ million and $10 million. In sterling/dollar transactions, it is usual to deal for a round number of pounds; in other foreign exchange transactions, it is usual to deal for a round number of dollars.

The difference between the buying and selling rate is the dealer's margin (also called the 'bid/ask' or 'bid/offer' spread). Thus a quote of $1.8015–1.8025 for the sterling/dollar rate is a spread of $0.0010 or ten points. A point is a unit of decimal, the fourth place to the right of the decimal point (0.0001). A pip is the fifth place to the right (0.00001). One point is one ten thousandth of a dollar. Thus 100 points becomes one cent. Which decimal place is implied by a point varies from currency to currency.

The spread fluctuates according to the volatility of the market and the currency at that time, the location of the market and the volume of transactions in the currency. Higher spreads are caused by higher uncertainty, lower volumes of trade and the remoteness of the market in relation to its currency. Conversely, lower spreads occur with stable conditions, a high volume of trade and an actively traded currency.

Deals within the market could proceed as follows. As already mentioned each price-making bank is in frequent contact with one or more of the brokers. Perhaps one price-making bank in London quotes the brokers a sterling/dollar rate of 2.3995–2.4005. Another bank, keener than the first to buy sterling, may quote 2.4000–2.4010; while a third, keener to sell, may quote 2.3993–2.4003. Indeed, the second bank may quote just the bid (2.4000) and the third just the offer (2.4003). The prices are understood to be good until a certain time has elapsed, and for a certain amount and for a certain category of counterparty, unless the bank stipulates otherwise. The broker recognises these factors when presenting his clients with the best bid and offer available – in this example 2.4000–2.4003.

When approached by a bank seeking to deal, the broker must give the fullest possible information without revealing the identity of the bank (or banks) whose prices he is quoting until a deal is ready to be completed. For example, the best bid may have come from a bank prepared to do more or less than the standard amount, and the offer from a bank abroad; and the broker will make this known. In general, the broker will aim to keep all his clients, price-making banks and others, informed about the prices at which the most recent deals have been done, telling them whether price-making banks are tending to be offered sterling or to be bid for it, thus indicating the next likely movement in the exchange rate. Having brought about a deal – a sale of sterling, perhaps, by another bank to the bank which was bidding 2.4000 – the broker will reconstruct a two-way price by taking the unchanged offer and what was the previous second-best bid, in this example 2.3995–2.4003. If the deal had left no bid for sterling in the market, the broker would have said so.

Dealers quote their selling price first (for the $/£ rate the selling rate for dollars); this means the lower number. Dealers are in such a rush they abbreviate as much as possible – a price will not be spelt out more than anyone who is well informed about the going market rate will need. So a rate of 2.1010/20 might be called 'ten twenty on ten' or simply 'ten twenty'. Round numbers in hundreds of points are the figure – 2.0990/00 would be 'ninety the figure'. 2.100/10 would be 'figure ten'.

Many price-making banks publicise their rates on video screens, although in order to avoid frequently changing rates and making the kind of qualification about size, category of counterparty, etc. with which a broker would be familiar, such rates are normally for information and are not rates at which the bank will feel obliged to deal. Nevertheless, the bank's reputation would suffer if it regularly refused to deal near these rates with first-class counterparties.

QUOTATION AND INTERPRETATION OF FORWARD EXCHANGE RATES

A forward exchange contract is an agreement to deliver a specified amount of one currency for a specified amount of another currency at some future date.

The important point is that the exchange rate is agreed upon *now* although the currencies are exchanged in the future. Forward exchange rates are normally quoted with a buying and a selling rate for periods of one, two, three, six and twelve months for the major trading currencies, e.g. the dollar, pound sterling, Deutschmark, Swiss franc, etc. Up to these maturities the market is fairly 'thick', i.e. trading does not lead to wide rate fluctuations. Beyond these maturities the market is fairly 'thin' and large single transactions can produce wide rate fluctuations. Although specific maturity dates are normally given, if one is not sure when a foreign currency may be needed it is possible to arrange forward option contracts which permit delivery at periods within a month. Normally, these are more expensive than fixed maturity date contracts.

Before looking at how rates are quoted and how the market can be used it is necessary to examine the forces influencing the forward market. Under normal market conditions the forward rate is determined by international interest rate differentials. Interest rate arbitrage is the process of moving funds from one currency to another currency in order to take advantage of higher rates of interest. Uncovered interest arbitrage is where an investor transfers funds from one currency to another and bears the risk that currencies with high interest rates tend to be prone to devaluation. Covered interest arbitrage is where an investor transfers funds and takes out a corresponding forward contract which, at a cost, guarantees that he has no exchange risk.

Whether or not covered arbitrage is profitable depends not only on the additional interest that might be gained by so doing, but also on the relation of the two currencies in the spot and forward markets. If, for example, a US investor is considering investing money in UK Treasury bills because the interest rates are higher than on US Treasury bills, it is necessary first to convert dollars into pounds. While he holds sterling Treasury bills he runs an exchange risk in that at the end of three months the pound may be worth a lot less than at the beginning of the period and this could wipe out any increased interest he receives. In order to eliminate any exchange risk the US investor could sell pounds forward, i.e. buy dollars forward. Whenever the amount of a currency being sold forward outweighs the amount being bought forward the forward price of that currency will go down, and whenever the amount of a currency being sold forward is less than the amount being bought forward the forward price of that currency will go up.

If a currency is at a discount this means that the forward value of that currency is lower than the spot value. If a currency is at a premium this means that the forward value of that currency is higher than the spot value. In the above example, since there are more forward sellers of pounds sterling the pound is at a discount and the dollar is at a premium. By definition, if two currencies are quoted against each other and one currency is at a discount the other currency must be at a premium.

When examining how forward rates are quoted it will be seen that whether one adds or subtracts the premium or discount depends on which of the two possible ways that exchange rates can be quoted is used. The theory of forward exchange holds that under normal conditions the forward discount or premium on one currency in terms of another is directly related to the difference in interest rates prevailing in the two countries. The currency of the higher interest-rate country would be a discount in terms of the currency of the lower interest-rate country. Similarly, the currency of the lower interest-rate country would be at a premium in terms of the higher interest-rate currency. The forward exchange rate is said to be at interest parity whenever the interest differential and the forward discount or premium (expressed in per cent per annum) are equal. This relationship is explained diagrammatically in Appendix I.

In practice, forward rates are determined under normal conditions by differences in Euro-rates. Thus, the forward rate of sterling against the dollar depends on the difference between the rate on Eurosterling and the rate on Eurodollars. Essentially, the Euromarkets are free markets and can be freely used by non-residents. Unless the arbitrage condition held almost exactly there would be a rapid and heavy movement of funds to profit from the difference. This would change interest rates and exchange rates in a direction that would eliminate the differential. In order to convert pips into percentage differences the following formula is used:

$$\frac{\text{Forward rate-spot rate} \times \text{number of days in the year} \times 100}{\text{spot rate} \times \text{lifetime of the operation in days}}$$

Consider the following example:

	Bid	Offered	
Eurodollar market (six months)	$5\,5/8\%$	$5\,3/4$	
Eurosterling market (six months)	15	$15\,1/8$	
Spot £	1.6860	1.6850	
Six months forward cover	1.6080	1.6090	
	780	760	discount

Applying the formula gives:

$$\text{Percentage per annum} = \frac{1.6080 - 1.6860 \times 360 \times 100}{1.6860 \times 180} = 9.25\% \text{ p.a.}$$

which is almost identical to the difference between the Eurodollar and Eurosterling rates.

To convert percentage premia or discounts into 'pips' the formula is simply reversed:

$$\frac{\text{spot rate} \times \text{percentage difference in Euro-rates} \times \frac{\text{lifetime of the operation}}{\quad}}{100 \times \text{number of days in the year}}$$

$$= \frac{1.6860 \times 9.25 \times 180}{100 \times 360} = 0.779 \text{ or } 779 \text{ pips}$$

Note that for most foreign exchange transactions it is assumed that there are 360 days in the year and 30 days in a month.

These formulae indicate the close relationship between discounts/ premiums and Euro-interest rate differentials. Indeed, when a quote for a eurocurrency is required by a client the broker will often simply give the eurodollar rate plus the relevant discount (or minus the premium) on the currency involved.

If sterling is at a discount of 9.25% the dollar is at a premium of 9.25%. This means a UK importer from the USA selling sterling forward to pay for his dollars will lose an annualised 9.25%. He must then decide whether he expects the future decline in spot sterling to be greater or less than this in deciding whether to purchase forward cover.

Forward rates are quoted as being at a discount or premium to the spot rate. As already stated, a currency is at a premium where its future value is greater than the spot value against the base currency and, conversely, a discount means that the future value will be lower than the spot value.

The discount or premium is expressed in points and the future rate is calculated by subtracting or adding the points from or to the spot rate. Where the method of quoting the rate is in units of foreign currency to one unit of base currency, the premium is subtracted from the spot rate and the discount is added, e.g. the closing spot exchange rate for the pound against the dollar, taken from the *Financial Times* and reproduced below, was 1.9090–1.9110 (see Table 1.1). The one month premium of the dollar was 0.35–0.25c. This gives the following:

1.9090–1.9110	Spot rates
0.0035 0.0025c	Premium (to be subtracted)
1.9055 1.9085	Outright forward rate

Table 1.1

The Pound Spot and Forward

Jan 4	Day's spread	Close	One month	% pa	Three months	% pa
US	1.9040–1.9180	1.9090–1.9110	0.35–0.25	1.88	0.80–0.70 pm	1.57
Canada	2.2000–2.2750	2.2650–2.2670	0.20–0.05c pm	0.66	0.30–0.10 pm	0.35
Netherlands	4.69–4.74	4.69–4.71	$1\frac{7}{8}$–$1\frac{1}{8}$c pm	4.15	$5\frac{1}{2}$–5 pm	4.47
Belgium*	73.20–73.30	73.30–73.50	30–60c dis	−7.36	55–95 dis	−4.09
Denmark	13.90–14.05	13.93–13.95	$3\frac{3}{4}$–$2\frac{1}{4}$ore pm	2.80	$5\frac{1}{4}$–$3\frac{5}{8}$ pm	1.27
Ireland	1.2060–1.2130	1.2070–1.2090	0.24–0.34p dis	−2.00	0.75–0.96dis	2.83
W. Germany	4.28–4.32	$4.28\frac{1}{2}$–$4.29\frac{1}{2}$	$1\frac{7}{8}$–$1\frac{3}{8}$pt pm	4.54	$5\frac{1}{4}$–$4\frac{3}{4}$ pm	4.66
Portugal	124.00–125.25	124.25–124.75	25–190c dis	−10.36	75–410 dis	−7.79
Spain	183.50–185.50	183.50–184.00	10–40c dis	−1.63	55–105 dis	−1.74
Italy	2,288–2.302	2,291–2,293	12–16 lire dis	−7.33	45–50 dis	−8.29
Norway	11.04–11.14	11.06–11.08	$2\frac{3}{8}$–$2\frac{3}{4}$ ore pm	1.69	$5\frac{1}{8}$–$3\frac{5}{8}$ pm	1.58
France	10.86–10.93	10.87–10.89	$\frac{1}{4}$c pm–$\frac{3}{4}$ dis	−0.27	$3\frac{1}{2}$–$4\frac{1}{2}$ dis	−1.47
Sweden	10.51–10.69	10.53–10.55	$2\frac{1}{4}$–$1\frac{1}{4}$ ore pm	1.99	3–7 pm	2.85
Japan	416–423	419–420	3.45–3.05 y pm	9.30	9.15–8.60 pm	8.46
Austria	30.00–30.20	30.02–30.12	$14\frac{1}{2}$–$9\frac{1}{2}$ gro pm	4.79	43–33 pm	5.05
Switzerland	3.43–3.45	3.43–3.44	$1\frac{1}{8}$–$1\frac{5}{8}$c pm	6.55	$5\frac{3}{8}$–$4\frac{3}{4}$ pm	5.97

Source: *Financial Times*.

* Belgian rate is for convertible francs. Financial franc 81.00–81.10.

Six month forward dollar 0.35–0.75c pm. 12-month 1.05–0.85c pm.

Thus the foreign exchange market will buy pounds sterling one month forward, i.e. sell dollars at $1.9055, and will sell pounds one month forward, i.e. buy dollars at $1.9085 (see Table 1.2).

Having given an example of a currency at a premium against sterling, we turn to give an example of a currency which is at a discount against sterling. Take, for example, the Portuguese Escudo. The Portuguese Escudo is quoted as being at a discount of 25–190c one month forward. This gives the following outright rates:

124.25–124.75		Spot rates
0.25	1.90c	Discount (to be added)
124.50	126.65	Outright forward rate

Thus the foreign exchange market will buy pounds sterling one month forward for 124.50 escudos and will sell pounds forward for 126.65.

The *Financial Times* also quotes spot and forward rates against the dollar (see Table 1.2). The same principle as above holds since there is still the system of quoting the rate in units of foreign currency to one unit of base currency, i.e. the dollar.

Table 1.2

The Pound Spot and Forward

Jan 4	Day's spread	Close	One month	% pa	Three months	% pa
UK	1.9040–1.9180	1.9090–1.9110	0.35–0.25c pm	1.88	0.80–0.70 pm	1.57
Ireland*	1.5790–1.5840	1.5765–1.5795	0.67–0.57c pm	4.71	1.75–1.65 pm	4.31
Canada	1.1858–1.1890	1.1865–1.1870	0.08–0.11c dis	−0.86	0.20–0.37 dis	−1.13
Netherlands	2.4608–2.4750	2.4600–2.4675	0.60–0.50c pm	2.68	1.90–1.70 pm	2.92
Belgium	38.35–28.58	38.41–38.43	25–35c dis	−9.37	50–76 dis	−6.25
Denmark	7.3100–7.3325	7.3110–7.3210	par–0.40 ore dis	−0.33	1.80–2.00 dis	−0.98
W. Germany	2.2420–2.2580	2.2465–2.2475	0.58–0.48 pt pm	2.83	1.82–1.72 pm	3.15
Portugal	65.00–65.50	65.10–65.35	26–106c dis	−11.96	65–236 dis	−9.20
Spain	97.08–97.70	97.15–97.36	20–35c dis	−3.39	55–75 dis	−2.67
Italy	1,190–1,202	1,190–1,193	8½–10 lire dis	−9.31	22–30 dis	−9.73
Norway	5.8000–5.8125	5.8000–5.8100	0.50 ore pm–par	0.52	0.50 pm–par	0.17
France	5.6900–5.7200	5.6975–5.7025	0.90–1.00c dis	−1.89	4–4½ dis	−2.93
Sweden	5.5250–5.5450	5.5250–5.5350	0.35–0.15 ore pm	0.54	2.20–2.00 pm	1.52
Japan	219.20–220.00	219.65–219.75	1.45–1.30y pm	7.51	3.90–3.75 pm	6.96
Austria	15.71–15.78	15.73–15.75	5.30–4.10 gro pm	3.53	18¼–13½ pm	3.81
Switzerland	1.7800–1.8050	1.7995–1.8005	0.80–0.65c pm	4.83	2.15–1.96 pm	4.55

Source: *Financial Times*.

* UK and Ireland are quoted in US currency. Forward premiums and discounts apply to the US dollar and not to the individual currency.

To take an example of a currency at a premium against the dollar, e.g. the Deutschmark, this gives:

Bid Offered	
2.2465–2.2475	Spot rate
0.0058 0.0048	Premium (to be subtracted)
2.2407 2.2427	Outright forward rate

In this case the foreign exchange market will buy dollars (sell Deutschmarks) one month forward at DM 2.2407 and will sell dollars (buy Deutschmarks) at DM 2.2427.

Again, take the example of a currency at a discount against the dollar, e.g. the French Franc; this gives:

Bid Offered	
5.6975–5.7075	Spot rate
0.0080 0.0100	Discount (to be added)
5.7055 5.7175	Outright forward rate

In this case, the foreign exchange market will buy dollars (sell French Francs) one month forward at FF 5.7055 and will sell dollars (buy French Francs) at FF 5.7175.

To compare forward discounts or premia with interest rates they must be expressed in per cent per annum terms. Using the formula on page 16 we can see that this is given by:

$$\frac{\text{discount/premium in points} \times \text{time} \times 100}{\text{spot rate}}$$

Note that time can be expressed as:

$$\frac{\text{number of months in the year}}{\text{number of months forward}} \quad \text{or as} \quad \frac{\text{number of days in the year}}{\text{number of days forward}}$$

Of course, this only works because of the convention in the market that there are 360 days in a year and 30 days in the month.

Assume a UK exporter to the USA is receiving dollars in one month; he is able, if he wishes, to sell these forward: applying the formula he can calculate that he 'gains' (he gains since the dollar is at a premium against sterling). Take the mid-closing spot rate from Table 1.2.

$$\frac{0.0025 \times 12 \times 100}{1.9100 \times 1} = 1.57\% \text{ p.a.}$$

The UK exporter to the USA can be said to have gained 1.57% by dealing in the forward market rather than the spot market. A UK importer from the USA will be paying sterling in one month which he can sell forward. In this case he loses, since sterling is at a discount against the dollar:

$$\frac{0.0035 \times 12 \times 100}{1.9100 \times 1} = 2.20\% \text{ p.a.}$$

The UK importer can be said to have lost 2.20% by dealing in the forward market over that which he would have received by dealing in the spot market.

The *Financial Times* quotes are the mid-point of the discount or premium. Therefore, they show 1.88% for the one month percentage premium of the dollar against sterling in Table 1.2.

Now assume a US company is importing in one month from Holland: in this case the US company loses since the guilder is at premium against the dollar. Using the mid-closing rate of 2.4637 from Table 1.2 the calculation is as follows:

$$\frac{0.0050 \times 12 \times 100}{2.4637 \times 1} = 2.44\% \text{ p.a.}$$

In the converse case of a US company exporting in one month to Holland, where it will benefit from the premium, the calculation is:

$$\frac{0.0060 \times 12 \times 100}{2.4637 \times 1} = 2.92\% \text{ p.a.}$$

Again the *Financial Times* gives an approximate middle rate of 2.68%.

In these examples the term 'gained' or 'lost' is used in the sense of the difference between dealing forward or dealing spot. As we shall see below, the true cost of using the forward market depends on actual developments in future exchange rates and is a less clear-cut concept.

Examples of how companies can use the forward exchange market are given in Chapter 3. Appendix II illustrates an alternative way of calculating the cost of forward cover.

An important concept to be familiar with in the foreign exchange market is the '*swap*'. A swap is the simultaneous buying and selling of a currency for different maturities (e.g. a spot purchase against a forward sale or spot sale against a forward purchase.) The swap is easiest to understand by considering how a bank might cover a forward exchange transaction.

Suppose that a US company approaches a bank to buy Deutschmarks which it needs to pay for German goods in one month's time. If there were no outright forward market the bank would cover its sale by buying the DM at once in the spot market. However the bank does not need these for one month when the company takes delivery so it places them on deposit earning one month's DM interest.

However the bank also has to pay out dollars immediately in order to settle the spot transaction but does not receive dollars for one month. It therefore borrows them in the market. Suppose the bank earns 5% on its DM but has to pay 10% for the dollars. In this case the bank will charge the company more for the one month Deutschmarks than on the spot date to compensate for the cost of coverying its position.

OPTION DATE FORWARD CONTRACTS

We have seen that traders (and others) can buy or sell currencies with a specified date in the future for delivery. However, it is more usual for traders to be uncertain as to exactly when they expect to pay or receive foreign exchange. In these circumstances a fixed contract would not be suitable and the alternative, an option forward deal, would be relevant. An option forward contract can be defined as: 'an agreement to buy or sell foreign exchange with delivery in the future *between* agreed, specified dates, at exchange rates determined at the outset'. The way companies can use option date forward contracts is discussed in Chapter 3.

FOREIGN EXCHANGE FUTURES CONTRACTS

A foreign exchange futures contract can be defined as an agreement to buy or sell a standard quantity of a specific financial instrument at a future date and at a price agreed between the parties through open outcry on the floor of an organised exchange. What do these different terms mean?

Standard quantity — Each contract for a given type of financial instrument is for the same standard quantity, e.g. $1 million.

Specific financial instrument — The contract specification lays down the type of financial instrument, e.g. a 3 month US dollars.

Future date — The delivery of the amounts specified in the contract must take place during a specified month in the future.

Open outcry — All transactions must be executed on the floor of the exchange and prices are instantly available to all participants.

Thus a financial future is a legally binding contract to buy or sell a fixed amount of a financial commodity at an agreed price on a specified day in the future. It is important to realise that the exposure to profit or loss is total, unless the trade is reversed, and this is in contrast to an 'option' where the risk is limited to the price that you pay for the 'option'.

Foreign exchange futures are traded on the International Monetary Market (IMM) and the London International Financial Futures Exchange (LIFFE.) The basic unit of foreign exchange on the IMM and on LIFFE is the currency futures contract. The futures contract, as already indicated, provides for the future delivery of a specified amount of a foreign currency at a particular date, time and place. Fulfilment of a contract depending on whether one is a buyer or seller, is satisfied by accepting or by making delivery of the specified currency on the value date of the contract. A buy or sell position can also be closed out by making an offsetting purchase or sale of an equivalent contract prior to the expiration of trading for the contract.

Every futures contract must be backed by a margin deposit. Margin is simply a security deposit that guarantees performance on one's side of a contract. The exchange sets initial margin requirements and subsequent maintenance levels based on the price volatility of the various commodities. An adverse price movement greater than the difference between the initial margin and the maintenance margin would require the trader to bring his account balance up to the initial margin level.

Foreign exchange trading on the IMM is limited to 8 major currencies with contract sizes and minimum and maximum daily price fluctuations specified by the exchange. Foreign exchange futures on LIFFE are limited to four currencies. Full details of both markets are outlined in Tables 1.3 and 1.4

Table 1.3
The London International Financial Futures Exchange

SUMMARY OF CONTRACTS

March 1985

Contract	Unit of trading	Contract standard	Delivery months	Delivery day	Last trading day	Quotation	Minimum price movement (Tick size & Value)	Daily price limit (Value)	Initial margin (Straddle)	Trading hours
Sterling currency	£25,000	Delivery of the designated currency	March June September December	Second Wednesday of delivery month; from December 1985 onwards third Wednesday of delivery month	10.31 Second business day prior to delivery	US $ per £	0.01 cents per £ ($2.50)	5 cents ($1,250)	$1,000 ($100)	08.32–16.02
Deutschmark	DM 125,000	Delivery of the designated currency	March June September December	Second Wednesday of delivery month; from December 1985 onwards third Wednesday of delivery month	10.32 Second business day prior to delivery	US $ per DM	0.01 cents per DM ($12.50)	1 cent ($1,250)	$1,000 ($100)	08.34–16.04
Swiss franc	SFr. 125,000	Delivery of the designated currency	March June September December	Second Wednesday of delivery month; from December 1985 onwards third Wednesday of delivery month	10.33 Second business day prior to delivery	US $ per SFr.	0.01 cents per SFr. ($12.50)	1 cent ($1,250)	$1,000 ($100)	08.36–16.06
Japanese yen	Yen 12,500,000	Delivery of the designated currency	March June September December	Second Wednesday of delivery month; from December 1985 onwards third Wednesday of delivery month	10.30 Second business day prior to delivery	US $ per 100 Yen	0.01 cents per 100 Yen ($12.50)	1 cent ($1,250)	$1,000 ($100)	08.30–16.00
FT-SE 100	Valued at £25 per full index point (e.g. value £25,000 at 1000.0)	Cash settlement	March June September December	First business day after the last trading day	11.20 The last business in the delivery month	FT-SE-100 Index + 10 (e.g. 100.00)	0.05 (£12.50)	5.00 (£1,250)	£1,500 (£250)	09.35–15.30

* For the US Treasury Bond contract, a business day in the delivery process is defined as a day when banks in New York and Chicago are open for business as well as LIFFE. The last trading day is defined to coincide with the last trading day for the Chicago Board of Trade US Treasury Bond futures contract, where this is a LIFFE trading day.

The above information is an abbreviation of the Contract Terms and Trading Procedures and reference should be made to these documents for full details. Reproduced by kind permission of the London International Financial Futures Exchange Limited. Registered Office: The Royal Exchange, London EC3V 3PJ.

Table 1.4
C.M.E. Futures Contract Specifications

Size	Hour	Months	Minimum fluctuation in price	Limit	Last day trading	First del. day	Min. margin
Swiss franc 125,000	7:30 1:16X (9:16)	Jan. Mar. Apr. Jun. Jul. Sep. Oct. Dec. & Spot Month	.001 (1 pt) ($12.50/pt) ($12.50)	.0150%% (150 pt) ($1,875)	2nd bus. day bef. 3rd Wed.	3rd Wed.	I $2,000 M $1,500
Mexican peso 1,000,000	7:30 1.18X (9:17)	Jan. Mar. Apr. Jun. Jul. Sep. Oct. Dec. & Spot Month	.00001 (1 pt) ($10.00)	.00150%% (150 pt) ($1,500)	2nd bus. day bef. 3rd Wed.	3rd Wed.	I $3,000 M $2,500
Deutsch mark 125,000,	7:30 1:20X (9:18)	Jan. Mar. Apr. Jun. Jul. Sep. Oct. Dec. & Spot Month	.0001 (1 pt) ($12.50/pt) ($12.50)	.0100%% (100 pt) ($1,250)	2nd bus. day bef. 3rd Wed.	3rd Wed.	I $1,500 M $1,000
Canadian dollar	7:30 1:26X	Jan. Mar. Apr. Jun. Jul. Sep. Spot Month	.0001 (1 pt) ($10.00)	.0075%% (75 pt) ($750)	2nd bus. day bef. 3rd Wed.	3rd Wed.	I $900 M $700
Pound sterling 25,000	7:30 1:24X (9:20)	Jan. Mar. Apr. Jun. Jul. Sep. Oct. Dec. & Spot Month	.0005 (5 pt) ($2.50/pt) ($12.50)	.05%% (500 pt) ($1,250)	2nd bus. day bef. 3rd Wed.	3rd Wed.	I $1,500 M $1,000
Japanese yen 12,500,000	7:30 1.22X (9:19)	Jan. Mar. Apr. Jun. Jul. Sep. Oct. Dec. & Spot Month	.000001 (1 pt) ($12.50/pt) ($12.50)	.000100%% (100 pt) ($1,250)	2nd bus. day bef. 3rd Wed.	3rd Wed.	I $1,500 M $1,000
French franc 250,000	7:30 1:28X (9:22)	Jan. Mar. Apr. Jun. Jul. Sep. Oct. Dec. & Spot Month	.00005 (5 pt) ($2.50/pt) ($12.50)	.00500%% (500 pt) ($1,250)	2nd bus. day bef. 3rd Wed.	3rd Wed.	I $1,200 M $900

* 'I' refers to initial margin; 'M' to maintenance margin; 'S' to speculative positions; 'H' to hedge positions; 'C' to changer positions; 'CM' to margin required to be maintained with Clearing House for S&P 500; 'Mem' to member rate.

Source: Chicago Mercantile Exchange, October 1894

FOREIGN CURRENCY OPTIONS

A currency option is the right to buy or sell a currency against delivery of a base currency at an agreed exchange rate. The buyer of the option has the right to exercise this option at any date up to and including an agreed date, but he has no obligation to do so. The buyer of the option pays a premium for the provision of this rate.

Currency options are true options and are different in kind from option date forward contracts which provide an option only as to the date when exchange shall take place but require exchange at sometime within the option period. True options may be regarded as 'whether to exchange' options as opposed to 'when to exchange' options.

Foreign currency options are traded on the Philadelphia Stock Exchange (Phlx), the International Monetary Market (IMM) and the European Options Exchange (EOE), as well as in Montreal and Vancouver.

More recently currency options have become available from certain banks in London and New York. Bank options may be made more flexible than those traded on exchanges as they can be tailormade to particular strike prices, expiration dates and amounts to suit the customer, and need not be constricted by any externally defined contract specification.

The unit of trading for each foreign currency option varies depending upon the specific currency underlying each option. The following are the units of trading for foreign currency options on which trading is currently authorised on the Philadelphia Stock Exchange:

Underlying foreign currency	*Unit of trading*
British pounds	12,500 British pounds
Canadian dollars	50,000 Canadian dollars
Deutschmarks	62,500 Deutschmarks
Japanese yen	6,250,000 Japanese yen
Swiss francs	62,500 Swiss francs
French francs	125,000 French francs

The exercise price of a foreign currency option is the price at which the underlying foreign currency may be purchased or sold upon exercise of the option. The exercise price is stated in US cents per unit of foreign currency other than Japanese yen. Exercise prices for Japanese yen are expressed in hundredths of US cents per unit of foreign currency. Therefore in order to determine the exercise price per contract, it is necessary to multiply the stated exercise price by the unit of trading of that foreign currency option.

Options can be either 'call' or 'put'. Using the dollar as the base currency, the call holder has the right to buy sterling at the exercise price anytime before the expiration date. The holder of a put option has the right to sell sterling at any time before the expiration date. The seller (or writer) of a call option must sell sterling if the call holder exercises the call option. The seller of a put option must buy sterling if the put holder exercise the put option. It is useful to summarise the circumstances under which one would choose between these four options.

(1) One would buy a call option when:
- speculating that the £ will rise (or the $ will fall);
- receiving a $ payment in the UK in order to lock in a high £ value for the incoming $;
- a US company is importing UK goods and wants to lock in a low price for the £ needed to finance the imported goods.

(2) One would sell a call option when:
- speculating that the £ will fall (or the $ will rise);
- holding £ deposits – as a means of generating additional income (interest) on the deposits;
- a bank grants an 'over-the-counter' call option to a corporate client.

(3) One would buy a put option when:
- speculating that the £ will fall (or the $ will rise);
- receiving a £ payment in the US in order to lock in a high $ value for the incoming £;
- a UK company is importing goods and wants to lock in a low price for the $ needed to finance the imported goods.

(4) One would sell a put option when:
- speculating that the £ will rise (or the $ will fall);
- holding $ deposits – as a means of generating additional income (interest on the deposits);
- a bank grants an 'over-the-counter' option to a corporate client.

ALTERNATIVE MEASURES OF EXCHANGE RATES

From a business planning point of view, it is important to distinguish between different measures of changes in the exchange rates. Nominal changes in exchange rates arise when the rate of inflation differs between countries. For instance, if the rate of inflation in the United Kingdom is persistently above that of its trading partners and the German rate of inflation persistently below that of its trading partners, then there would be, in the absence of offsetting capital flows, pressure for the pound sterling to depreciate and the deutschmarks to appreciate against the countries of their trading partners at a rate reflecting the relevant inflation differentials. The reason for this is that investors continuously reshuffle their portfolios by shifting out of assets denominated in currencies that are weak and into assets that are strong in terms of expected purchasing power. Changes in the spot rate of exchange between currencies of two countries are called *nominal spot exchange rate changes* if they reflect nominal sources: diverging inflation rates between countries. Changes in the spot rate of exchange rate are called real if they reflect real sources: diverging developments in technology, resources, institutions and trading patterns between countries.

So nominal changes in the exchange rate are due to different inflation rates, or expected inflation rates between countries, while real changes take place because of diverging structural developments between countries. An example will make this clear. If we take the example of the discovery of North Sea oil in the UK, that will cause the pound to appreciate in real terms against all other currencies. The way this works depends on whether the exchange rate is fixed or whether it is floating.

Under fixed rates the required real appreciation of the pound would eventually take place via a lower rate of inflation relative to inflation elsewhere, whilst under a floating rate as the demand for sterling has risen (from sales of oil) the spot exchange rate rises. The importance of using the real exchange rate when making business pricing decisions is illustrated in Chapter 8.

As is explained in Chapter 4, in the 25 years from 1946 to 1971 exchange rates for most of the major currencies of the world were fairly stable. Usually, only one major currency changed its par value at any one time, and the dollar did not change its parity. Since August 15 1971, however, all major currencies have fluctuated by differing amounts. Widespread floating since 1971 has created a situation where changes in the rate against the dollar does not accurately indicate the overall change in the exchange rate for a currency.

It is in order to overcome this problem that effective exchange rates have been developed. They use changes in a country's trade balance as a proxy for exchange rate changes. The objective is to calculate an index which expresses the observed change in any currency against several others as the exchange rate change necessary to achieve the same effect on the trade balance as that of the observed change. Effective exchange rate calculations assume that all other currencies remain unchanged. If there is a 10% effective depreciation, for example, in the pound sterling this means that this is the size of the depreciation which would have been required had all the other currencies remained fixed *vis-à-vis* one another to produce the same effect on the trade balance of the UK as the exchange rate changes that actually did occur.

A country's competitive position may be thus thought of as being determined by the value of its currency in terms of a trade weighted basket of its competitors' currencies (*the effective spot exchange rate*) as well as by the country's tradeable goods price level relative to a trade weighted average of its competitors tradeable goods prices (the effective price ratio). If the effective value of a country's spot exchange rate rises at the same speed at which its tradeable goods prices fall relative to those of its trading partners, or vice versa, nothing happens to its competitive position (*the effective real exchange rate*) *vis-à-vis* its trading partners. So the effective real exchange rate is the trade weighted exchange rate adjusted for inflation rate differentials.

EXCHANGE RATE REGIMES

During the twentieth century the world economy has been characterised by alternating periods of fixed and fluctuating exchange rates.

As shown in Table 1.5, the 1930s, 1950s and 1970s and early 1980s were, by and large, periods of exchange rate flexibility, whereas the 1940s and 1960s were characterised by greater rigidity.

Table 1.5

	Flexibility	*Rigidity*
1930s	Gold parities abandoned Fluctuating exchange rates	
1940s		Wartime controls Reaction to post-war inflation Bretton Woods
1950s	Trade liberalisation and freeing of markets Relaxation of monetary regulations Most countries rigidly fixed to the dollar	
1960s		Controls on capital flows US balance of payments strains Inadequate adjustment to balance of payments deficits and surpluses
1970s	Smithsonian agreement 'Managed' floating exchange rates Extreme currency volatility	
1973 to the present	Dollar flexibility Yen/Sterling/Swiss franc flexibility	European snake 1979 – EMS

Four main types of exchange rate regime can be distinguished, all of which have operated in one form or another. Proposals for alternative exchange rate regimes fall within one or other of the four main categories of regime distinguished, though some schemes comprise features of more than one of the main types. The four main types of regime that we shall discuss briefly are as follows:

(i)   rigidly fixed exchange rates epitomised by the gold standard;

(ii) flexible rates, of which we will discuss three variants:

    (a) the adjustable peg or par-value system, which was the system which governed international monetary relations between 1944 and the early 1970s, and was sometimes referred to as the gold exchange standard. A par value system, known originally as the 'snake' and later developed into the European Monetary System was established in 1979;

   (b) a wider bands system
   (c) a crawling peg system
 (iii) managed exchange rate flexibility;
 (iv) multiple exchange rate systems;
 (v) freely floating rates.

1. The gold standard *

The international monetary system which was generally adopted among major industrialised countries before the First World War is referred to as 'the Gold Standard'. On a full gold standard the money of the country concerned, be it dollars, pounds, francs or whatever, consists of a fixed weight of gold of a definite fitness; the price of gold is fixed by law; and there is complete freedom to buy or sell gold, to import it or to export it. When Great Britain was on the gold standard before the First World War the Bank of England was legally obliged to buy gold at £3 17s. 9d. and to sell gold at £3 17s. 10½d. per standard ounce.

In the international field the gold standard provides stability of exchange rates between different currencies, for the exchange rate cannot fluctuate beyond the limits of the gold points (discussed below). In addition in international dealings the gold standard provides, assuming a country keeps to the rules, an automatic solution to its balance of payments adjustment problem. Certain preconditions are necessary for the successful operation of a gold standard. First, since in theory gold would be the only form of internationally acceptable money, domestic monies must be freely convertible into gold in order to permit international trade. Second, individuals must have complete freedom to import and export gold. Third, Central Banks must stand ready to buy and sell unlimited amounts of their own currency at a fixed gold price. Finally, each country's gold stock has to form the reserve base of its domestic money stock, thereby ensuring that domestic financial policies are dependent on any gold inflows and outflows.

Each country in the system would have a fixed gold price for its currency. Exchange rates between different currencies would therefore be automatically determined if for example, the Bank of England fixed the price of £1 at 112.982 grains of pure gold, whilst the US authorities set $1 = 23.2 grains, then the sterling-dollar exchange rate would be £1 = $4.87 (i.e. 112.982/23.2). This would be known as the mint par rate. On either side of this value would be a gold import point and a gold export point. The gold import point is the exchange rate above which gold flows into a country and the gold export point is the exchange rate below which gold flows out of a country. The precise locations of these points would be determined by the cost of shipping and

* The gold standard is discussed in more detail in *Gold*, Brian Kettell (Graham & Trotman, 1982).

insuring gold bullion. Suppose the costs of shipping and insuring gold were 1 per cent, i.e. 1 cent per dollar, then the gold import point would be $4.92, the gold export point $4.82. The sterling-dollar exchange rate would be kept strictly within these limits by the profit seeking activities of arbitrageurs. At any rate below $4.82 gold flows out and at any rate above $4.92 gold flows in. An example will help to illustrate how this would be accomplished.

Assume for instance that an excess supply of sterling temporarily pushes the exchange rate to $4.70 in London. Under such circumstances, it would profit an American arbitrageur to convert $4.70 into £1, use the £1 to purchase 112.892 grains of gold from the Bank of England, then resell the gold to the US treasury at the fixed price $1 = 23.2 grains. For his 112.982 grains, the arbitrageur would therefore receive $4.87, which yields him a net profit of 12 cents on the transaction (17 cents less 5 cents costs incurred in transporting the gold from London to New York). The incentive for arbitrageurs to shift gold from London to New York remains as long as the transport costs involved are less than the price differential between the two markets. The increased demand for sterling forces up the sterling/dollar exchange rate until sterling reaches $4.82. At this stage the incentive to shift funds from the United States to England is removed. ($4.87 minus 5 cents gives $4.82.) Similarly $4.87 plus 5 cents gives a rate of $4.92 at which gold imports would be unprofitable.

Thus the authorities do not intervene in the foreign-exchange market, they merely stand ready to buy and sell domestic money at a fixed gold price; it is the profit-seeking activities of gold arbitrageurs which maintains the exchange rate between the gold import and export points.

During the First World War all countries left the gold standard, and many of the main belligerent countries had substantial inflation. There was a general attempt to restore the old system after the war – the British government in particular maintained strong deflationary policies during the early 1920s in order to be able to return sterling to its pre-war parity with gold, under the impression that such a move would restore not only the prosperity of the world economy but the financial supremacy of London as well. However, the world slump which originated in the US in 1929 led to the collapse of the restored gold standard and initiated a period characterised by the breakdown of international cooperation, increasing protection, bilateral trading arrangements and a series of competitive depreciations by the major countries in an attempt to reduce unemployment at each other's expense.

2(a) The adjustable peg or par-value system

It was against this background that the major allied powers met at Bretton Woods (in New Hampshire in the United States) in 1943 and 1944 to construct an international monetary system for the post-war period. The negotiations were complex, but certain principles were generally accepted by the countries attending the Bretton Woods conference: the desirability of a system of multilateral trade and convertible currencies; the desirability of internationally agreed fixed exchange rates; and the need for a means of increasing the world stock of gold and foreign exchange reserves so that countries would not be forced to meet short-run balance of payments deficits or surpluses by disrupting their domestic economies.

The agreement at Bretton Woods in 1944 re-established fixed (but adjustable) exchange rates between currencies in the form of so-called 'par values' defined in terms of gold. Countries were obliged to intervene in the foreign exchange market to maintain the exchange rate within 1 per cent either side of its par value. The system which evolved was a gold bullion standard in which domestic currencies were not convertible into gold as under a gold standard, but in which the monetary authorities undertook to buy and sell the currency of another country which was itself operating a gold bullion standard. Under the Bretton Woods system national currencies were convertible into the dollar, and the dollar itself was convertible into gold at $35 per ounce. In effect the dollar replaced gold as the reserve asset of the international monetary system.

In the Articles of Agreement of the Bretton Woods system, however, it was clearly recognised that internal flexibility could not be relied on and that if provisions were not made it would be income and employment that would bear the brunt of adjustment, as in the inter-war years. Two provisions were made to safeguard full employment. First, a country in temporary disequilibrium could borrow from the IMF to tide it over its difficulties without having to pursue internal adjustment policies which threatened employment. The mechanics of borrowing are discussed in detail in Chapter 4. Second, provision was made for exchange rate adjustment – in practice this was rarely used.

The general reluctance to change exchange rates was attributable to several things. There was a general fear that devaluation might preserve or even exacerbate inflation, and not merely correct its effects on the balance of payments. Memories of the inter-war years were important. Surplus countries' governments were wary of the deleterious consequences of revaluation or appreciation on profits and employment in industries producing tradeable goods. In Britain's case, opposition to devaluation in the 1960s was also based on considerations of political prestige, a belief that there was a moral obligation to countries holding their reserves in sterling, and worries that the role of sterling as a trading and reserve currency, and the invisible earnings thought to depend on this, would be undermined. Another worry was that a devaluation would be followed by another one and this would provoke further speculation. The breakdown of the Bretton Woods agreement is discussed further in Chapter 4.

2(b) (c)   Wider bands and crawling peg systems

In an attempt to preserve the virtues of pegged exchange rates, while avoiding the speculative pressure that can build up with the threat of devaluation, several schemes have been developed by economists which might make the adjustable peg system workable by introducing more flexibility into it. One such scheme is the *crawling peg*. Under the crawling peg a country would maintain its pegged exchange rate within agreed margins at a level equal to the moving average of the market exchange rate over an agreed previous time period. This would allow a country's currency to drift gradually lower if circumstances warranted, and at the same time would avoid both the upheaval of devaluation under the adjustable peg system and the possibility of excessive depreciation under free floating.

Other objective indicators, other than a moving average of the past rates of exchange, could be used to introduce more flexibility into exchange rates while preserving some semblance of order. Changes in the level of reserves, the domestic rate of inflation, the level of employment, etc., could all be used to trigger off exchange rate changes according to agreed rules. All the proposals would involve automatic adjustment of a pegged rate according to some agreed formula.

3. Managed floating

Under managed floating there are no pegs and no parities that the authorities are obliged to preserve. Instead the currency is free to float but the authorities intervene to avoid what they regard to be undesirable consequences of excessive appreciation or depreciation. A weak currency may lead to excessive depreciation which the authorities may wish to avoid because of its repercussions on the domestic price of imports and the internal cost structure. Alternatively, countries with a strong currency may wish to avoid excessive appreciation. To operate a managed float requires that the monetary authorities add to the supply of or demand for foreign exchange as circumstances warrant in order to achieve the exchange rate desired. The limits to which a country can manage a floating rate depends on the volume of reserves it has (to defend a depreciating currency), and its ability to control the money supply, if need be, as it accumulates reserves (to prevent an appreciating currency). This latter effect occurs when with a fixed rate and currency inflows, the country is obliged to supply its own currency (thereby raising the local money supply) in exchange for foreign currency.

4. Multiple exchange rate systems

Under such systems, and there are many types of them, no single rate or parity, either in fact or in effect, is applicable to all transactions; instead, two or more are applicable to a given group of transactions. Thus a country might have two official parities, a lower one in terms of the domestic currency that is applicable to exports and a higher one that is applicable to imports. Such a system would encourage exports and discourage imports.

Multiple exchange rate systems are usually designed to encourage some transactions and discourage others. During 1984, as in 1983 and 1982 about one third of the IMF's members engaged in multiple currency practices.

5. Freely floating exchange rates

Under freely floating exchange rates the exchange rate is left to find its own level in the market without any official intervention. Balance of payments equilibrium is supposed to be achieved automatically. In an economic system in which the authorities are indifferent to the exchange rate, there is no need for international reserves. In practice, however, countries are not totally indifferent to the value of their currency in relation to others, and in the recent past free floating has never been adopted for any length of time as an exchange rate regime. Freely floating rates stand at the other end of the spectrum to the rigidly fixed parities of the old gold standard.

APPENDIX I

Interest arbitrage and the determination of the forward exchange rate

An important factor determining the forward exchange rate is interest rate differentials. In order to understand the importance of interest arbitrage let us take an example.

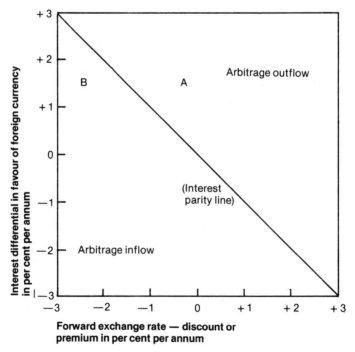

Fig. 1.4 Covered Interest Arbitrage

Plotted on the vertical axis of Figure 1.4 are interest rate differentials, with a plus (=) differential indicating a higher interest rate in the 'foreign' country than in the 'home' country.

Plotted on the horizontal axis are the discounts (minuses) or premiums (pluses) on the forward exchange of the 'foreign' country, expressed in per cent per annum. Any combination of these two variables can be expressed as a point on the chart. The 'interest parity' line joins together those points where the forward exchange rate is in equilibrium with the interest rate differential. Moving along the interest parity line, if interest rates in the foreign country are 2% higher than in the USA, the currency of that country is at a 2% per annum discount in the forward market; if foreign interest rates are 1% below the USA rates, the foreign currency is at a 1% premium. When the forward exchange rate is at its interest parity, movements of short-term funds between the two centres with exchange risks covered are not profitable, since the gain to be made from the higher interest rate abroad is exactly offset by the cost of covering the exchange risk in the forward market.

When the forward exchange rate gets out of line with its interest parity (either because of developments in the exchange market or because of changes in interest rates) it becomes profitable for short-term investors to shift funds from one centre to another, i.e. an 'interest arbitrage incentive' emerges.

Point A on Figure 1.4 indicates a position where interest rates in the foreign country are 1.5% higher than in the home country while the forward discount on the foreign currency is only 0.5%; a transfer of funds abroad with exchange risks covered would consequently return an additional yield of 1% per annum.

The actual movement of funds abroad tends to restore interest parity because:

(i)   selling the home currency spot and buying it back forward respectively raise and lower the spot and forward exchange rates, thereby increasing the cost of forward cover;

(ii) withdrawing funds from the domestic market raises interest rates at home, whilst investing funds abroad reduces foreign interest rates.

Point B also illustrates a position where interest rates abroad are 1.5% above those in the home country, but in this case the forward discount on the foreign currency is 2.5% per annum. Despite the higher interest rates abroad, there would be no incentive to move funds there for investment with the exchange risk covered. On the contrary, it would be profitable to move funds from abroad despite the fact that the investment of these funds would bring a lower yield, since the interest loss of 1.5% would be more than compensated for by the 2.5% gain on the forward exchange transaction. The movement of funds from abroad would again tend to restore interest parity, however, by: (a) reducing the forward discount on the foreign currency as the result of an increased supply of spot exchange and the demand for forward foreign exchange by the arbitrageur abroad; and (b) lowering the interest rate differential as funds are transferred from the foreign money market to the home market.

This theory indicates that forward rates fluctuate closely around their interest parities. However, there are several reasons why this theory may not work in practice; the supply of funds able to arbitrage freely may not be unlimited; there may be a shortage of suitable short-term investments in some countries. In the case of potential institutional investors there may be legal restrictions on investing abroad with exchange control limiting the ability of residents to move funds to where they wish. Finally investors may have reasons to fear that funds may become blocked if they are placed in certain currencies. This suggests that the supply of arbitrage funds may be highly responsive (or 'elastic') within certain limits. Beyond this the supply of funds becomes less responsive and apparently profitable opportunities will attract only a limited amount of funds.

APPENDIX II

How to measure the cost of forward cover*

The way the cost of forward cover is measured depends on the way exchange rates are being quoted. As already discussed exchange rates can be expressed either directly or indirectly. In making a forward contract the price of the currency concerned is likely to differ from its current (spot) price. The purpose of the cost of forward cover is to take account of any difference and to express it as annual interest cost of the current price of the currency on a percentage basis, that is per £100, per $100, etc. This latter point is important since we need to ensure that the prices, spot and forward, used in the formula are quoted in the appropriate manner.

In general the relationship is usually written

$$\text{Cost of forward cover} = \left[\frac{FR-SR}{SR}\right] \times T \times 100 \qquad (i)$$

where   FR, SR are the forward and spot per unit price of foreign currency respectively, (in terms of domestic currency), and T is time required to bring period up to one year.

Note that from the UK viewpoint since the cost of forward cover is expressed in terms of £100 units we must ensure that the exchange rates express the *sterling* cost of foreign currency.

This means we need to quote indirect or pence rates of exchange.

In other words, instead of £1 = $1.80 we need 1$ = 1/1.80 (= £0.555); in general we need to replace FR with 1/FR and SR with 1/SR in the formula, thus we get:

---

* This appendix is based on work undertaken by Alan Munro of the City of London Polytechnic.

$$\text{Cost of forward cover} \quad \left[\frac{\dfrac{1}{FR} - \dfrac{1}{SR}}{\dfrac{1}{SR}}\right] \times T \times 100$$

$$= \left[\frac{SR - FR}{FR}\right] \times T \times 100 \tag{ii}$$

Note that the reason we have the forward rate in the numerator is because of the method of exchange rate quotation and the need for our formula to express the interest cost in *sterling terms*. Hopefully we can also see that looking from the US viewpoint whose exchange rate is indirect the formula in equation (i) is appropriate since it reflects the *dollar* cost of sterling and therefore any difference in *dollar* percentage interest rates.

There are then two possible forms in which the formula may appear, depending on the method of exchange rate quotation:

(a) For direct (UK) method $\left[\dfrac{SR-FR}{FR}\right] \times T \times 100$ (i)

i.e. with the forward rate in the denominator

(b) For indirect e.g. (US and most other countries) $\left[\dfrac{FR-SR}{SR}\right] \times T \times 100$ (ii)

i.e. with the spot rate in the denominator

Uses and interpretation of the cost of forward cover

It is possible to use the formula in different ways, e.g. comparison of a spot settlement/payment against a forward settlement/payment for exporters and importers, or a forward contract against the interest costs of a foreign currency borrowing/lending (exchange control permitting), or in calculating the net covered yield on funds held in money market assets denominated in different currencies. With each of these there will be an appropriate spot and forward buying and selling rate, but in interpreting the *sign* of the cost of forward cover we need to remember that our conclusion will be dependent on whether we are buying or selling forward. An example might illustrate the point giving the following market rates:

	Selling $	Buying $
Spot	·1.82(15)	1.82(25)
3 month forward	1.81(95)	1.82(15)

and applying the formula in equation (ii) we have for a UK importer and a UK exporter in the simplest case, considering a spot or forward operation:

Importer   Cost of forward cover $= \dfrac{\$1.82(15) + \$1.81(95)}{\$1.81(95)} \times 4 \times 100$

$$= \dfrac{\$ .00(20) \times 4 \times 100}{\$1.81(95)}$$

$+ 0.439\%$ p.a.

Exporter   Cost of forward cover $\dfrac{\$1.82(25) - 1.82(15)}{\$1.82(15)} \times 4 \times 100$

$+ 0.219\%$ p.a.

Both of these results produce a + ve cost of forward cover. Clearly in the first case since the dollar is at a small forward premium, the importer *buying* forward as opposed to spot has a + ve cost since he is getting less foreign currency, in fact, he had to *pay* 43.9 pence more per £100 of foreign currency he buys forward than if he had bought spot. However, for the exporter who is *selling* forward as opposed to spot he is gaining and the + ve sign reflects a gain. This gain on an annual basis is 21.9 pence per £100 of foreign currency he sells forward over its spot value. Since the sign depends upon whether there is a forward premium or discount we can summarise the possibilities as shown in Table 1.6

Table 1.6
Cost of forward cover's sign

		+ve	−ve
Forward operation	Buying foreign currency	Cost	Gain
	Selling foreign currency	Gain	Cost

If we now reverse the situation to examine the US importer and exporter undertaking a similar operation, using the same rates and applying equation (i) we find the sign for both cases is −ve. This indicates as we would expect, that since £ is relatively cheaper forward than spot, for the importer a forward operation has a gain and for the exporter a loss.

Chapter 2
International Financial Flows

One of the most important concepts to grasp in understanding the foreign exchange market developments is that of the balance of payments. Indeed a glance at any financial newspaper would reveal widespread discussion about world trading developments and about changes in a country's balance of payments. But why do countries trade and is it desirable that they do so. Again, what is the balance of payments and why is it important?

WHY DO COUNTRIES TRADE?

Most international *trade* can be explained in terms of *four aspects*: cost of factors of production, technology, tastes, and incomes.

1. Cost of factors of production

A country will tend to import products which require a relatively high input of those factors of production with which it is relatively poorly endowed. For example, the UK imports lamb and butter from New Zealand despite transport costs, because these products require much land relative to labour, and because New Zealand has an abundance of land relative to its labour force, when compared to the UK. The abundance of land will tend to make it relatively cheap, and this would give rise to relatively low costs for such products. Similarly, a country with little capital per man compared to other countries may tend to import products which are capital-intensive in production, again because the relative abundance of capital abroad may make such products relatively cheaper.

2. Technology

Another reason may be technology: Britain imports, for example, television sets from Japan, some pharmaceutical products from Switzerland, and several types of aeroplane and computers from the United States. In each case, the exporting country generally has a relative technical lead in their manufacture; indeed, because of the heavy costs of small-scale production, patents, and other obstacles to the international transmission of knowledge, these commodities may not even be produced in Britain at all.

Both differences in costs of factors of production and technology will cause differences in product prices, but the crucial question is whether they generate different *relative* prices. In order to understand this point, it is necessary to distinguish between absolute and comparative advantage.

Adam Smith, in *The Wealth of Nations*, published in 1776, argued that if one of two countries could produce one product more efficiently and more cheaply and the other country could produce a second product more efficiently and more cheaply, then it would be natural for them to trade and both would benefit from doing so. Countries would gain from specialising in the production of, and exporting, the product in which they had an absolute advantage and importing other products in which they had an absolute disadvantage.

David Ricardo, in *Principles of Political Economy and Taxation*, took the argument a bit further. He showed that it was comparative, not absolute, advantage that mattered. Suppose, to take Ricardo's example, that if no trade took place the production of a certain quantity of cloth and a certain quantity of wine in England and Portugal would require the following number of hours of labour:

	Cloth	Wine
England	100	120
Portugal	90	80

Portugal would have an absolute advantage in both wine and cloth since it could produce both more efficiently than England. However, Portugal would be relatively more efficient in wine which it could produce for two-thirds of the hours of labour required in England, which in cloth it would need nine-tenths of the hours required in England; thus Portugal would have a comparative advantage in wine. England on the other hand would have a comparative advantage in cloth, which it could produce with 111% of the hours required in Portugal (100 · 90), whereas it would need 150% of the time taken in Portugal to make wine (120 · 80). Now countries could gain if each specialised in the product in which it had a comparative advantage and trade took place between them. England could specialise in making and exporting cloth and obtain wine more cheaply by importing it from Portugal, which in its turn would specialise in making wine and import cloth. If for example the international price ratio were 1 unit of cloth for 1 unit of wine, Portugal would be able to obtain a unit of cloth for 80 hours instead of 90 hours of labour, while England could get a unit of wine for 100 hours instead of 120 hours.

The relative price of exports to imports is known as the terms of trade – the ratio of a price index of exports to a price index of imports. This therefore represents the import purchasing power of a given volume of a country's exports. A rise in the terms of trade is known as an 'improvement', and implies that fewer exports have to be sold to obtain the foreign currency necessary to purchase a given volume of imports. Less work is required, therefore, to obtain the imports, and this represents a rise in the standard of living.

Demand factors can also influence relative prices of products, and this leads us to the other main influences on trade – tastes and income.

3. Tastes

The third possible cause lies on the demand side. The size of British imports of tea, port, sherry, and champagne is partly explained by the lack of domestic production (for climatic reasons), but partly also because of a traditionally high level of consumption in comparison with many other European countries, reflecting different tastes.

In each example, the foreign country is a cheaper source of supply than Britain. By and large, the lower the level of foreign costs and prices, the greater the probability that a particular commodity will be imported, and – if it is already imported – the greater the volume of imports.

4. Income

In addition to these price and cost influences on imports, there is the powerful effect of changes in aggregate demand at home. In a boom, with incomes rising, the demand for most commodities rises. In the early stages many domestic producers can increase their own sales and output roughly in pace, so imports as a whole rise little faster than demand itself. In a few sectors, however, the boom may start to eat into stocks of materials, and attempts by producers to re-stock lead to sharp rises in imports. As the boom progresses, more and more bottlenecks appear: steel, bricks, machine tools, consumer durables all run short, as the limits of current domestic production are reached. Further rises in demand then begin to spill over almost entirely into imports. After the boom breaks, and demand starts to ebb away, the ratio of imports to national income stops rising and often starts to drop back.

WHAT IS THE BALANCE OF PAYMENTS AND WHY IS IT IMPORTANT?

Information about the balance of payments assists a country in determining its relative strength in the world economy. Data on the balance of payments will give companies an important indicator as to the direction of pressure on a country's exchange rate. A continual deficit is a useful indicator of a likely fall in a country's exchange rate. In addition the data can be used to forecast changes in macro-economic policy, which may seriously affect future corporate sales, in the economy. A continued deficit is a valuable indicator of likely deflationary policies. Also, balance of payments data may help a company to foresee changes in exchange controls which could seriously hinder a company's ability freely to move funds in or out of a country. In this Chapter we examine the case of the United Kingdom balance of payments but it must be stressed that the principles are identical for any country.

The object of the balance of payments accounts is to identify and record transactions between residents of the United Kingdom and residents overseas (non-residents) in a way that is suitable for analysing the economic relations between the UK economy and the rest of the world. The transactions may involve a flow of real resources, that is, of goods, services or property income, between the United Kingdom and the rest of the world; a change in the United Kingdom's foreign assets or liabilities; or a transfer payment.

In interpreting the balance of payments accounts it is important to be aware of what is known as the 'sign convention', i.e. whether items are credits or debits in the accounts. The basic principle is that transactions which result in there being a demand for sterling (the home currency) in the foreign exchange market are listed as credits and transactions which result in there being sterling (the home currency) selling in the foreign exchange market are listed as debits.

Exporting, falls in foreign assets held by the United Kingdom (explained below) or increases in the United Kingdoms liabilities to non-residents are all positive entries. The process of exporting requires the buyers to pay in such a way that either he or the seller will buy sterling. An example of a fall in foreign assets held in the UK would be if there were sales of US Treasury bills for sterling. An example of an increase in UK liabilities to non-residents would be if non-residents purchased gilts, placed deposits in UK banks or took over British companies. Similarly importing, increases of the UK's foreign assets or decreases in the UK liabilities to non-residents are debit entries.

PRINCIPLES OF THE ACCOUNTS – WHY THE BALANCE OF PAYMENTS ALWAYS BALANCES

The balance of payments accounts are a summary of all transactions between UK residents and non-residents over a given period. Each transaction, whether it be, for example, the sale of a good to a non-resident or the purchase of stocks and shares from a non-resident, involves both a credit and a debit to the UK. The balance of payments accounts is thus an amalgam of credits and debits, indicated by appropriate signs, which ensures that the total of the whole account is always zero for each period provided all transactions are measured accurately (the reason for this is explained below). In practice errors and omissions enter the recording process and in presenting the accounts a balancing item is included to compensate for this.

Under this system, and with the sign convention employed, the whole account always sums to zero, but the sum of credits and debits will not necessarily net out to zero for each individual group within the accounts. The sum of transactions in each group produces a balance for that group, for example the sum of exports of goods (exports carry a positive sign) and the imports of goods (negative) is the balance on visible trade.

A simple way to appreciate why total debits and credits must be equal is to realise that a country, like an individual, cannot buy goods and services worth more than what it sells unless it either:

(i) reduces its cash reserves (gold, foreign exchange and bank accounts abroad);

(ii) sells off some of its investments;

(iii) receives repayment of debt owed to it;
(iv) borrows/or receives credit;
(v) receives gifts or indemnities.

Conversely, a country cannot sell more than it buys in goods-and-services transactions unless it engages in matching debit transactions by accumulating cash reserves, investing, lending, paying off debt, or making gifts.

To clinch an understanding of the balance of payments concept, it is worthwhile to draw the analogy between a country and a single family. Examples of *credits* in the family's balance of payments might be: (1) sales of goods, such as crops grown or goods produced by members of the family, (2) provision of lodgings to tourists, (3) work done by wage-earning members of the family, (4) earning of interest and dividends on bank accounts and bonds and stocks, and earning of profit from a family-owned business, (5) receipt of gifts, perhaps from relatives or from public-relief authorities, (6) new borrowing, including the obtaining of hire purchase credit from sellers of goods, (7) undoing loans and investments previously made, including, for example, selling stocks, cashing in savings bonds, spending, spending wads of currency kept in the mattress, and drawing down bank accounts and (8) sale of gold coins from a collection. *Debits* might include: (1) purchase of groceries and other goods, (2) travelling, staying in hotels and eating in restaurants, (3) buying medical and legal and repair services, (4) incurring interest on money previously borrowed, (5) making gifts, (6) repayment of borrowing, including payment of instalments on credit purchases, (7) purchases of stocks and bonds and increases in bank accounts and hoards of currency and (8) purchase of gold coins. The family clearly cannot be spending more than it earns on current account (items 1 to 4) without at the same time receiving gifts, borrowing, drawing down bank accounts and hoards of cash, otherwise recovering old loans or selling off investments or selling gold. Coversely, a family cannot be earning more than it spends on current account without lending, investing, making gifts, accumulating cash and bank accounts, or the like.

The necessary balance of debits and credits is a matter of sheer definitions and arithmetic and gives no guarantee of 'equilibrium' in any reassuring sense of the word. Total debits would equal total credits even for a family or a country in terrible economic straits.

Thus, like family, unless there is some transaction on the credit side a country could not be running the deficit in the first place. A country simply cannot be importing more goods and services than it can pay for in some way or other. If debits and credits are equal one may wonder why the existence of a deficit creates a 'problem'. The problem occurs whereby the deficit is financed in a merely stopgap way, as by drawing down bank accounts abroad, selling off gold or investment assets, receiving stopgap loans from abroad, or receiving gifts granted by foreigners precisely in order to tide the country over the crisis. The worry is that such stopgaps cannot go on for ever: eventually, foreign bank accounts and gold and other saleable assets will be exhausted, and foreigners will become tired of making bad loans and unrequited gifts. The deficit country may suddenly be caught up by the unpleasant need to live within its income. A persistent current-account deficit may indicate the impending need for sudden unpleasant readjustments.

Even borrowing in a non-stop gap way can involve difficulties. High interest payments may have to be made for foreign currency inflows. If borrowings are from the International Monetary Fund, discussed in Chapter 4, severe 'austerity' conditions may be attached to the loans.

THE STRUCTURE OF THE BALANCE OF PAYMENTS

At a high level of aggregation, the UK balance of payments can be arranged into four main groups. The first of these is called the *current account* and it covers exports and imports of goods and services, interest profits and dividends and current transfers. The balance on the current account has been described as 'an indicator of whether the nation is paying its way'. *Capital* transfers form the small second group of transactions. These comprise compensatory payments to holders of sterling under the Sterling Agreements introduced in 1968 and terminated in 1974. 'Investment and other capital flows', the third group, covers such things as *official long-term* capital transactions, external lending or borrowing by UK banks, overseas investment and trade credit. The second and third groups make up what is known as the 'capital account'. The fourth group, *official financing*, consists of changes in the UK official reserves of gold and foreign currency and other transactions concerned with their management through the Exchange Equalisation Account (EEA).

In the standard presentation of the balance of payments accounts, these four groups are listed in the above order and the balance for official financing, the dividing line across the accounts, is the aggregate balance for the first three groups. The fourth group, official financing, is sometimes said to be 'below the line' and completes the accounts. The structure of the accounts may therefore be summarised in the form of a table:

Table 2.1

	Net credit or debit
Current account	A
Capital transfers	B
Investment and other capital flows*	C
Balance for official financing	A + B + C
Official financing	− (A + B + C)
Total	0

* In practise the balancing item (see above) is included here to compensate for the extent that the sum of the three autonomous groups as measured does not match the total of official financing transactions – which, as defined, is known exactly.

The reasoning behind the presentation of the accounts is that transactions in the first three groups, which are often designated 'autonomous', contribute to the balance for the official financing which is financed by the items below the line which are included as the fourth group in the accounts, official financing.

When analysing the balance of payments it can be useful to make a distinction between autonomous and accommodating external transactions. Autonomous transactions are undertaken for private gain, e.g. as would occur with a capital inflow by private individuals wishing to benefit from high interest rates. This can be contrasted with accommodating external transactions, transactions undertaken or induced specifically to finance a gap between autonomous credits or debits. This distinction is not altogether satisfactory as the government can, by manipulating UK interest rates, create an inflow of short-term capital to accommodate a given current account deficit even though, from the point of view of individuals or banks buying and selling the assets, the transactions are autonomous. However, as will be discussed later, the autonomous – accommodating distinction provides a useful starting point for discussing the concept of balance of payments 'equilibrium'.

The balance of payments can be said to be in equilibrium when, at the existing exchange rate, autonomous credits are equal to autonomous debits over a period of good and bad years, without involving:

(i)   departures from full employment or price stability;
(ii) departures from the desired rate of economic growth;
(iii) adoption of tariffs or subsidies inconsistent with accepted international obligations.

We can now discuss the major constituent items in the balance of payments: the current account, the capital account and official financing.

1. The current account

This includes visible trade, i.e. exports and imports of goods: and also invisibles, namely services; interest, profits and dividends, and most transfer payments (goods, services or financial items that are rendered without a reciprocal flow).

The visible balance is simply the difference between the value of exports and imports, a positive or negative sign indicating a net inflow or outflow of currency respectively. The difference between the value of exports and the value of imports is known as the balance of trade.

2. The capital account

The current account quantifies how well a particular country performs in the buying and selling of goods and services with the rest of the world, whereas investment and other capital flows records capital transactions.

Before discussing individual items, it is· useful to make some general comments about the types of flows in the capital account. First, there is the distinction between official and private transactions, the former being carried out by government or governmental agencies and the latter by the rest of the community. Secondly, most capital movements can be classified into those which are long-term and therefore more permanent in nature, and those which are short-term and more easily reversible. Long-term transactions are usually carried out after consideration of the general prospects for profitability in other countries, whereas short-term transactions are determined more by interest rate differentials or by the prospect of capital gains or losses from potential exchange rate movements. Finally, a distinction is often made between direct investment and portfolio investment, even though the former is generally long-term and the latter short-term in nature. Direct investment includes capital expenditure abroad on factories, equipment, and the like but portfolio investment takes the form of stocks, shares, and other financial assets. Usually, direct investment is long-term in nature.

3. Official financing

The composition of official financing shown in the balance of payments accounts in any period, summarises the way that the UK monetary authorities have reacted to the net demand for, or accommodated the net supply of, foreign currency at whatever exchange rate prevailed. The direct effects are drawings on or accruals to the official reserves; the other official financing transactions represent the effects of directly reconstituting or supporting the official reserves by borrowing or similar arrangements. Historically such arrangements have been with overseas monetary authorities (including the IMF) but in the 1970s HM Government borrowed on the euro-currency and New York securities markets and, since 1969, public corporations and local authorities have borrowed foreign currencies under the exchange cover scheme. Under the scheme, public bodies are able to borrow in foreign currencies from abroad with the guarantee of the Treasury that the foreign currency required for interest payments and capital repayments will be available at the same cost in sterling terms as at the time that the loan was raised. The public bodies require sterling to finance domestic projects and the foreign currency supplements the United Kingdom's official reserves.

The sources of official financing are threefold:
1. net transactions with overseas monetary authorities;
2. foreign currency borrowing;
3. official reserves.

4. Balancing item

As we have stressed throughout this Chapter, because a flow in one direction (say an export of goods) must be offset by another (say, an inflow of foreign currency), with the conventional use of plus and minus signs, in principle, all entries should sum to zero. In practice, however, a balancing item is included to offset the sum of errors and omissions.

The UK balance of payment statistic for 1972 to 1983 are given in Table 2.2.

THE ADJUSTMENT PROBLEM

If all transactions have been recorded correctly, the overall balance of payments must balance exactly. An excess of expenditure over income implies more foreign currency going abroad than is received from abroad. The extra foreign currency must either come from borrowing or from the reserves, or both. Each of these generates a surplus on the capital account which offsets the deficit generated by the excess expenditure.

However some form of adjustment will inevitably be required if a country persistently faces the problem of finding official finance, given that the official reserves are finite and given that borrowing may not be possible, be expensive or involve onerous 'conditions' attached to the loans.

Adjustments can take place on either the current account, the capital account or both. Two types of adjustment policies can occur, automatic adjustment and discretionary adjustment. The basic difference is that automatic adjustment comes about by itself as a result of prevailing economic forces, whereas discretionary adjustment requires policy actions to rectify the disequilibrium. Two groups of discretionary policies are possible; expenditure reducing policies and expenditure switching policies. These will all be discussed in turn.

1. Automatic adjustment

An optimistic school of thought maintains that balance of payments deficits are usually transient phonemena and that automatic forces are brought into play to reverse deficits or surpluses. Thus automatic adjustment may come about when, with imports being greater than exports, an economy suffers a fall in incomes and prices, imports (income related) fall and exports (price related) rise. In addition with a fall in the money supply interest rates would rise, attracting capital inflows and thereby improving the capital account.

To be more precise there are three ways in which a balance of payments disequilibrium can be 'cured' automatically. To correct a deficit (and conversely) a surplus each of these involves a fall in home money income in line with the fall in foreign money income (as exports fall). First there could be a fall without any decline in the physical volume of domestic production and employment if there was a fall in prices and wages at which goods and services were valued. This would stimulate exports and reduce imports. Secondly, home income could fall through a shrinkage in the physical volume of goods and services produced with prices and wage rates unchanged. Again as fewer domestic goods are bought then domestic incomes fall thereby reducing the demand for foreign goods. Thirdly, home income could fall if there was a decrease in the exchange rate making domestic goods more competitive abroad and foreign goods more expensive at home.

Which mechanism or combination of these mechanisms operates depends on the international financial arrangements amongst the various countries. Under a gold standard or fixed exchange rate standard requiring governments

Table 2.2
United Kingdom Balance of Payments

Summary

£ million ....

Seasonally adjusted ....

| | | Visible trade (balance) | Invisibles (balance) .... | | | | Current balance |
			Services	I.P.D.	Transfers	Total	
1972		−748	+701	+538	−268	+971	+223
1973		−2 586	+786	+1 257	−436	+1 607	−979
1974		−5 351	+1 075	+ 415	−417	+2 073	− 278
1975		−3 333	+1 515	+773	−468	+1 820	− 513
1976		−3 929	+2 503	+1 365	−775	+3 093	−836
1977		−2 284	+3 338	+116	−1 116	+2 338	+54
1978		−1 542	+3 816	+661	−1 777	+2 700	+1 158
1979		−3 449	+4 071	+1 090	−2 265	+2 896	−553
1980		+1 513	+4 267	−51	−2 079	+2 137	+3 650
1981		+3 652	+4 249	+1 338	−1 967	+3 620	+7 272
1982		+2 384	+3 874	+1 402	−2 109	+3 167	+5 551
1983		−500	+4 389	+480	−2 320	+2 549	+2 049
1975	1	−944	+369	+201	−73	+497	−447
	2	−713	+380	+142	−146	+376	−337
	3	−1 030	+365	+180	−112	+433	−597
	4	−646	+401	+250	−137	+514	−132
1976	1	−524	+581	+294	−194	+681	+157
	2	−1 048	+561	+350	−167	+744	−304
	3	−1 227	+674	+369	−188	+855	−372
	4	−1 130	+687	+352	−26	+813	−17
1977	1	−933	+751	+123	−245	+629	−304
	2	−917	+842	−11	−279	+552	−365
	3	−166	+856	−11	−321	+534	+368
	4	−268	+879	+15	−271	+623	+355
1978	1	−562	+914	+72	−531	+455	−107
	2	−159	+845	+237	−388	+694	+535
	3	−557	+1 027	+185	−462	+750	+193
	4	−264	+1 030	+167	−396	+801	+537
1979	1	−1 433	+1 013	+410	−506	+917	−516
	2	−479	+954	+107	−503	+558	+79
	3	−723	+1 056	+401	−610	+847	+124
	4	−814	+1 048	+172	−646	+574	−240
1980	1	−404	+1 101	−56	−462	+583	+179
	2	−247	+1 067	−26	−594	+347	+00
	3	+889	+1 015	+16	−579	+452	+1 341
	4	+1 275	+1 084	+115	−444	+755	+2 030
1981	1	+1 814	+1 129	+259	−504	+884	+2 698
	2	+1 333	+ 080	+410	−527	+963	+2 296
	3	+90	+1 014	+322	−637	+699	+789
	4	+415	+1 026	+347	−299	+1 074	+1 489
1982	1	+471	+1 096	+29	−489	+636	+1 107
	2	+211	+1 052	+385	−621	+816	+1 027
	3	+588	+807	+398	−556	+649	+1 237
	4	+1 114	+919	+590	−443	+1 066	+2 180
1983	1	+203	+1 121	+291	−521	+891	+1 094
	2	−460	+1 273	−172	−678	+423	−37
	3	−248	+959	+299	−357	+901	+653
	4	+	+1 036	+62	−764	+334	+339

Reproduced by kind permission of the Controller of Her Majesty's Stationery Office.
Source: *Economic Trends*, March 1984.

Table 2.2 continued

Not seasonally adjusted ....

Current balance	Capital transfers	Investment and other capital transactions	Allocation of SDRs and gold subscription to IMF	Official financing	Balancing item
+223	—	−673	+124	+1 141	−815
−979	−59	+178	—	+771	+89
−3 278	−75	+1 602	—	+1 646	+105
−1 513	—	+154	—	+1 465	−106
−836	—	−2 975	—	+3 628	+183
+54	—	+4 166	—	−7 361	+3 141
+1 158	—	−4 263	—	+1 126	+1 979
−553	—	+1 835	+195	−1 905	+428
+3 650	—	−1 455	+180	−1 372	−1 003
+7 272	—	−7 352	+158	+687	−765
+5 551	—	−3 258	—	+1 284	−3 577
+2 049	—	−2 044	—	+816	−821
−642	—	+103	—	+326	+213
−353	—	+101	—	+572	−320
−467	—	+264	—	+213	−10
−51	—	−314	—	+354	+11
−111	—	−543	—	+678	−24
−342	—	−1 734	—	+1 955	+121
−151	—	−658	—	+861	−52
−232	—	−40	—	+134	+138
−628	—	+1 620	—	−1 913	+921
−454	—	+14	—	−908	+1 348
+701	—	+1 254	—	−2 608	+653
+435	—	+1 278	—	−1 932	+219
−408	—	−153	—	−173	+734
+335	—	−203	—	+1 494	+374
+604	—	−454	—	−210	+60
+627	—	−1 453	—	+15	+811
−883	—	+460	+195	−879	+1 107
−138	—	+738	—	−758	+158
+568	—	+123	—	−297	−394
−100	—	+514	—	+29	−443
−208	—	−501	+80	−689	+1 218
−119	—	+371	—	−246	−6
+1 557	—	+192	—	−279	−1 470
+2 420	—	−1 517	—	−158	−745
+2 708	—	−3 911	+158	−319	+1 364
+1 793	—	−2 002	—	+165	+44
+842	—	−1 164	—	+709	−387
+1 929	—	−275	—	+132	−1 786
+1 216	—	−132	—	+31	−1 115
+360	—	+131	—	+661	−1 152
+1 214	—	−1 032	—	−247	+65
+2 761	—	−2 225	—	+839	−1 375
+1 021	—	−477	—	+616	−1 160
−687	—	+539	—	−132	+280
+663	—	+831	—	+5	−1 499
+1 052	—	−937	—	+327	+1 558

to fix their exchange rates the first and second mechanisms operate together. The gold standard was a particular form of fixed exchange rates within which the price of gold was fixed in terms of domestic currency, and therefore the exchange rate was determined for all countries adhering to this standard by the ratios of gold prices specified in domestic currencies. Since the exchange rate was fixed, a balance of payments surplus would be met by inflows of international specie (gold). This approach, known as the price-specie flow mechanism, was especially linked with the work of David Hume. With the domestic money supply based on gold, the inflow of gold induced by a balance of payments surplus would cause in its turn an expansion of the domestic money supply. In line with the traditional quantity theory discussed in Chapter 1 it was believed that this would drive up the domestic price level. If the rate of increase of the domestic price level was faster than the rate at which the rest of the world price level was increasing, then imports would expand and exports contract until such time as the balance of payments surplus was eliminated. Conversely, a balance of payments deficit would entail an outflow of gold, which would result in a decrease in the domestic money supply and the domestic price level; and the falling prices would be expected to improve the balance of payments. Thus the important prediction of this approach was that there was an automatic adjustment mechanism which would lead to the correction of balance of payments disequilibria. Naturally the extent to which automatic adjustment occurred would depend on the extent to which there was this degree of wage and price flexibility.

If the countries had flexible exchange rates the third mechanism would operate. The mechanism and limitations of relying on exchange rate changes to cure balance of payments problems automatically are discussed further on pages 121–22.

2. Discretionary adjustment

Proponents of the need for discretionary adjustment (i.e. government induced) maintain that automatic adjustments, if they occur, operate with a long time lag during which time the country risks losing its entire foreign exchange reserves and/or paying unacceptable cost(s) of foreign borrowings and that therefore governments need to take action to ensure that the appropriate adjustments occur.

ADJUSTMENT POLICIES – EXPENDITURE-REDUCING AND EXPENDITURE-SWITCHING

The two major types of adjustment policies are known as '*expenditure-reducing*' and '*expenditure-switching*'. The former policy is based on the observation that the level of imports is related to domestic national income. Fiscal and monetary policies designed to reduce domestic demand (and thereby incomes) should improve the current account by reducing the volume of imports. Exports should not be affected as much because they are related more to overseas demand.

Expenditure-reducing policies include cuts in government expenditure, increases in taxation, and changes in monetary variables such as interest rates and the money supply.

The policy of expenditure-reducing is often referred to as deflation. Deflation affects expenditure and production by reducing the money supply, forcing money incomes and possibly prices down, and making new expenditure, particularly on investment less attractive. Expenditure on foreign goods is reduced along with expenditure on domestic goods.

The problem with deflation is that it imposes *high adjustment costs* to external disequilibrium (i.e. balance of payments deficits). Prices respond only slowly to a lower level of demand because of rigidities in the goods and labour markets: deflationary policies therefore impose a high cost in terms of foregone output and high unemployment in the period of adjustment. In addition, if investment is curtailed because of the fall in demand, this may impair the efficiency of industry and hence its future capacity to compete in world markets. Finally there may be politically undesirable consequences of high unemployment. It is for this reason that expenditure-switching policies are frequently introduced.

Expenditure-switching policies are policies which induce a switch of expenditure towards home-produced and away from foreign-produced goods. Two types of expenditure-switching policies can be distinguished. One is devaluation, which by making the country's goods relatively cheaper compared with foreign goods will tend to switch both domestic and foreign expenditure towards domestically-produced goods. The other is by the introduction of protectionist measures. These are usually designed to reduce imports and can take various forms. They include tariffs, quotas, 'voluntary' restraint, orderly marketing arrangements, administrative delays, government purchasing schemes and subsidies, among others, and are discussed further on pages 52–53.

1. Devaluation

Devaluation is defined as a downward alteration in the exchange rate. One objective of devaluation is to alter the foreign selling price of a product. The foreign selling price of a commodity is its internal price multiplied by the rate of exchange. Clearly the lower the rate of exchange, the lower may be the foreign selling price and the greater may be a country's exports. The domestic selling price of an imported good is the foreign selling price multiplied by the exchange rate. A devaluation means that one requires less of the foreign currency to buy the home currency. Similarly, one requires more of the home currency to buy the same amount of foreign currency. Since a devaluation increases the amount of domestic currency needed to obtain the same amount of foreign currency, then the effect is to raise the price of, and consequently (hopefully) reduce the demand for, imports. This will become clearer with a numerical example. It is convenient to illustrate the effect of devaluation by using the sterling exchange rate with the dollar, but the same effects hold for other major currencies.

On November 18 1967 the UK devalued the pound sterling from US$2.80 £1 to US$2.40 £1. What does this devaluation mean in terms of export prices and profitability and of import prices? A UK exporter who sold goods for US$280 in the USA before devaluation received £100 for them. After devaluation three options are open to him:

1. Continue to sell the goods in the USA for US$280; then he will receive not £100 but £116.66 and thus have a really big increase in profit per unit.
2. Sell the goods for US$240, when he will receive £100 as before but can expect an increase in his total sales because his selling price is now one-seventh (14.3%) less than before. The size of the increase in demand and sales depends on the response of demand (the elasticity), but unless this is zero, there will be some increase in sales.
3. Sell the goods at an intermediate price between US$280 and US$240, in which case his profit per unit will rise (but not as much as in the first instance) and his sales increase (but not as much as in the second instance). Thus devaluation makes exporting easier and more profitable.

The purpose of a devaluation is to enable a country to earn more foreign currency on exports and spend less foreign currency on imports. Devaluation encourages exports because exports have become cheaper or exporting has become more profitable or a combination of the two; this applies to both visible and invisible exports.

On the import side the effect of a devaluation is to raise import prices in terms of the domestic currency. An import from the USA priced at US$280 which cost £100 before devaluation costs £116.66 afterwards, a rise of nearly 17%. This higher price is designed to discourage imports and encourage the substitution of home produced goods, which are now relatively cheaper, for imports. This reasoning applies also to invisible imports; thus, for example, devaluation not only encourages foreigners to take holidays in the devaluing country because these are cheaper, it also encourages nationals to holiday at home because domestic holidays have become cheaper relative to holidays abroad.

A caveat

It should be stressed that one of the purposes of devaluation is to make exporting more profitable. It does not follow that if a firm retains its pre-devaluation price in terms of foreign currencies (i.e. puts up prices in terms of its own currency), this is necessarily contrary to the purpose of devaluation. For example, the additional profit margin might be more effectively used for a sales campaign than by offering lower prices; if demand is unresponsive to price, i.e. inelastic, more foreign currency would be earned by retaining the previous price in terms of foreign currency than by lowering it. Earnings of foreign currencies are only increased from lower export prices if sales expand more than proportionately to the reduction in price (i.e. if the price elasticity of demand is greater than one and supply is elastic – this is discussed further below).

Limitations of the text book model of devaluation

This devaluation approach to analysing balance of payments adjustment is, however, subject to some major limitations. The first major limitation in the analysis is that domestic wage earners are unlikely to accept readily a reduction in their real incomes at the same time as a redistribution of domestic incomes towards profits is taking place. Hence it can be difficult to control internal costs, so that the benefit of the devaluation is quickly eroded. Trade unionists may demand higher wages to offset rising import costs in turn forcing the manufacturer to raise his foreign selling price and placing him at a competitive disadvantage.

The second main limitation in the elementary analysis of how devaluation is expected to work is that clear-cut advantages are presumed to appear automatically across most of industry, shifting demand towards the devaluing country's goods. That view is based upon two false assumptions – first that non-price factors are unimportant and secondly that small scale firms dominate production. By non-price factors is meant that factors other than price may be all-important in influencing sales so that even if the product is cheaper there will not be an increased market for it. Non-price factors are considerations such as after-sales service, reliability, delivery times, etc.

The second false assumption is that small firms dominate production. In fact some 60% of world trade takes place between the subsidiaries of multinational companies. Their decisions as to where to sell products may be unresponsive to the potential benefits of devaluation and will reflect broad corporate considerations. So international firms in important export sectors tend to divide up their international markets between different subsidiaries and to avoid large-scale direct competition between subsidiaries in different foreign markets. For this reason the increased export competitiveness, which would be possible for a national firm decreasing its prices in line with a national devaluation, may be ruled out by a multinational company for those markets in which it has other subsidiaries with which the increased exports would compete.

This is quite apart from the fact that multinational companies tend to operate in oligopolistic markets in which a few companies influence the prices on a world of regional scale. For various reasons these companies tend to earn 'super-normal' profits of a kind which allows them considerable room for manoeuvre if either their costs rise or their prices fall in relation to other currencies, following a devaluation. In general, they make considerable efforts to avoid a price war with their principal regional or world competitors which may leave them all worse off in the longer run. Consequently, multinational companies may tend not to reduce export prices by the full extent of a devaluation.

A third flow in the analysis entails a consideration of what is known as the J-curve. The J-curve is caused by prices changing more rapidly than traded volumes can change. A country's import bill in terms of its own currency is, as already discussed, increased overnight by a depreciation in its currency. The revenue from its exports is initially unchanged. Its trade balance initially gets worse at a stroke. But then higher priced imports are progressively replaced by cheaper home-produced substitutes. Exports expand because they are cheaper in foreign currency terms on overseas markets. The trade balance gradually improves.

Figure 2.1 The J-curve

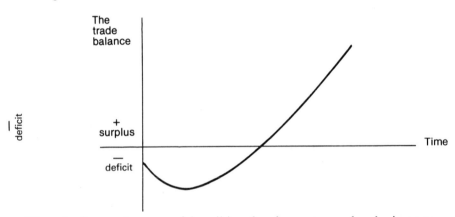

Thus the J-curve is a way of describing the phenemenon whereby imports are less price-elastic than exports (which is the case for most industrial countries) causing the effect of devaluation on prices to be unfavourable. However, with high price elasticities, increased volumes of exports in due course occur, overcoming the adverse price effect. Hence both the dip and the rising right side of the J. For the various reasons mentioned above, in particular with relation to export volumes, the trade balance, however, may not improve even some time after a devaluation.

2 Protectionist measures

There are a variety of means by which one country may limit or prohibit the inflow of foreign produced goods into the domestic economy: such policies go under the collective name of 'Protectionism'. When adopting such a strategy, the government is employing tools which either make it more difficult, or more expensive, or impossible, for the purchase of imported goods. The most widely known of import controls are tariffs and quotas.

Tariffs — are a tax on foreign produced goods. Levied at varying percentages they result in the sellers of the imported commodities having to raise their domestic purchase price. The impact on domestic consumers and on their demand for imports then has two facets. First, there is the income effect. The higher post-tariff price of imports effectively cuts the real income of consumers, and their demand for imports falls. Secondly, there is the substitution effect. With imports higher in price after the imposition of the tariff, consumers may deem it rational to switch to cheaper, home-produced alternatives. This will stimulate demand, production and employment domestically at the expense of the country producing the imports.

Quotas — are quantitative restrictions on imports. By stating a limit on the volume of categories of goods which may be imported within a given period (usually a year) the government exerts a direct control on the flow of imports and the level of import expenditure. This direct rationing of imports contrasts with the tariff system which is dependent upon the mechanics of the price system and the rationality of consumer choice. At its most extreme, a quota of zero may be imposed on categories of goods or upon the goods made within a specific country. This is termed an embargo, and is usually applied only under specific political (as opposed to economic) circumstances. A recent example is the embargo on trade imposed by many Western economies against Iran in 1980.

Other types of protectionism some of which were discussed earlier include:

Health and safety standards — demanded for imported goods. By imposing strict safety standards on certain goods (in the name of consumer well being) imports would be curbed by the inability of foreign producers to meet the required specifications. With large-scale production methods, the necessary changes may only be effected over the long run. It is only when the final goods meet the stipulated health and safety standards that import licences are granted for the overseas produce. The limited penetration of British-made cars into the Japanese market has been ascribed to such safety and health standard protectionism, applied by the Japanese government.

Exchange controls — Imports must eventually be paid for in the currency of the producer country (e.g. Datsuns paid for in yen). Placing limits on the amounts of domestic currency which may be exchanged for foreign currencies; or even denying convertability between domestic and certain foreign currencies, will lead to a cut in import levels.

Government subsidies to domestic industry — may be viewed as an indirect form of protectionism when such subsidies are paid to import competing firms. Such subsidies will facilitate a cut in the final price of the domestically produced goods, allowing them to undercut the imported goods.

Informal agreements between importing and exporting countries — The most notorious example of these is the agreement between Japan and Britain on the export of Japanese cars to the British Isles. By negotiation a level of 10–11% of the British market was assigned to Japanese-produced cars for the period 1976–1980.

Chapter 3
How Companies can use the Foreign Exchange Market

As we discussed in the Introduction and the previous chapters if companies, when faced with fluctuating exchange rates, do not endeavour to take advantage of the insurance facilities offered by the foreign exchange market they are liable to substantial risks. This chapter deals with the practical mechanics of how companies can measure the size of exchange rate changes and how they use the forward market and the option date forward market to obtain this insurance. We then move on to illustrate what companies can do when events occur to prevent the completion of a forward contract. This involves discussion of close-outs, extensions and new contracts.

After this we discuss the corporate use of some newer hedging techniques, foreign exchange futures and foreign exchange options. Finally we stress the fact that foreign exchange controls can limit free usage of these various markets.

MEASURING THE SIZE OF AN EXCHANGE RATE CHANGE

There is often confusion as to the exact amount by which a currency has been devalued or revalued. As already discussed in Chapter 1 the exchange rate between two currencies, say the dollar and the pound, can be expressed in two ways, as dollars per pound or pounds per dollar. When measuring percentage movements in an exchange rate, it can matter a great deal to the numerical result which way the rate is expressed. If, for example, the pound depreciates from \$2.40 to \$1.80, the percentage fall is 25%. This is equivalent to an appreciation of the dollar from 0.4167 pounds to 0.5555 pounds which is an appreciation of 33.33% in the dollar

In order to calculate the percentage change we take the new rate (X_1) subtract the old rate (X_0) and divide by the old rate (X_0) for the situation where the devaluation is expressed in so many units worth one dollar, i.e.

$$\frac{X_1 - X_0}{X_0}$$

An example should make this clear. Suppose the lira has been devalued from 400 to the dollar to 500 lira. From the standpoint of the number of lira required per dollar a 25% devaluation has taken place, i.e.

$$\frac{500 - 400}{400} = 25\%$$

When currencies are expressed in terms of their dollar values the formula becomes

$$\frac{X_0 - X_1}{X_1}$$

Using the same example but looking at the percentage decline in the dollar value of the lira the lira has declined in value from $-25c$ to $-20c$. Using the formula we have

$$\frac{400 - 500}{500} \text{ which equals } 20\%$$

So it is correct to state a 25% or a 20% devaluation of the currency has taken place. Care must be used in interpreting exchange rate changes.

HOW COMPANIES CAN USE THE FORWARD EXCHANGE MARKET

Having seen how the forward market works and how to interpret discounts and premiums we turn now to the benefit to a company of the forward market to see what constraints affect its use and to understand how the company can decide when it is worthwhile to cover forward and when it is not.

By entering into a forward foreign exchange contract a UK importer or exporter can:

(i)   fix at the time of the contract a price for the purchase or sale or a fixed amount of foreign currency at a specified future time;

(ii) eliminate his exchange risk due to future foreign exchange rate fluctuations;

(iii) calculate the exact sterling value of an international commercial contract despite the fact that payment is to be made in the future in a foreign currency.

A premium of the foreign currency shows that the currency is 'stronger' than sterling in the forward market. This means that when entering into a forward contract:

(i)   the UK exporter will receive more sterling for his currency export proceeds at the future date than at the current spot rate at the time the contract is taken out;

(ii) the UK importer will have to pay more sterling to settle his currency debts at the future date than at the current spot rate at the time the contract is taken out.

A discount of the foreign currency shows that the currency is 'weaker' than sterling in the forward market. This means that when entering into a forward contract:

(i)   the UK exporter will receive less sterling for his currency export proceeds at the future date than at the current spot rate at the time the contract is taken out;

(ii) the UK importer will have to pay less sterling to settle his currency debts at the future date than at the current spot rate at the time the contract is taken out.

In deciding whether to use the forward market a company has to make an assessment of what the future spot rate is likely to be. The essential point can be clarified by the example given in Chapter 1. Assume that the company has a one-month forward payment of dollars to make, i.e. it wants to sell forward pounds sterling. The company has two choices: firstly, it can sell pounds forward now; secondly, it can wait for one month and then sell pounds spot. If it sells pounds spot, the company receives $1.9090 per pound. If it sells pounds forward it receives $1.9055 per pound. It now has to decide whether in the future the pound will be worth more or less than this forward rate. Suppose that the future one-month spot value of the pound were 1.9075. The difference between the future one month spot rate and the current spot rate would be 0.0015, i.e. 1.9090 minus 1.9075 which, substituting into the formula, gives:

$$\frac{0.0015 \times 12 \times 100}{1.9100 \times 1} = 0.94\%$$

Alternatively, assume that the future value of the pound is 1.9010. Again the difference between the current and the future spot rate is 0.0080, i.e. 1.9090 minus 1.9010 which, substituting into the formula, gives:

$$\frac{0.0080 \times 12 \times 100}{1.900 \times 1} = 5.02\%$$

Bearing in mind that the cost of forward cover is 2.19% the company has to decide what action to take. If it expects a future spot of $1.9075, i.e. a loss of only 0.94%, the company would expect to benefit by dealing future spot. However, if the company expects a future spot rate of $1.9010, i.e. a loss of 5.02% the company would expect to benefit by dealing forward. In deciding whether or not to take out forward cover the company needs to take a view as to the likely future spot rate.

Companies operating on high turnover and small profit margins would be strongly advised to take out forward cover. If the company does not take out a foward contract and the 5.02% decline in the future spot rate occurs the company's total profits may be wiped out simply because of an exchange rate movement.

Since the advent of floating exchange rates there has been some controversy about how to calculate the cost of forward cover. Robert Ankrom, Treasurer of Chrysler (Europe) contends that while the forward premium or discount is a known, easily calculable number, it is totally misleading as a measure of 'cost'.

The true cost is rather the difference between the forward rate and the spot rate at the time the forward contract matures. For a company the important factor in hedging is not the past spot rate but the spot rate which will occur on the day a foward contract matures. Assume that a US manufacturer with a £1 million exposure wants to hedge by selling sterling forward and the current spot rate is $1.77 with a current forward rate of $1.76. The one cent forward discount on £1 million is $10,000. This discount is what was referred to earlier as the cost of cover. Ankrom goes on to ask what happens when the foward contract matures. The hedging company has contracted to deliver £1 million against $1,760,000. If the company does not have sterling, it will be compelled to buy sterling at the spot rate in effect at the time the forward rate matures. The cash outlay the company will have to make or the cash inflow it will enjoy on the closing of the foward contract will depend on that future spot rate.

Assume the future spot rate is $1.75 or less than the forward rate of $1.76: to buy £1 million the company needs $1,750,000. On closing the forward contract, the company will enjoy a cash inflow of $10,000. Assume the spot rate is $1.76 or exactly equal to the forward rate: there will be no cash inflow or outflow on the closing of the contract.

If it is assumed that the spot rate is $1.77 or exactly equal to the spot rate at the time the forward contract was taken out, the company will have to find $1,770,000 in order to buy the sterling and will have an additional cash outlay of $10,000. It is apparent that the cash outlay equals the forward discount only in the last case, where the spot rate does not change.

Ankrom claims that hedging is analogous to insuring only in that it limits the exposure. A company will receive the forward rate no matter what happens to the spot rate, but the cost of limiting the exposure is not analogous to an insurance premium, for the cost can only be determined after the fact.

HOW COMPANIES CAN USE OPTION DATE FORWARD MARKET

Suppose a UK importer places an order for goods to be delivered and paid for within six weeks of placing the order on (say) October 3. Payment is to be in Dutch guilders and the rates are:*

October 3   Spot £1 = DG4.51 − 4.52
             1 months forward   1½ − 1c pm
             2 months forward   2½ − 2c pm
             3 months forward   4⅛ − 3⅝ pm

If the importer knew that he would pay in (say) two months' time he could buy guilders, two months fixed forward at 4.48½ (after deducting 2½c from the spot bank selling rate of 4.51).

* The author would like to thank L. Waxman of the City of London Polytechnic for permission to reproduce this and the following section from his book, *Finance of International Trade* (Graham & Trotman, 1985).

However, all he knows is that he may be called upon to pay at *any* time from October 3 to November 14 (six weeks). In order to ensure that the bank will release guilders to him as and when he will need them, he can buy guilders six weeks *option* forward. However, as our rates show only one, two and three months forward, he can buy guilders two months option forward between October 3 and December 3. This deal gives the importer the flexibility of obtaining guilders any time between the two aforementioned dates.

Suppose, for example, that payment is called for on October 28; he can ask his bank to sell him the guilders *on that day* as it is within the option period. However, should he not require the currency until *after* the last day of the option period then he will suffer the same fate as if he had purchased a fixed forward deal – namely, a close-out (see later in this Chapter).

Option exchange rates

But what rate will the bank quote for an option deal? The answer is simple:

'banks will quote the worst rate from the customers' point of view selected from all the rates within the option period'.

Look at the guilder rates again. If the importer buys guilders two months option forward the relevant bank selling rates are:

October 3	spot	DG4.51
	one month	DG4.49½
	two months	DG4.48½

By giving him the right to acquire guilders anytime during this period the bank will have to protect itself by quoting the rate which would have applied if the customer had purchased guilders two months fixed forward, i.e. DG4.48½.

However, unlike a fixed deal, the importer can receive guilders from the bank at this exchange rate at any time up to two months from October 3. These forward rates are at a premium on spot. Does it make a difference if they were at a discount? The answer is 'yes'.

For example, suppose the bank selling rates were:

October 3	spot	DG4.51
	one month	DG4.52
	two months	DG4.53

The importer wishing to buy guilders two months option forward will now be quoted *DG4.51*.

The same principle applies; the customer could ask for the guilders almost at once (spot) and the bank protects itself by quoting the rate that applies to its most exposed position.

Principle one — When banks are selling currency and forward rates are at a premium, option deals will tend to be at rates at the furthest end of the time range; when rates are at a discount, option deals will tend to be at spot rates.

The examples so far have been of customers wishing to *buy* currency forward. What is the case when they wish to *sell* currency forward?

Let us suppose that the *bank buying rates* are:

October 3   spot   DG4.52
            1 month forward   DG4.51
            2 months forward DG4.50

Note that forward rates are at a *premium* on spot. If the customer wishes to *sell* guilders two months option forward, the bank will quote *DG4.52.*

If the rates were at a discount, for example:

October 3   spot   DG4.52
            1 month   DG4.53
            2 months   DG4.54

then the bank will quote *4.54* for selling guilders to a customer two months option forward.

Principle two — When banks are buying currency and forward rates are at a premium, option deals will tend to be at spot rates; when rates are at a discount, option deals will tend to be at the furthest end of the time range.

Note that Principle Two is a mirror image of Principle One.

The best way to ensure the correct option forward quote is to remember that the bank will compare the rates at the beginning and the end of the option period and select the one *least* advantageous from the customer's point of view.

Combined fixed and option deals

Finally, we have to consider cases where currencies need to be bought and sold forward where:

(i)   an option is called for and

(ii)   the option period starts *after* day 1.

For example:

Suppose an exporter knows that he will receive Dutch guilders not later than in three months' time, but he also knows that they will not arrive within the first month. This is shown in Figure 3.1.

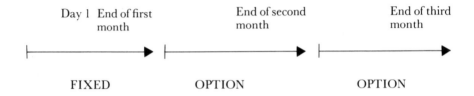

Fig. 3.1 Determination of Forward Rates with a Part Fixed & Part Option Contract

Figure 3.1 illustrates that the option period starts *after* the end of the first month; thus, using our principle again, we have to select the rate at the beginning of the option period, namely, the one-month rate, and at the end of the option period, namely, the three-month rate.

If the rates are:

Day 1	Spot	DG4.47½ – 4.48½	
	One month forward	4.45⅞	4.47⅜
	Two months forward	4.44	4.46½
	Three months forward	4.42⅛	4.44⅝

Thus, the selection will be from DG4.47⅜ with the *former rate being quoted*.

Note that this is a better rate for the exporter than he would receive if he wanted a *full* three months option deal; this would have been at DG4.48½. However, had the rates all been at a forward *discount*, or had the customer been *buying* forward currency, then this advantage would not apply.

It is a matter for the trader's own decision whether to go for a fixed or option deal, and if the latter, whether to have a full or part option and part fixed contract. His decision will depend on:

(i)   the expected timing of his receipts or payments;
(ii) the forward rates;
(iii) his willingness to speculate.

Note – within the time span of a forward contract there can be variations of the combinations of part fixed and part option.

For example:

Given a six month's forward deal there can be:

(i)   one month fixed and five months options
(ii) two month fixed and four months options
(iii) three month fixed and three months options
(iv) four month fixed and five months options
(v)   five month fixed and one month options

Each of these combinations will command a unique exchange rate.

CLOSE-OUTS, EXTENSIONS AND NEW CONTRACTS

We now turn to the question of what happens to a forward contract when events occur to prevent its proper completion. The first point to note is that a forward contract is legally binding on both parties. If a trader agrees to buy forward, buy he must! If a bank agrees to sell forward, sell it must! There is no 'option' to the honouring of this contract.

What happens, however, when a customer *cannot* honour his forward deal? Suppose, for example, a customer agrees to sell a currency forward but due to matters beyond his control, he is unable to deliver the currency in the forward period (option or fixed). This could be due to the receipts failing to arrive as planned perhaps because of a dispute with the party remitting the funds.

In *all* cases where a customer cannot meet his forward liabilities he will suffer what is called a 'close-out'.

Definition of a close-out

A close-out is defined as 'an effective honouring of a forward commitment by use of a spot transaction'.

In other words, to take our example of a customer not having the currency to deliver as planned, he will have to purchase that currency in the then spot market at the then current rate, and deliver the same under his forward contract.

Let us take an example. Suppose an exporter has agreed to sell Portuguese escudos two months forward, and at the end of the two months he has not received the escudos from his Portuguese buyer. He is locked into a rate of £1 = PE185.25.

He will then have to purchase escudos in the spot market (say) at £1 = PE181.75 and deliver them as per his forward agreement, losing PE3.5 for every £1's worth of business. His loss has been due to the new spot £1 being at a *depreciated* level relative to his forward rate. Had the £1 moved the other way (say) to PE187.50 then a gain of PE2.25 per £1 would have been made.

This puts a close-out into proper perspective. It is a situation where the customer can lose or gain, in complete contrast to the 'hedging' concept of a forward deal.

In other words, a closed-out forward contract is a *negated* contract, leaving the customer in a *speculative* position as if he had never covered forward at all! A close-out is hedging in reverse.

In a situation where an importer buys a forward currency and then for one reason or another finds that he has no need for the currency in the time span of the forward deal, he too can be closed-out, i.e. he can take delivery and then sell it spot making a gain or loss as in the previous example.

Under UK Exchange Control Regulations which were abolished in October 1979, currencies purchased forward had to be for acceptable commercial purposes (like buying imports). If they were not, in fact, needed, they *had* to be sold spot.

However, it is now quite legal for UK residents to hold foreign currency accounts and therefore close-outs are no longer binding. The alternative in this last case is simply to put the currency receipts to the credit of the existing currency account, or to open a new currency account.

In the case of the UK exporter, he can now borrow the relevant currency in the Euro-market, and deliver that to his forward contract.

In other words, the alternative to a close-out is:

(i) lending a currency (e.g. opening a currency account);
(ii) borrowing a currency (e.g. taking out an overdraft.

The factors that will determine whether to select a 'close-out' are:

(i)   expectations of future exchange rates;
(ii) current and future rates of interest;
(iii) commercial need to hold currency balances.

These factors are discussed in detail later in this Chapter. (See Interest Arbitrage.)

Extensions and new contracts

What happens when a 'close-out' has occurred and the customer still wants further forward cover? The answer is that he can obtain either an extension to his previous contract or a completely new contract.

A new contract

Quite simply the customer enters into a new forward deal for the same or different value to that of the first, but of course, at current forward rates. For example: suppose a customer sells $200,000 one month fixed forward.

The rates are: spot   £1 = $1.5230 − 1.5240
                 one month forward   0.05 −   .10c dis.
                 giving forward rates of $1.5235 − 1.5250

He will be quoted $1.5250 for the one month deal giving a sterling receipt of £131,147−54.

At the end of one month he does not have the dollars to deliver so he is closed-out. The following new rates apply:

New spot $1 = $1.5325 − 1.5335
one month forward   0.50 −   1.00c dis.
giving forward rates $1.5375 − 1.5435

The close-out rate is $1.5325 (bank selling spot dollars). That is he buys $200,000 spot at $1.5325 giving a sterling cost of £130,505.76.

He now enters into a new forward contract to sell $200,000 for one month fixed at $1.5435 yielding a sterling receipt of £129,575−63. The results are summarised in Table 3.1.

Table 3.1
Customers' forward transactions

	Debit		Credit	
	$s	£s	$s	£s
Original forward contract at maturity				
'Close-out'. Customer buys $200,000		130,505−70	200,000	
$200,000 delivered as per orignal contract	200,000			131,147−54
New forward contract at maturity				
$200,000 received from abroad			200,000	
$200,000 delivered as per new contract	200,000			129,575−63
Net receipts				£130,217−47

In fact, his final sterling receipt is £903.07 less than his original forward contract if completed would have yielded. This is because although the close-out spot rate is favourable, this is more than offset by the unfavourable new forward rate.

Extensions

Where a bank regards a customer highly, or where the volume of business warrants it, a customer may receive a special new forward exchange rate which is more favourable than under a new contract. This would apply when a bank is prepared to offer a customer an extension to his existing forward contract to cover problems of the timing of the delivery of the currency, as an alternative to a new contract.

For example: using the above rates, instead of the bank quoting $1.5435 as it did under the new contract method, it will quote a more favourable rate which is found as follows:

New spot   £1 = 1.5325 – 1.5335
one month forward   0.50 –   1.00c dis.

As the customer wishes to extend by *selling* $200,000 one month forward, the rate is calculated by taking the spot bank buying rate of $1.5335, but instead of adding the bank buying discount of 1.00 cents, the bank selling discount of 0.50 cents is added instead.

This gives a one month rate of $ 1.5335
                    plus   0.50c dis.
                    gives $ 1.5385

This is a more favourable rate for the customer as he now sells $200,000 one month fixed forward at $1.5385 giving a sterling receipt of £129,996–75 which is £421–12 more than under the new contract method.

Note — this concession is achieved by 'crossing-over' from the bank *buying* spot rate and adding the bank *selling* forward discount. Of course, the method works just as well if the customer is buying forward or if the forward rates are at a premium. Extension rates *always* give more favourable results to the customer.

In fact, although in theory both methods involve new forward contracts, the bank will, actually, simply increase or decrease the sterling credit or debit accordingly at the end of the day. The customer will have been *deemed* to have carried out these deals.

HOW COMPANIES CAN USE FOREIGN EXCHANGE FUTURES

The hedger uses the futures market as a management tool for fixing the exchange rates that affect his business activities. For the hedger, the currency futures contract works as an insurance policy. For speculators futures offer the potential for large profits due to the highly leveraged nature of futures trading. Since margin requirements on the Chicago Mercantile Exchange are typically about 5% of the value of a contract, it is possible to control large amounts of currencies with relatively little capital. For example, a contract for delivery of 125,000 Deutschmarks, may be controlled for $US1,500. If a speculator bought a Deutschmark contract at a price of $.5,000/DM, a rise in the value of the DM of 2% would result in a profit to the speculator of $1,250. However the same leverage could lead to equally substantial losses.

Like a forward contract, a currency futures contract can be used by a company to fix the level of an exchange rate. Using the same example as above, DM125,000 has a current value of $62,500. An importing company needing DM125,000 three months from now would purchase a contract through a broker after depositing a minimum initial margin of $1,500. The value of the contract would fluctuate daily based on the movement of the exchange rate as determined in the market.

Suppose the Deutschmark begins to rise in value relative to the dollar on the world's foreign exchange markets. The futures price on the IMM would typically move in sympathy with the movement of the spot exchange rate. Suppose that the price of the Deutschmark for delivery in March rises from $.5000/DM to $.5060/DM, the maximum daily fluctuation permitted under the rules of the exchange. As a result of the appreciation, the value of the DM125,000 contract is now $63,250, $750 higher than the initial price of $62,500.

If the price of the Deutschmark remains at the level until March, the individual who sold the contract to the importer unless he already held DM must spend $63,250 to purchase the amount of marks he contracted to deliver. The clearing member through which the contract was sold will require him to add $750 (the amount by which the value of the contract has increased) to his account. The money is then channelled through the Clearing House to the broker who arranged the contract for the import company. Such settlements take place daily based on price fluctuations that occur as the contract progresses to maturity.

Suppose that, at the time the contract matures, Deutschmarks can be purchased on the world's spot foreign exchange market at an exchange rate of $.6000/DM. The import company has two options: (1) take delivery, i.e. the seller of the contract to deliver DM125,000 to the company for $62,500 as contracted; (2) give delivery, i.e. it can liquidate the contract on the last trading day. Choosing the latter option, the company would 'sell back' or liquidate the contract by obtaining from the broker the deposit (less some agreed-upon commission) plus the $12,500 that the broker collected from the seller as the value of the contract appreciated.

The company then enters the spot market and purchases the DM125,000 it needs at a cost of $75,000. This is $12,500 more than the same amount of marks cost three months ago when the rate was at $.5000/DM. The increase in cost exactly matches the amount that the company received from the resale of the contract ($75,000–$62,500 = $12,500). By using a futures contract, the company has achieved its goal of protecting itself against a possible loss arising from a fluctuation in the exchange rate in essentially the same way as if it had purchased the currency for future delivery in the forward market.

The differences between futures markets and forward markets are discussed in the next section.

THE DIFFERENCES BETWEEN FUTURES MARKETS IN FOREIGN CURRENCIES AND FORWARD MARKETS

Again it can be instructive to compare futures markets in foreign currencies with forward markets. While the principle of protection against currency price fluctuations is the same in the future and forward markets, there are two major features that differentiate the two markets. First, the forward market offers contracts for specific amounts of currencies tailored to particular needs, while the futures market offers only standardized contracts in the predetermined amounts noted in Table 1.4 above. As a result, a customer wanting to protect his account payable of, for example, DM200,000 could only cover a portion of the risk (DM125,000) in the futures market but could arrange for full coverage in a single contract in the forward market.

The second difference concerns the maturities of forward and futures contracts. A forward contract can be written for the exact date when the foreign currency is needed or is to be disposed of. The futures contract has a standardised delivery date. If a user wishes to lift his hedge before the expiration date of the futures contract, he must be prepared to assume some risk of a currency price fluctuation between the time when the foreign currency is actually needed for the settlement of the transaction and the delivery date of the contract.

Several other differences arise from the particular structural features of the futures and forward markets. First, most forward contracts are settled by actual delivery of a specific currency on the value date of a contract. In contrast, since the futures market offers only four major delivery dates each year, most futures contracts are liquidated prior to their expiration dates. Secondly, the futures market, unlike the forward market, has a central clearing body. Customer's accounts are settled daily upon the conclusion of trading to reflect real profits or losses. Debt exposure is limited to one day's market fluctuations. Moreover, the exchange, either LIFFE or the IMM, guarantees performance on all contracts. However, this guarantee is to the member, *not* the user. Consequently users must be careful as to which member they deal with. Performance on a forward contract is contingent upon the financial integrity of the party assuming the opposite side of the contract. Thirdly, information costs to the members may be lower in the futures market than in the forward market. For example, if a bank is asked to write a forward contract for a customer, he might contact several different banks and brokers in search of the best exchange rate. In the futures market, however, a customer need not search for the best rate since the market rate on the most recent futures transaction is the best rate available to the customer at that time.

HOW COMPANIES CAN USE
FOREIGN CURRENCY OPTIONS

In essence, an option may be likened to foreign exchange insurance. It grants the holder the right, but not the contractual obligation, to deal at a given exchange rate for a specific period of time. For such flexibility the option buyer pays to the seller, or writer, a premium or fee upon initiation of the contract. A call option grants the buyer the right to buy foreign currency and a put option the right to sell foreign currency.

The most significant advantage which the currency option has over the forward exchange contract, discussed earlier, is that whilst unlimited profits may be enjoyed if the currency purchased actually appreciates, loss in the event of a decline is restricted to the option premium. Let us consider the circumstances where an option is preferable to a forward exchange contract.

Consider the position of a UK importer purchasing paper from the USA at a price of $520,000. It is August and payment is due in December. Exchange rates both spot and outright to December are 1.5160. The importer cannot afford to take the risk of having no cover, yet feels the dollar may weaken by year end. He decides that he could accept a limited downside of a cent or so in the exchange rate and decides to cover using call options in dollars. (A dollar call option is a sterling put option so this example written from a US perspective would refer to sterling puts.)

His sterling costs if he were to cover in the forward market would be $520,000/1.5160 = £343,008 no matter what the exchange rate was in December. This would eliminate all downside risk, but would also eliminate any upside potential.

Being prepared to accept a worse case of 1.50 (and possible planning to set his UK selling prices based on a rate of 1.50 in any case) he takes out a US dollar call option against sterling for $520,000 at a strike price of 1.50 with an expiration date of December 31. Premium is set at, say, £5,000.

If the dollar weakens to say 1.6160 the option expires worthless, and he takes advantage of the better exchange rate to buy his paper more cheaply. His cost will now be $520,000/1.6160 = £321,782 plus £5,000 cost of the option = £326,782; a saving of £16,226.

If the dollar strengthens to, say, 1.4160, he uses the option to buy at 1.50. In this case his cost will be 520,000/1.50 = £346,667 plus the £5,000 cost of the option = £351,667; a net cost of £8,659. But this is his worst case, even if the dollar were to strengthen further, this cost cannot worsen.

Many companies will find this combination of containable and often affordable downside protection plus retention of all the upside potential to be a very attractive proposition.

But there is a further argument in favour of the option route which perhaps owes more to human frailty than cool business logic but is no less important for that. In the situation above, had it been hedged with forward contracts then the business would have no risk at all. If the dollar rose, the cost rose, but this was offset by the gain on the forward contract; if the dollar fell, the cost fell, but this was offset by the loss on the forward contract. All in all, then, a successful hedge.

Yet in the latter case it is only human to ask the treasurer to account 'his' loss on 'his' forward contracts. The firm would have been better off without them would it not? What is his advice for next time? And so on.

Some other examples of when options are useful include the following. A machinery exporter fears that should the pound recover from say, the 1.45–1.50 area, his high export sales will decline. He knows that in all probability, he will sell 100 units in the fourth quarter of the year, but because orders are made only three months ahead in his business, he cannot safely cover outright in the forward exchange market in case his sales forecasts are not met, and he is left uncovered on surplus foreign exchange. His remedy is to sell the requisite amount of dollars in the form of a foreign exchange option, which will both protect his export sales against the impact of the sterling recovery and in the event of a sterling decline, will not impair his foreign exchange conversion beyond the cost of the option premium.

Since the holder of an option is not obliged to exercise it, options are particularly suitable for covering contingent cash flows. The classic 'ideal' use for currency options is the 'tender situations'. Here, a firm makes an offer to supply at a fixed currency price and holds this offer open for a period of time. During this time the firm is at risk to currency movements, but cannot economically take out forward cover – to do so could give rise to a loss if the order were lost. Effectively the tenderer gives his potential customer a currency option for as long as the offer remains open; the only way he can achieve precise cover is by the use of another, offsetting option.

In the UK 'tender to contract' cover is provided by ECGD. However, ECGD as well as covering losses, also take the profits. Options enable the profits to be kept by the company.

Another example would be a *treasurer* with large hard currency assets who has seen a dramatic increase in the value of those assets when translated into sterling. His financial year end may be some weeks or months away, but the financial effect on his balance sheet at that time and the prevailing exchange rate may make him wish to fix a rate for his overseas assets. This will give him both the benefit of the approximate current levels, and the possibility of disregarding the option and effectively translating his overseas assets into sterling at a more favourable rate, should the exchange rate further shift in his favour.

Yet another example would be a *fund manager* who has, over a period of time, acquired a large portfolio in the United States, and is now considering whether to retain or dispose of the holding. Having gone out of sterling into dollars at above $2.00 to the pound, he is now facing a substantial net gain both in his individual dollar securities and in his currency translation. He does not wish to lose the advantage of this currency gain, but at the same time does not yet wish to dispose of his US holding. By purchasing a call option on a declaration date sufficiently far forward to cover his possible disposable date, he has isolated and locked in the currency gain and can judge the US securities entirely on their own merit.

Again, take the example of a *foreign travel operator* who is required to print and publish his prospectus for sales for summer 1985 during the early autumn of 1984. To be able to quote his foreign holidays at fixed prices in sterling, he is forced into the position of having to take a view on the probable exchange rate for mid-1985. If he takes forward cover outright in the forward market against his probable sterling cash flows, he runs the risk that one of his competitors may take a more speculative view and take no action. If the exchange rate subsequently declines, his competitor will be strongly advantaged and will be in a position to undercut his prices.

Table 3.2

Comparisons of Options Market, Forward Market and Futures Market

	Options	*Forward*	*Futures*
Nature of transaction	Buyer of a call (put) has the right to take (make) delivery if he so desires. Seller has contractual obligation	Contractual obligation for buyer and seller	Contractual obligation for buyer and seller
Size of contract	Standardized	Determined in each transaction	Standardized
Delivery date	Expiration date standardized, but can deliver at any time before expiration	Determined in each transaction	Standardized
Method of transaction	Open auction market at a registered securities exchange	Direct contact between buyer and seller by telephone or telex	Open auction market at a registered commodities exchange
Issuer and guarantor	The Options Clearing Corporation	None	Exchange clearing-house
Participants	Approved PHLX participating organizations and public customers through accounts carried by such organizations	Primarily a corporate and institutional market	Member organizations of a registered commodities exchange and public customers through accounts carried by such organisations
Security deposits	Buyer pays premium only. Seller margined based on daily mark to market	None, but established relationship with bank and credit line must exist	Set amounts for original margin with daily mark to market for maintenance

Source: Philadelphia Stock Exchange

By covering the requisite amount of foreign exchange through the medium of an option, the travel operator protects himself against any major move in the currency rate in an unfavourable direction, and also eliminates the risk of an over-optimistic forecast from his marketing department, resulting in an over-exposure in the foreign exchange market.

Whenever a supplier makes an offer to a prospective customer in ordinary trading the company is exposed. All currency price lists come into this category and can be covered with options.

The common theme in all these examples is that a currency risk is incurred which is contingent in nature; cover is required which is similarly contingent in nature, i.e. there if required but not otherwise.

Table 3.2 illustrates the similarities and differences between currency options forwards and futures.

Figure 3.2 illustrates how a US company needing to pay Japanese yen can use currency options. If the yen rises the company exercises the option and gains. If the yen falls the company does not exercise the option and buys the yen at the future spot rate, again gaining. If the yen remains the same the company loses the cost of the option. So the company is hedged against losses but is also able to take advantage of the exchange rate moving in its favour.

It is useful to compare this with a forward transaction. Assume that the company buys the yen forward at the rate of 240. It arranges to pay $10 million for 2.4 billion yen. If the rate at maturity of the contract is 240 yen the company has neither won nor lost. If the dollar rises to 260 yen, the company is still obligated to buy the yen at 240 and forgoes any gain it would have enjoyed. At 260 yen on the spot market the company would have had to spend only $9.23 million to buy its 2.4 billion yen, so the forward contract cost it an extra $770,000. But if the dollar drops to 220, it would have had to pay $10.91 million for the 2.4 billion yen on the spot market. The forward contract has protected it against a $910,000 loss. The company is hedged against losses but does not benefit from the future spot rate moving in its favour.

As is illustrated in Figure 3.2, if the future spot rate is 240 and the company has taken out an option the premium paid becomes a cost of the transaction above what the forward contract would have cost. But if the exchange rate is 260 after the three months, then the company could let its options contract expire unexercised and lose the $200,000 premium, then buy the 2.4 billion yen for $9.23 million, a big saving. If the dollar has fallen to 220 yen, though, the company exercises the contract at the more advantageous 240 rate. The maximum sum at risk at all times is the premium. With the forward exchange contract maximum losses are eliminated but so are maximum gains. Naturally, if the premium costs more than the difference between the locked in options rate and the future spot rate then an overall loss is incurred.

The advantages of options over forwards are summarised in Figure 3.2

Fig 3.2 Hedging Against Exchange Rate Fluctuations Using Options

A hypothetical example of an American manufacturer making a purchase paid for in Japanese yen.

An American manufactuer purchases Japanese goods worth $10 million at the current exchange rate of 240 yen per dollar. The manufacturer knows that when the bill for the goods comes due in three months he will owe the Japanese company 2.4 billion yen no matter what happens to the yen-dollar exchange rate.

The American buys a foreign currency option – which gives him the right, but not the obligation – to buy 2.4 billion yen at 240 yen per dollar. The option carries a premium, or cost, of $200,000.

If the Yen Rises

- After the three months the yen rises to 220 yen per dollar.
- Since the dollar buys fewer yen the American company must pay almost $10.9 million to purchase 2.4 billion yen.
- The American company excercises the option and purchases the necessary 2.4 billion yen at 240 yen per dollar.
- Savings: about $700,000 (the $900,000 in added cost because of the higher yen exchange rate, less the $200,000 cost of the option).

The Yen is Stable

- After three months the yen stays at 240 yen per dollar, then the American company's purchase price stays at $10 million.
- The manufacturer allows the option to expire unexercised.
- The cost of the transaction is increased by the $200,000 cost of the foreign currency option.

If the Yen Falls

- After three months the yen falls to 260 per dollar.
- Since the dollar buys more yen, the American company can now buy 2.4 billion yen for about $9.2 million.
- The Americans buy the yen at the more advantages rate in the spot market.
- Savings: about $600,000 (the $800,000 savings in the purchase price less the $200,000 cost of the option).

Source: J. Sterngold, *New York Times* August 2 1984.

THE ADVANTAGES OF CURRENCY OPTIONS COMPARED WITH FORWARD MARKETS

(1) Where cash flow is hedged by a forward contract, the company achieves protection against adverse currency movements, i.e. the downside risk is eliminated. Unfortunately, this method also eliminates any upside potential that otherwise would have accrued to the company if exchange rates had moved in its favour.

By contrast, a principal advantage of an option is that it provides protection against downside risk in the same way as a forward contract, but since there is no obligation to exercise the option, the upside potential is retained.

(2) The option buyer knows at the outset what his 'worst case' will be; having paid the premium no further expense is payable. When the main objective is simply to limit downside risk, this is a powerful advantage. In many commercial applications, the option premium can be built in to the pricing process, thus fixing minimum profit margins.

(3) Since there is no obligation to exercise an option, options are ideal for hedging contingent cash flows which may or may not materialise, such as in tenders.

(4) Options may be used as a 'ratchet' to lock up profit to date on a currency position while retaining any remaining upside potential.

FOREIGN EXCHANGE CONTROLS

In order to prevent currency speculation and to protect their reserves, many ·countries impose foreign exchange controls. These controls are designed to limit an individual's ability to freely convert one currency into another currency. Normally, there has to be proof of an underlying economic transaction, i.e. exporting or importing, before permission to exchange the currencies is given. Details of different types of foreign exchange controls can be found in the *Annual Reports on Exchange Restrictions*, published by the IMF.

In exchange control-free countries, there are no regulations for resident firms concerning forward dealings and they may undertake forward exchange commitments whenever and wherever they desire. Where there are exchange control systems, three types of restrictions generally apply. First, contracts are restricted to legitimate commercial transactions evidenced by appropriate documentation. Secondly, contracts must be concluded with local 'authorised' banks. Thirdly, the final terms of any such contract is also limited, usually to match the existing limits on export or import credit terms. This is to control what is called 'leading' and 'lagging' (see Chapter 7).

Chapter 4
The International Monetary System 1945 – Present

WHAT IS INTERNATIONAL LIQUIDITY?

In order to understand the current nature of the international monetary system it is essential to grasp the concept of international liquidity. By international liquidity is meant the stock of internationally acceptable assets available for the settlement of debts between individuals, corporate bodies and trading nations. These international assets can take various forms, the qualifications for continuous use being that they be liquid, easily transferable, readily acceptable and that they have a stable and predictable value. International liquidity, like national money, serves at least three potential functions: it is a medium of exchange, a unit of account, and a store of value. Individuals and corporate bodies are likely to hold international money to finance trade, for investment and for speculative purposes. Central banks' demand for reserves are likely to be motivated by two conceptually separable forces, a desire to defend the value of their currency on the foreign exchange market and a precaution against the possibility that they will have to finance a balance of payments deficit. Private demand for international liquidity stems from transaction and speculative motives while central banks' demands from precautionary motives.

Historically international monies have taken three broad forms: commodity money, fiat money and credit money. In the context of international trading relations gold has been the principal form of commodity money. Commodity monies were used, both domestically and internationally, and among these commodities precious metals, and particularly gold, acquired pre-eminence and eventually drove out competitors. Gold, as a relatively scarce precious metal, was acceptable in international transactions because it fulfilled the function of a medium of exchange and store of value. Over time, however, with a continuous expansion in world trade and a shortfall in gold supplies, the need to economise on existing gold stocks became increasingly apparent. Despite the obvious advantages of paper money (cheaper to produce, more convenient to hold in cash form, etc.) international trust was not sufficient to accept it on its own. Money that has intrinsic value because it is made of a precious metal can be contrasted with fiat money which has value because the public has 'faith' that it will be accepted as legal tender. It was quickly realised that the advantages of fiat money could be reaped if it were backed by something with intrinsic value. Consequently, fiat money backed by gold came to be used in international transactions. The countries whose currencies were used were those which were important trading nations, had a stock of gold with which to back their currency, and were prepared to run balance of payments deficits in order to supply the rest of the world with such liquidity. Thus, prior to the Second World War, the pound sterling was the principal form of fiat money, whereas since the Second World War the US dollar has dominated international monetary relations.

Increasing sophistication of, and confidence in, the domestic economy usually results in an increasing dependence on credit money. This is also the case with the international economy. Thus, over the past decade there have been increased attempts to develop a form of credit money as a further attempt to economise on the use of national currencies. This development has been particularly evident in attempts to increase the role of Special Drawing Rights.

International reserves are conventionally defined as official holdings of gold, foreign exchange, and International Monetary Fund-related assets. Apart from gold, these reserves are made up of currencies suitable for intervention in the foreign exchange market and for direct payment of foreign obligations and of financial assets that can be converted into such currencies on short notice at a generally moderate risk of loss.

In understanding developments in international liquidity it is necessary to first understand the role and importance of the International Monetary Fund as a supplier of international liquidity. We then move on to discuss other sources of international liquidity, foreign exchange, central bank gold holdings and Special Drawing Rights.

ROLE OF THE INTERNATIONAL MONETARY FUND

The International Monetary Fund originated from the overall economic mistakes in the 1930s. The combination of worldwide depression and rising unemployment induced many countries to protect their domestic industries by trade barriers which ultimately made the depression even worse.

With this background representatives of the Allies met at Bretton Woods in 1944 in order to plan the international monetary and trade environment. A forum for collaboration was thereby created. One of the major fears at the time was that the currency instability and competitive depreciation of the 1930s would recur and there was a widespread desire to stabilise exchange rates. Fixed exchange rates were introduced with countries agreeing to fix their rates to the US dollar and the US dollar in turn being fixed against gold.

In recent years this fixity of exchange rates has been modified with countries now free to choose the exchange rate which they feel is most desirable.

When a country joins the Fund, it is assigned a quota that fits into the structure of existing quotas considered in the light of the member's economic characteristics relative to those of other members of comparable size. The size of the member's quota determines, among other things, the member's voting power, the size of its potential access to Fund resources, and its share in allocations of SDRs. Quotas are reviewed at intervals of not more than five years to take account of changes in the relative economic positions of members and the growth of the world economy. Initial subscriptions, and subscriptions associated with increases in quotas, are paid mainly in the member's own currency, and a small portion, not exceeding 25%, in reserve assets (SDRs or other members' currencies that are acceptable to the Fund).

The principal way in which the Fund makes its resources available to members is by selling to them the currencies of other members or SDRs in exchange for their own currencies. A member to which the Fund sells currencies or SDRs is said to make 'purchases' (also referred to as 'drawings') from the Fund. The purpose of making the Fund's resources available to members is to meet balance of payments needs.

As already mentioned the quota provides the basis upon which voting rights and drawing rights are assessed. Each member pays a subscription to the Fund equal to the value of its quota; 25% of this was originally paid in gold, the remaining 75% in the country's own currency. With effect from the ratification of the Second Amendment to the IMF's Articles of Agreement, in 1978, members were no longer required to pay gold to the Fund in connection with any transaction or operation. The IMF therefore acquires stocks of currencies from its members which can subsequently be lent to nations facing balance of payments difficulties. Any country facing payments difficulties can borrow an amount of foreign currency from the Fund up to the value of its quota. The loan (plus service charges) is repaid over a specified time period (three to five years). The use of the Fund positions forms a relatively small percentage of total reserves.

In addition to these automatic drawing rights any member can further draw on its credit tranche. Here the member can borrow up to 125% of its quota in five slices or 'tranches'. The first drawing (the 'reserve tranche') is unconditional. The remaining four tranches are, however, conditional, the conditions imposed becoming more stringent with each successive drawing. Because of the conditionality element these are not usually included in calculations of countries' foreign exchange reserves. A country's ability to draw on the IMF depends on the IMF's holdings of the drawing country's own currency.

In addition to the reserve and credit 'tranches' other borrowing facilities are available to IMF members. First there is the Compensatory Financing Facility which was devised for countries which for various reasons, such as the weather, suffered temporary set backs in their export earnings. Secondly there is the 'Extended Fund Facility' which was established to assist countries with longer term structural economic problems. Thirdly there is the 'Trust Fund' which uses funds obtained from profits from the IMF's gold sales programme.

Fourthly there is the 'Supplementary Financing Facility' also called the 'Witteveen Facility' which is designed to help members to cope with balance of payments problems caused by the rising oil price. Finally there is the 'buffer stock facility' which provides loans for countries to finance commodity stocks.

The compensatory financing facility, which was established in February 1963, is to assist members, particularly primary producing countries, experiencing balance of payments difficulties attributable to shortfalls in earnings from merchandise exports and invisibles that are both temporary and due largely to factors beyond their control. In May 1981, the Fund decided to extend financial assistance to members facing balance of payments difficulties produced by an excess in the cost of their cereal imports. This assistance was integrated with assistance available under the compensatory financing facility in respect of temporary shortfalls in export receipts.

The buffer stock financing facility, which was established in June 1969, is to provide assistance to members with a balance of payments need related to their participation in arrangements to finance approved international buffer stocks of primary products.

The extended facility, which was established in September 1974, is to make resources available for longer periods and in larger amounts than under the credit tranche policies, to members that are experiencing balance of payments difficulties owing to structural imbalances in production, trade, and prices, or that are unable to pursue active development policies because of their weak balance of payments positions.

The oil facilities, which were set up in June 1974 and April 1975, were to assist members with balance of payments difficulties due to the rise in oil prices.

The supplementary financing facility was established in February 1979 to provide assistance to members facing payments difficulties that are large in relation to their economies and their Fund quotas.

FOREIGN EXCHANGE AS A COMPONENT OF INTERNATIONAL LIQUIDITY

Foreign exchange includes monetary authorities' claims on foreigners in the form of bank deposits, treasury bills, short-term and long-term government securities, and other claims usable in the event of a balance of payments deficit.

When currencies like sterling and dollar act as international money they are often referred to as reserve currencies. The motivation for their increasing use is fairly well known. They are less costly to produce than gold, they are more convenient to hold for foreign exchange intervention purposes, they are easier to acquire, and they usually yield income in the form of interest payments.

The mechanism for creating convertible currency reserves differs from that for gold. With gold it is necessary to rely on increased production from South Africa or sales to the West from the USSR. With convertible currency reserves it is necessary to rely primarily on the key currency countries running balance of payments deficits. In other words, the rest of the world runs a balance of payments surplus with the key currency countries by selling them goods and services in exchange for stocks of their currencies which, because of their international acceptability, can then be used as reserves.

Between 1938 and 1949 the United States economic power was rapidly leading to the US dollar replacing the pound sterling as the world's premier currency. (See Fig. 4.1.)

Fig. 4.1 Share of World Trade

Source: IMF

The post-war dominance of the dollar combined with the overall acceptance of fixed exchange rates ultimately led to the dollar collapse in 1971. As US liabilities increased, by 1964 (See Fig. 4.2), they were greater than US assets. The process of stimulating the US economy and financing the Vietnam War had greatly expanded the number of overseas dollar holders.

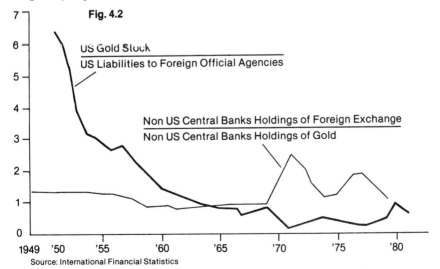

Fig. 4.2

US Gold Stock
US Liabilities to Foreign Official Agencies

Non US Central Banks Holdings of Foreign Exchange
Non US Central Banks Holdings of Gold

Source: International Financial Statistics

The dollar was devalued in 1971 and has moved up and down in value considerably since then. It has, however, retained its role as the world's dominant currency. This is largely due to the liquidity of dollar denominated paper based on the lack of US exchange controls and on the depth of US financial markets. The dominance of the dollar in official reserves can be seen from Table 4.1. In addition the reduction in the importance of sterling is also highlighted.

CENTRAL BANK GOLD HOLDINGS*

The use of gold as a monetary unit is long lived. Following the demise of the international gold standard which had been adopted prior to the First World War the role of gold in international monetary relations went into secular decline. Gold's role at the Bretton Woods Conference (1944), however, was reasserted despite Lord Keynes' protestations about the metal being a 'barbarous relic'. Throughout the 1950s and early '60s, gold's role declined. However, the late '60s and particularly the late '70s saw a great resurgence in the importance of gold. Following the adoption of the basket measurement of the SDR (see Table 4.2) gold ceased to have any relevance as a unit of account; a state of affairs underscored, in 1976, by the abandonment of the official gold price. Gold remains a reserve asset but its price is allowed to fluctuate with the pressure of the free market supply and demand. Central banks are no longer prevented from buying or selling the metal on the open market.

SPECIAL DRAWING RIGHTS (SDRs)

The late 1960s were characterised by increasing uncertainty as to how future increases in the demand for international reserves could be satisfied. It was against this background that the International Monetary Fund decided to create a new international reserve asset. The supply of, and confidence in, this new asset would be independent of any one country's domestic economic policies. The new type of reserve asset which was created to help improve the functioning of the international payments system was the Special Drawing Right (SDR), and came into existence in 1970. SDRs were created as book-keeping entries and were essentially given to all IMF member countries electing to receive them. These bookkeeping entries were designed to be transferred directly between central banks in settlement of balance of payments deficits, with the IMF originally guaranteeing their value in terms of a fixed amount of gold. Actual holders of SDRs have included only the central banks and Treasuries of IMF member countries which have agreed to accept them and the IMF itself.

---

* These are discussed in detail in *Gold* Brian Kettell (Graham and Trotman, 1982).

Table 4.1

Share of National Currencies in Total Identified Official Holdings of Foreign Exchange, End of Selected Years 1973–83*

(In per cent)

	1976	1977	1978	1979	1980	1981	1982	1983	Memorandum: 1983 ECUs treated separately†
All countries									
US dollar	76.5	77.9	75.6	72.8	66.7	69.4	68.5	69.1	58.8
Pound sterling	1.8	1.7	1.7	2.0	3.0	2.2	2.5	2.6	2.4
Deutschmark	9.0	9.2	11.0	12.6	15.1	13.2	12.5	11.9	10.6
French franc	1.6	1.3	1.2	1.4	1.7	1.4	1.4	1.2	1.0
Swiss franc	2.3	2.4	2.3	2.7	3.2	2.8	2.7	2.4	2.2
Netherlands guilder	0.9	0.9	0.9	1.1	1.3	1.2	1.0	0.8	0.7
Japanese yen	2.0	2.3	3.2	3.5	4.2	4.1	4.2	4.2	3.8
Unspecified currencies	5.9	4.3	4.2	4.0	4.8	5.7	7.2	7.8	20.5
	100.0	100.0	100.0	100.0	100.0	100.0	100.0	100.0	100.0

Sources: Various Fund publications and Fund staff estimates.

* The detail in each of the columns may not add to 100 because of rounding. Starting with 1979, the SDR value of European currency units (ECUs) issued against US dollars is added to the SDR value of US dollars, but the SDR value of ECUs issued against gold is excluded from the total distributed here.

† This column is for comparison and indicates the currency composition of reserves when holdings of ECUs are treated as a separate reserve asset, unlike the earlier columns starting with 1979 as is explained in the preceding footnote. The share of ECUs, amounting to 13.5% for the total and 25.0% for the industrial countries, respectively, has been added to that of unspecified currencies.

Table 4.2

SDR Basket of Currencies Payments

	July 1 1974		*July 1 1978*		*January 1† 1981*
	Units of currency included	Weight %	Units of currency included	Weight %	Weight %
US $	0.40	33.0	0.40	33.0	42
Deutschmark	0.38	12.5	0.32	12.5	19
£ sterling	0.045	9.0	0.05	7.5	13
French franc	0.44	7.5	0.42	7.5	13
Japanese yen	26.0	7.5	21.0	7.5	13
Dutch guilder	0.14	4.5	0.14	5.0	—
Italian lira	47.0	6.0	52.0	5.0	—
Canadian $	0.071	6.0	0.07	5.0	—
Belgian franc	1.60	3.5	1.60	4.0	—
Saudi riyal	—	—	0.13	3.0	—
Swedish krona	0.13	2.5	0.11	2.0	—
Iranian rial	—	—	1.70	2.0	—
Spanish peseta	1.10	1.5	1.50	1.5	—
Austrian schilling	0.22	1.0	0.28	1.5	—
Norwegian krone	0.099	1.5	0.10	1.5	—
Australian $	0.012	1.5	0.017	1.5	—
Danish krone	0.11	1.5	—	—	—
South African rand	0.0082	1.0	—	—	—

Source: IMF

† Units of currency unchanged since July 1 1976.

The SDR was valued at the par value of the US dollar, i.e. SDR 1 = US dollar 1 until November 1971, SDR 1 = US dollar 1.08571 from December 1971 until January 1973, and SDR 1 = US dollar 1.20635 from February 1973 to June 1974. At the beginning of July 1974, the value of the SDR was determined daily by the Fund on the basis of a basket of currencies with each currency assigned a weight in the determination of that value. In the derivation of the SDR value, the currencies of the basket are valued at their market exchange rates for the US dollar and the US dollar equivalents of each of the currencies are totalled to yield the rate of the SDR in terms of the US dollar. The method of calculating the US dollar/SDR exchange rate remains the same, although the number and weights of currencies in the SDR basket have changed over time.

At the beginning of January 1 1981, the SDR valuation basket consisted of the currencies of the five members having the largest exports of goods and services during the period 1975 to 1979, i.e. the US dollar, Deutschmark, French franc, Japanese yen, and pound sterling. The weights for the five currencies (US dollar 42%, Deutschmark 19%, French franc, Japanese yen and pound sterling 13% each) broadly reflect the relative importance of these currencies in international trade and finance, based on the value of the exports of goods and services of their members issuing these currencies and the balances of their currencies officially held by members of the Fund over the five year period 1975–79. The weights remain the same today.

THE BREAKDOWN OF THE BRETTON WOODS SYSTEM

The Bretton Woods agreements were intended to construct an international monetary system conducive to the growth of world trade and to growing international prosperity. To be efficient in this way the Bretton Woods system required three things: first, provision for the appropriate amount and growth of international *'liquidity'* (i.e. reserves of gold and foreign exchange), since countries needed reserves to stabilise their exchange rates against short-run fluctuations; secondly, a high degree of *confidence* in the arrangements made, to prevent destabilising speculative capital movements; and thirdly, an effective *adjustment* mechanism to remedy long-run balance of payments deficits and surpluses without countries being forced to adopt policies such as trade controls or domestic deflation which would be injurious to the growth of world trade and prosperity.

1. The liquidity problem

Countries' rights to draw on the IMF were initially small and though quotas were subsequently increased they made only a small contribution to international liquidity. The addition to countries' reserves of gold was determined by the amount of new gold produced less the (additional) demand for gold to be used industrially or held privately for speculative purposes; it was essentially arbitrary, and small. Significant growth in world reserves could therefore come only from increased holdings of 'reserve currencies' – held by the central banks of other countries. Because of the increasing weakness of the UK economy and recurrent fears of sterling devaluations, holdings of sterling made only a small contribution to the growth of world reserves. So the major source of new liquidity was increased holdings of dollars.

During the 1960s there were growing doubts about the system's role in the creation of international liquidity which, as already discussed, had come to depend upon the US deficit channelling dollars into other countries' reserves. In 1964 dollar liabilities of the US to foreign official institutions exceeded US gold holdings for the first time. As long as US balance of payments continued, a run on the US gold reserves became possible. The Vietnam War increased external holdings of US dollars thereby raising the possibility of this run. The obverse of the 'liquidity' problem was the 'confidence' problem.

2. The confidence problem

One aspect of what was called the 'confidence problem' in the Bretton Woods system was that, with a system of fixed but adjustable exchange rates, speculation on exchange rate changes was a one-way gamble: if speculators moved their funds out of sterling in anticipation of a devaluation either they would make a profit, if devaluation did take place, or they would not make a loss, if it did not. A second, and ultimately more important, aspect of the problem was the co-existence of gold and the dollar as reserve assets. The system, as already discussed, depended on US balance of payments deficits for the growth of international liquidity but these deficits necessarily involved a decline in the gold backing of US dollar liabilities which could eventually lead to a decline in confidence in the dollar.

The large overall US balance of payments deficit slowly undermined confidence in the dollar. This highlighted the problem of how balance of payments adjustment was to be achieved when the key currency itself was weak. If the link between the key currency and gold was to be maintained, essential if the dollar's role was to continue, other countries would have to revalue against the dollar. They were unwilling to do this. The question of how countries were to alter their exchange rates became known as the 'adjustment problem'.

3. The adjustment problem

The failure to define 'fundamental disequilibrium' combined with US desire to maintain the strength of the dollar meant that countries with balance of payments deficits could not easily devalue and adjustment had to take place via deflationary fiscal and monetary policies. With surplus countries simply accumulating reserves, the pressure for adjustment was on deficit countries. The US was not subject to the same pressures as other countries as when it had a balance of payments deficit it was not losing gold and foreign exchange reserves as other countries were but simply increasing the amount of dollar liabilities held by other countries.

A persisting lack of confidence in the dollar finally precipitated the suspension of dollar convertibility in August 1971. In effect, this removed the cornerstone of the system and all the major currencies then floated for the first time since the 1930s, with most of them appreciating quite sharply in terms of the dollar. This episode concluded with the Smithsonian realignment of December 1971, which represented a final attempt to reverse the generalised trend towards floating. It incorporated a 10% devaluation of the dollar, and a consequent appreciation of other currencies, via an increase in the official price of gold (to US $ 38 an ounce). But a significant step towards greater flexibility was made by the wider (2¼%) margins of fluctuation permitted around the newly-set central rates. However, in an international economic environment characterised by widening inflation differentials and increased capital flows, the initiative failed when Britain, for one, decided not to maintain the value of sterling at its new level. In June 1972, the pound was allowed to float downwards. This, together with the more general adoption of floating following exchange rate problems early in 1973, marked the beginning of a new era of international monetary arrangements in which individual countries chose the exchange rate policies thought most appropriate to their domestic economic objectives from the variety of options available.

THE IMPACT OF OPEC ON THE INTERNATIONAL MONETARY SYSTEM

The activities of the Organisation of Petroleum Exporting Countries (OPEC) may be divided into five phases:

(i) The exploits of a widely dispersed group of countries to seize the opportunities given by the Yom Kippur war of 1973 to more than quadruple the price of crude oil from US $2.20 a barrel in October 1973 to US $9.84 a barrel in October 1974.

(ii) The period of hostility in the consuming countries, against the background that OPEC was a cartel and like all cartels was inherently unstable and would eventually disappear. There was, of course, another view that oil is an exhaustible resource and the price should be used to alert us to the need to conserve it.

(iii) The general acceptance by the industrialised countries that OPEC, and in particular Saudi Arabia, was a new force of world importance and that their new found wealth provided great opportunities for the exports of the industrialised countries and further that some OPEC member states, with small populations (called low absorbers) had accumulated vast current account surpluses which could be recycled – generally through the financial institutions of the industrialised countries – to borrowing countries, and in particular to the countries of the Third World. The acceleration of exports to the OPEC countries resulted in an OPEC balance of payments surplus being converted into a deficit.

(iv) The late 1979 early period was characterised by a further doubling of the oil price. The OPEC surplus rose to $114 billion in 1980 necessitating further recycling.

(v) The early 1983 phase until the present starting with the downturn in the price of oil and the consequential dent in the confidence of the weaker members of OPEC due to the oil glut. This is further exacerbated by the fact that for the first time in decades the non-OPEC oil exporters are producing more oil than the 13-member nations of OPEC. In addition OPEC is now in overall current account deficit.

In 1973, the world was rudely awakened to the fact that one of the main pillars of its economic structure, low cost energy from petroleum, was under attack. The supply of such energy was no longer secure, and its price has been high ever since, following the realisation that the monopoly power possessed by the Organisation for Petroleum Exporting Countries (OPEC) could be exploited.

What has happened is that OPEC has in effect levied a tax on oil-consuming countries. After spending some of the revenues for imports of goods and services, the OPEC nations put the surplus into foreign assets that they find attractive. In the aggregate the process appears to be automatic; the countries in surplus have no alternative to the purchase of claims on other countries. The rub is that the types and locations of claims are chosen by the oil producers, and most of the countries that pay the oil tax do not attract any OPEC investments directly. These countries – or entities in these countries – have to go out in the international capital market and borrow to cover their deficits.

For these borrowing countries, recycling is not automatic at all. It is an eventually painful process of piling up debts just to cover the higher cost of the same quantity of imported oil – debts that allow their economies to keep going but do not, in the absence of other adjustments, create new productive capabilities out of which the debts can be serviced in the years ahead. As discussed below, the burden of debt incurred by developing countries has become increasingly onerous.

Countries that attract OPEC investments – the stronger industrial countries in general and the UK in particular – wind up in effect as financial intermediaries. The countries themselves, or private institutions within them, take on the risks involved, for which they are paid through lending margins charged. Some of this intermediation takes the form of increased bilateral and multilateral official financing, but most of the increased financing required in the 1970s came from US and from foreign commercial banks that, in turn, added to their short-term liabilities to members of OPEC.

The oil shock of 1973–1974 came at a time of unsustainable world-wide demand pressures, an acute inflation problem (even apart from the escalation of oil prices) widespread speculation in commodities, and a build-up of inventories. Moreover, the international monetary system was going through an uneasy transition from the apparent stability of the Bretton Woods framework to a set of arrangements on which agreement had not yet been reached.

The effect on this fragile situation of the jump in oil prices – from $2.20 per barrel in June 1973 to $9.38 in June 1974 – was devastating. Economic activity slumped severely in 1974 and 1975, especially in the United States. In fact, gross national product (GNP) growth rates have never recovered to the average rate of over 5% achieved in industrial countries in the 1963–1973 period. Inflation rates rose from an already high average 8% rate in industrial countries in 1973 to the double digit range in 1974. The OPEC surplus jumped from $8 billion in 1973 to $70 billion in 1974 while the current account balance of nations in the Organisation for Economic Cooperation and Development (OECD) shifted from plus $10 billion to minus $27 billion, and the non-oil developing countries saw their deficit rise from $7 billion to $24 billion. Tables 4.3, 4.4, 4.5 and 4.6 illustrate the impact of the way different countries and the banking system reacted to the effect of OPEC.

Rising OPEC imports coupled with the declining real price of oil produced a fairly rapid reduction in the OPEC surplus. In fact, the OPEC surplus faded away much faster than many observers in 1974 thought possible. After the 1974 bulge, the surplus was in the $30–$40 billion range in 1975–77, and it dropped to less than $11 billion in 1978. The peak pressure on the external balance of the non-oil developing countries was in 1975, when they had a combined deficit of $32 billion. In the period 1976–78, their annual deficits averaged $20 billion – about 2.5% of their GNP and close to the average relationship prevailing before 1973. Industrial countries' current-account balances in the aggregate tended to vary with the cyclical situation – improving in 1975, registering moderate deficits in 1976 and 1977, and then moving into surplus in 1978. Within the total OECD, however, the US position deteriorated sharply with a cyclical upturn after 1976. Large US trade and current-account deficits in 1977 and 1978 helped to generate recurrent bouts of downward pressure on the dollar.

As the OPEC surplus declined, and the combined deficit of the non-oil developing countries stabilised, the financial stresses associated with the recycling problem seemed to ease. It also turned out that the international banking system was far more elastic than had been thought. The net size of the Eurocurrency market, through which much of the intermediation takes place, grew from $160 billion in 1973 to $970 billion by June 1983.

During the early part of the 1970s, the pressure on oil prices came mainly from the demand side, reflecting more than two decades of falling relative oil prices. Even after the 1973–74 quadrupling of oil prices many industrial countries, particularly the United States, failed to adjust effectively so that demand continued to be the major influence on oil prices. However, rising oil production from new areas (primarily the North Sea, Mexico and Alaska) kept the rate of oil price increases in nominal terms quite moderate during 1974–78. In fact they declined by 20% in real terms. It was not until the second shock in the wake of the 1979 Iranian revolution, which resulted in a doubling of real oil prices, that a more fundamental adjustment in oil demand took place.

This development is now known as the second oil shock. The average official OPEC export price for crude oil rose by 140% between the end of 1978 and the middle of 1980 (see Figure 4.3). The Organisation for Economic cooperation and Development has estimated that the rate of increase in consumer prices is about five percentage points higher in the twenty-four OECD member countries in 1980 than it would have been in the absence of the oil price increases.

The important difference between this oil shock and the original oil shock is that money supply targets were almost universally adopted by the industrial countries between 1975 and 1978. Since the original increase in oil prices, in order to reduce inflation and/or inflationary expectations, targets had been maintained, or in some cases tightened. With intensified inflationary pressures, this inevitably led to higher interest rates. Naturally, this fed through into the foreign exchange market, with those countries adhering to their targets, receiving capital inflows, and thereby having stronger exchange rates (and vice versa).

Fig. 4.3 Change in Oil Barrel Price

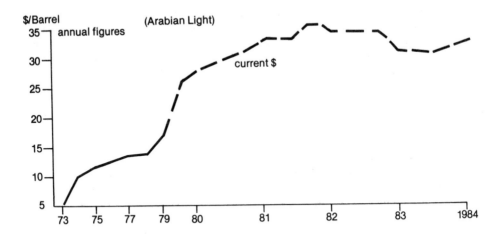

THE PRIVATISATION OF THE CREATION OF NEW INTERNATIONAL LIQUIDITY *

Increases in international liquidity have become increasingly dependent on the private sector banking system. So official organisations like the IMF, have been supplemented by the international capital markets as the primary sources of international liquidity. This is particularly true for less developed countries.

Lending through the international credit (Capital) markets comes in three principal forms: (1) suppliers' credits, (2) bond issues, and (3) bank credits.

1. Suppliers' credits occur when the manufacturer sells on deferred payments terms, borrowing from the home country bank to finance the period from shipment of the goods until payment is received. Official export credit agencies will often insure the exporter and, in many cases, additionally give a guarantee direct to the bank.

2. Bond issues represent fixed-term debt obligations issued by borrowers whose nationality is different from the country of the capital market in which an issue is made, and come in two varieties: (i) 'foreign' bonds, which are issued in a single national market, and (ii) 'Eurobonds', which are underwritten and sold in more than one market simultaneously. Foreign bonds and Eurobonds may be either 'publicly offered' (i.e. offered for sale to investors at large), or 'privately placed', and their maturities

---

* The ideas in this section are more fully developed in *The International Debt Game*, B. Kettell and G. Magnus. (Graham and Trotman, 1985)

tend to be relatively long-term – usually more than three to five years, frequently as long as 10 to 15 years.
3.   Bank credits consist of loans and lines of credit granted by banks to non-residents, either out of funds borrowed in the Eurocurrency market (Eurocurrency credits), or from domestic currency resources (domestic currency credits).

Until the 1970s, banks' involvement with LDC's was limited to the provision of short-term trade finance facilities, a few term loans to governments extended mainly in conjunction with IMF stabilisation programmes and often with gold as collateral, and a few project-related loans. Most of the finance raised by LDC's was acquired from governments (official development assistance), the World Bank (for economic development projects) and, as necessary, from the IMF (for balance of payments adjustment purposes). As of 1971, less than one-third of LDC debt was owed to banks and much of that took the form of suppliers' credits. In the preceding years, banks financed little more than 7% (on average) of the LDC's net external borrowing (see Table 4.3).

Table 4.3
Financing the Non-Opec LDC's 1968–73 ($bn)

	1968	1969	1970	1971	1972	1973
Current account deficit	6.8	5.9	8.7	11.4	9.2	9.9
Net external borrowing	5.0	3.8	7.1	8.2	10.5	10.2
of which, banks	0.3	0.4	0.4	1.2	2.1	3.7
suppliers credits	0.7	0.8	0.7	0.2	0.3	0.3
other private sources	—	-0.1	0.8	1.2	2.0	0.5
official sources	2.6	2.8	3.1	3.3	3.6	5.1
IMF	0.2	—	-0.4	—	0.4	0.2
short-term*	1.2	-0.1	2.5	2.3	2.1	0.4

*Including errors and omissions

Source: IMF, Annual Reports

In the immediate years before the first oil price shock, it can be seen that the role of banks in lending to LDC's was still rather small though beginning to become more important. Let us look at some of the reasons why banks and LDC's were beginning to form closer financing relationships.

First, during and after the second half of the 1960s, a number of LDC's began to open up their economies to foreign investment and trade and generate rapid economic growth and investment opportunities. To support the dynamism in these economies, governments and the multinational companies to which they played host now began to require increasing amounts of foreign debt.

Secondly, the growth of aid from official sources had begun to slow down and had, in any case, been redirected towards those LDC's with the lowest per capita income and the least flexible economies. As a result, the 'better-off'

LDC's turned to private commercial banks for more trade – and project-related financing. The fact that the gap between commercial and official interest rates was narrowing made commercial borrowing less unattractive and the fact that banks, unlike the IMF, could not impose conditions and could arrange loans rather more quickly made commercial borrowing more appealing.

Thirdly, the rapid growth in international banking and of the eurocurrency market in particular, allowed the supply of loanable funds to rise substantially. More and more banks were becoming active in international lending – around 60 new banks a year started to participate, including, it should be noted, many that had little or no experience in lending to LDC's or managing country risk.

Fourthly, the development and expansion of the syndicated loan market allowed more banks to become involved in lending to LDC's, to spread their risks geographically and to share in the perceived rewards resulting from the strong economic performance of the borrowers.

The banks were not passive agents in the formation of relationships with LDC's. It was part of, a perhaps informal, strategy to grow worldwide, to service their major customers in the developing world and to reap the rewards from an expanding economic environment in which LDC's were playing an increasingly important role. Though it was not the only concern, the drive to increase assets was the prevailing influence in bank strategies in the 1970s.

Lending from the first oil shock to 1981

The first watershed in international lending to LDC's arrived with the first oil price shock in 1973/74, which created a massive imbalance in the international balance of payments. The current account balance of oil exporting countries jumped from $7 billion in 1973 to $68 billion in 1974 and remained between $30 and $40 billion until 1977, while the current account balance of the non-oil LDC's deteriorated from -$11 billion in 1973 to -$37 billion in 1974 and -$46 billion in 1975 (see Table 4.4).

Table 4.4
Current Account Balances 1973–78 ($billion)

	1973	1974	1975	1976	1977	1978	1979	1980	1981
Industrial countries	20	-11	20	1	-2	33	-6	-40	1
Oil exporting countries	7	68	35	40	30	2	69	114	65
Non-oil LDC's	-11	-37	-46	-33	-29	-41	-61	-89	-108
Centrally planned Economics	-2	-2	-9	-7	-3	-5	-3	-4	-4

Source: BIS, OECD, IMF

At the time of the oil shock, there were dire predictions that the world would never be able to live with such large payments imbalances and that a major economic depression was likely since the oil price increases were seen as a sort of tax on the rest of the world that would not be offset by additional spending from the OPEC countries. The IMF and World Bank did not have the resources to lend to the rest of the world and the governments of the industrial countries had neither the willingness nor the ability to take the steps necessary to help the world economy to adjust. Almost by default, international banks took on the job of recycling the surpluses of the OPEC countries to the rest of the world, notably the non-oil producing LDC's.

As it happened, OPEC nations did spend rather more than had been expected and, being for the most part conservative investors, they deposited substantial funds at relatively short maturities in the eurocurrency market. Private financial institutions now found themselves awash with liquidity at a time when there was a large-scale demand for credit on the part of LDC's and when mechanisms existed to intermediate those surplus funds to LDC's. In recent years there have been frequent criticisms that after 1973/74 banks 'overlent' and/or that LDC's 'over borrowed'. Such criticisms are really rather academic and meaningless in the absence of qualification and are made with the benefit of hindsight. There is little question that the banks lacked proper tools and mechanisms for evaluating sovereign government risk and that LDC's borrowed partly, but not exclusively, for the purpose of sustaining consumption. However, had the banks not intermediated the so-called petrodollars in the way they did, LDC's would have been forced to curtail their development programmes sharply and economic activity in industrial countries would have fallen more dramatically and for much longer.

The most important development to be noted in and immediately after the 1973/74 period was the major change in LDC financing between private and official sources. Banks were now the most important players in the game, encouraged in part by the governments of industrial countries which at the very least, did nothing to interfere. Multilateral official institutions, notably the IMF, became in effect the lender of last resort to LDC's if private markets were unwilling to lend or accept the risks involved (see Table 4.5).

Table 4.5
Financing the LDC's[1] in the 1970s

	1971	1976	1978	1980
Total external debt[2] ($bn)	90	220	345	465
– financed by (%):				
Bank loans	12.2	29.1	30.4	33.3
Other private lending	10.0	7.3	8.4	7.6
Total private	22.2	36.4	38.8	40.9
Official sources	26.7	16.8	14.2	12.3
Multilateral sources	11.1	11.8	11.6	12.0
Export credits	30.0	23.2	24.6	24.5
Other[3]	10.0	11.8	10.7	10.3

[1] Including OPEC
[2] External term debt
[3] Includes lending by OPEC countries

Source: OECD, Development CO-operation 1982 Review

In 1979/80, the second oil shock generated new upheavals in the international economic system. The OPEC surplus rose from $2 billion in 1978 to $114 billion in 1980 and remained over $60 billion in 1981, while the non-oil LDC's increased their deficit from $41 billion in 1978 to $108 billion in 1981. This created a renewed major demand for recycling, which banks duly fulfilled but this time, the warnings of more serious problems were gathering. In 1979 Turkey was obliged to renegotiate its foreign debt and the Iranian crisis sent shock waves through the banking system. In both cases, however, the conventional wisdom was that these were isolated incidents and the result of specific domestic political upheavals. In the few years before the debt crisis finally 'broke' bank lending continued at a rapid pace (see Table 4.6).

Table 4.6
Bank Lending to Non-Oil LDC's, 1976–81

	1976	1977	1978	1979	1980	1981
Lending to all non-oil LDC's ($bn)	21	15	25	40	49	50
– as % current account deficit	64	52	61	66	55	46
Increase in bank claims (%)	28.7	14.9	19.3	26.6	26.2	22.2
Share of non-oil LDC's in total net bank lending (%)	30	21	28	32	31	30

Sources: BIS, IMF

There are two important aspects of banks' lending activities in this period which need to be highlighted. The first is the concentration of banks' exposure among a small group of countries. The second is the steady growth in the proportion of short-term debt, i.e. debt that falls due for repayment within 12 months.

From after the first oil price shock to just after the second one, the outstanding bank loans to the major LDC borrowers* grew at an average annual rate of 30%, compared with just over 22% for all LDC's. By 1982, this group accounted for 84% of all debt owed by LDC's to BIS banks. For US banks alone, the group acconted for 88% of LDC bank debt owed to the 9 largest US banks and 90% of the debt owed to all US banks. An increasing proportion of the debt contracted in the last few years was of a short-term character. This was deemed to be less risky than longer-term commitments to which lenders would be 'locked-in', but the rapid growth in short-term debt increased the vulnerability of borrowers to a sudden drop in the willingness of lenders to roll over that debt – an ominous development that occurred in 1982–83 – and it also made it more difficult for banks to extricate themselves from particular debt situations on the grounds that if all lenders withdrew credit lines, they would precipitate the very liquidity crisis they sought to avoid.

* 21 in all, comprising, Argentina, Brazil, Chile, Colombia, Ecuador, Mexico, Peru, Venezuela, Indonesia, Korea, Malaysia, Philippines, Taiwan, Thailand, Algeria, Egypt, Israel, Ivory Coast, Morocco, Algeria, Turkey.

FLOATING EXCHANGE RATES AND THE NEW ROLE OF THE IMF

One of the early purposes of the IMF was to promote foreign exchange market stability thereby avoiding competitive exchange rate depreciations. This policy was to be pursued alongside policies designed to facilitate the growth of world trade, promote high levels of employment and real income, and to reduce balance of payments disequilibria.

Members of the IMF (of which there are now 147) had to intervene in the foreign exchange market to maintain the value of their currencies within 1% of a centrally declared parity. Parity adjustments were only permitted if proof of fundamental disequilibrium could be established. When the fixed exchange rate rule book was thrown out in 1972 and 1973, the IMF found that it could no longer act as referee.

The IMF retained its important function of providing credit to countries that wished to intervene to support their currencies – most notably in the case of the UK in 1976 – and this enabled it to exert some influence over the economic policies of those countries. However, it was not until 1978, when everyone (including the IMF) recognised that there could be no return to the old system, that member countries were able to agree on a new code of conduct. This was enshrined in the Second Amendment of the Articles of Agreement of the IMF.

It gave member countries freedom to choose their exchange rate arrangements, except for a prohibition against maintenance of the value of a currency in terms of gold. At the same time, each country undertakes, under Article IV, 'to collaborate with the Fund and other members to assure orderly exchange arrangements and to promote a stable system of exchange rates', and the Fund is required to engage in continuous surveillance over members' exchange rate policies to ensure that they are consistent with this broad objective. In order to perform this function, the Fund adopted, in April 1977, a set of principles for the guidance of members' exchange rate policies, and principles and procedures for Fund surveillance over these policies, which became the basis for surveillance as soon as the Second Amendment came into force on April 1 1978.

The principles for the guidance of members' exchange rate policies were devised to ensure that each member country follows exchange rate policies that are compatible with its general obligations under Article IV:

A. A member shall avoid manipulating exchange rates or the international monetary system in order to prevent effective balance of payments adjustment or to gain an unfair competitive advantage over other members.
B. A member should intervene in the exchange market if necessary to counter disorderly conditions which may be characterised *inter alia* by disruptive short-term movements in the exchange value of its currency.
C. Members should take into account in their intervention policies the interests of other members, including those of the countries in whose currencies they intervene.

Table 4.7

Exchange Rate Arrangements as of March 31, 1984[1]

			Pegged			
	US dollar	French franc	Other currency	SDR	Other composite
Antigua and	Lao People's	Benin	Bhutan	Burma	Algeria[3]
Barbuda	Democratic Rep.	Cameroon	(Indian	Burundi	Austria
Bahamas[3]	Liberia	Central African	rupee)	Guinea[3]	Bangladesh[3]
Barbados	Libya	Republic	Equatorial	Iran, Islamic	Botswana
Belize	Nicaragua[3]	Chad	Guinea	Rep. of	Cape Verde
Bolivia	Oman	Comoros	(Sp. Pta)	Jordan	China,
Djibouti	Panama	Congo			People's Rep.
			Gambia, The	Kenya[7]	
Dominica	Paraguay	Gabon	(£ stg.)	Rwanda	Cyprus
Dominican	St. Lucia	Ivory Coast	Lesotho	Sao Tomé and	Fiji
Rep[3]	St. Vincent and	Mali	(SAR)	Principe	Finland[7]
Egypt[1]	Grenadines	Niger	Swaziland	Seychelles	Hungary
El Salvador[3]	Sierra Leone	Senegal	(SAR)		Kuwait
Ethiopia	Sudan[3]	Togo		Vanuatu	Madagascar
				Viet Nam	
Grenada	Suriname	Upper Volta			Malawi
Guatemala	Syrian Arab Rep.[3]				Malaysia[7]
Haiti	Trinidad and Tobago				Malta
Honduras	Venezuala				Mauritania
Iraq	Yemen Arab Rep.				Mauritius
					Nepal
	Yemen, People's				
	Democratic Rep.				Norway
					Papua New
					Guinea
					Romania
					Singapore
					Solomon
					Islands
					Sweden
					Tanzania
					Tunisia
					Zambia
					Zimbabwe

No current information is available relating to Democratic Kampuchea. All members whose currencies are pegged to a single currency do so at present within zero fluctuation margin. Members whose currencies are pegged to the SDR or "Other Composite" maintain their exchange rates within zero or very narrow margins, seldom exceeding ± 1% about the peg. Within the "Flexibility Limited" category the "Single Currency" subcategory lists those members that are observed to maintain an exchange arrangement such that their exchange rate fluctuates with a variability equivalent to 2.25% margins with respect to another member's currency. The subclassification "Cooperative Arrangements" lists the countries participating in the European Monetary System (EMS). With the exception of Italy, which maintains margins of 6%, these countries maintain 2.25% margins with respect to their cross rates, based on the central rates expressed in terms of the European Currency Unit (ECU). Members with exchange arrangements listed under the "More Flexible" category are divided on the basis of the extent to which the authorities intervene in the setting of exchange rates. In some instances the exchange rate is allowed to move continuously over time; if the authorities intervene at all they do so only to influence, but not to neutralize, the speed of exchange rate movement; the exchange arrangement is classified as "Independently Floating." Alternatively, the exchange rate may be set for a short interval, usually one day to one week, and the authorities stand ready to buy and sell foreign exchange at the specified rate (the "Managed Floating" group).

Table 4.7 continued.

	Flexibility Limited Against a single currency or group of currencies		More flexible		
Single currency[2]	Cooperative arrangements	Adjusted according to a set of indicators	Other	managed floating	Independently floating
Afghanistan[3]	Belgium[3]	Brazil		Argentina	Australia
Bahrain[4]	Denmark	Chile[3]		Costa Rica[3]	Canada
Ghana	France	Colombia		Ecuador[3][9]	Japan
Guyana	Germany, Fed.	Peru[3]		Greece	Lebanon
Maldives	Republic of	Portugal		Guinea	South Africa
Qatar[4]	Ireland	Somalia[5]		Bissau	
Saudi Arabia[4]	Italy[6]				United Kingdom
				Iceland	United States
Thailand	Luxembourg[3]			India[8]	Uruguay
United Arab Emirates[4]	Netherlands			Indonesia	
				Israel	
				Jamaica	
				Korea	
				Mexico[3]	
				Morocco	
				New Zealand	
				Nigeria	
				Pakistan	
				Philippines	
				Spain	
				Sri Lanka	
				Turkey	
				Uganda[3]	
				Western Samoa	
				Yugoslavia	
				Zaire	

[2] All exchange rates have shown limited flexibility against the US dollar.
[3] Member maintains dual exchange markets involving multiple arrangements. The arrangement shown is that maintained in the major market.
[4] Exchange rates are determined on the basis of a fixed relationship to the SDR within margins of up to ± 7.25%. However, because of the maintenance of a relatively stable relationship with the US dollar, these margins are not always observed.
[5] The exchange rate is maintained with overall margins of ± 7.5% about the fixed shilling/SDR relationship; however; the exchange rate will be re-evaluated when indicative margins of ± 2.25% are exceeded.
[6] Margins of ± 6% are maintained with respect to the currencies of other countries participating in the exchange rate mechanism of the EMS.
[7] The exchange rate is maintained within margins of ± 2.25%.
[8] The exchange rate is maintained within margins of ± 5% on either side of a weighted composite of the currencies of the main trading partners.
[9] Member maintains a system of advance announcement of exchange rates.

Source: IMF

The principles of Fund surveillance over exchange rate policies provide a list, which is not exhaustive, of developments that might indicate the need for discussions between the Fund and a member country. These developments include protracted large-scale intervention in one direction in the exchange market: an unsustainable level of official or quasi-official borrowing or lending for balance of payments purposes; various kinds of restrictions or incentives affecting current transactions or capital flows; abnormal encouragement or discouragement to capital flows through financial policies for balance of payments purposes; and exchange rate behaviour that appears to be unrelated to underlying economic and financial conditions.

When the Second Amendment came into effect all countries were required to notify the Fund of the exchange arrangements that they intended to apply after April 1 1978. They were also required to notify the Fund promptly of any changes in their exchange arrangements. The Exchange Arrangements as of March 31 1984 can be seen in Table 4.7.

Important as the floating currencies are (the principal ones being the US dollar, Japanese yen, Swiss Franc and pound sterling) the fact is that the vast majority of the world's currencies are still pegged in one way or another to one currency or a basket of currencies.

THE CURRENT NATURE OF THE INTERNATIONAL MONETARY SYSTEM

The key feature of the present international monetary system is that it is a form of international *laissez-faire*. First of all, it allows free play to the private market, not just to trade in goods and non-financial services but, above all, to the private capital market. Secondly, it allows free play to governments and their central banks to operate in the market and – if they wish and where they can – to influence and even fix its prices or its quantities. Thus it is a fairly free market where many governments, acting in their own presumed interests and not necessarily taking much account of the interests of other governments, are participants.

Governments are quite free to borrow and lend and to determine their own monetary policies. Above all, they are free to intervene as much or little as they wish in the foreign exchange market. From the point of view of the present discussion this is the most important way in which governments participate in the system. This latter freedom was clearly established in the Jamaica Agreement of January 1976 reached by the Interim Committee of the Board of Governors of the International Monetary Fund (IMF). The Jamaica Agreement in fact ratified the new system that had evolved since early 1973. It provided 'principles for the guidance of members' exchange rate policies' and for 'surveillance' of such policies by the IMF. But, for all practical purposes, countries could do what they liked. The proposed guidance was rather general and no element of compulsion was intended.

In practice, governments and central banks are subject to many constraints, whether constraints of credit-worthiness in the international capital market, ability to control their domestic monetary policies or self-imposed constraints on their exchange rate policies. They may choose to fix their own rates relative to some other currency, relative to a currency basket, or to the value of the Special Drawing Rights (SDRs). But, like the constraints which the members of the European Monetary System (EMS) have imposed on themselves, these are self-imposed and – above all – do not take into account the international system. The essential feature of the present system is thus *decentralisation* and absence of uniform, worldwide rules of any real significance.

In practice the world's trading currency remains the US dollar, largely based on the depth and liquidity of the US government securities market and bank deposit market. The system is increasingly back on a dollar standard. But unlike the 1950s and 1960s, it is within the context of a world of floating exchange rates.

Companies must therefore build in expectations of fluctuating exchange rates into their corporate decision making. Techniques for managing foreign exchange exposure are discussed in Chapters 8 and 9.

Chapter 5
The European Monetary System

THE EMS INTERVENTION SYSTEMS

At its meeting in Bremen in July 1978, the European Council composed of the heads of state and government of the member countries of the European Communities (EC), agreed that closer monetary cooperation between their countries should be promoted through the creation of the European Monetary System (EMS). The system went into operation on March 13 1979. At the same time, the European common margins arrangement (the 'snake') ceased to exist. All EC countries, except the United Kingdom, decided to participate in all aspects of the EMS, in particular the operational heart of the system, the exchange rate mechanism. Greece, which joined the EC in January 1981, is at present not a full member of the EMS. (although the diachma is now a component of the European Currency Unit).

According to the European Council, 'the purpose of the European Monetary System is to establish a greater measure of monetary stability in the Community'.

At the heart of the EMS is a system of fixed but adjustable exchange rates. Each currency has a central rate expressed in terms of the European Currency Unit (ECU). The ECU consists of a basket of fixed amounts of the ten currencies of all EC countries. These central rates determine a grid of bilateral central rates with fluctuation margins of plus or minus 2.25% (6% for the Italian lira). Intervention by the participating central banks to keep the exchange rates of their currencies within the margins is obligatory and unlimited, in principle in EMS currencies.

The ECU is a basket of fixed amounts of EC currencies – for example, it contains 8.78 pence sterling, which accounted on September 18 1984 for some 14.90% of the basket (see Table 5.1). The amounts of each currency in the basket are changed by agreement of the Council of Ministers if, for instance, the percentage weight of a currency in the basket comes to diverge too far from the country's relative importance in the Community, as measured by gross domestic product. In fact the weights were changed on September 18 1984.

Table 5.1

Composition of the European currency unit (September 18 1984)

	Amount of each currency in basket	Approximate weight of currency* at September 18 1984
Deutschmark	0.719	32.10
French franc	1.310	19.10
Pound sterling	0.0878	14.90
Dutch guilder	0.256	10.20
Italian lira	140.00	10.20
Belgian franc	3.71 ⎫	
	⎬3.85	8.60
Luxembourg franc	0.14 ⎭	
Danish krone	0.219	2.70
Irish punt	0.00871	1.20
Greek drachma	1.15	1.40
		100.0

* The exact weight of each currency depends on its current exchange rate, and changes continually.

The ECU performs several functions within the EMS. Exchange rate parities for participating currencies are all set relative to the ECU. For example, in the rates set on March 21 1983 ECU 1 = DM 2.24184, and ECU 1 = FF 6.87456. Central cross-rates are then derived by dividing these rates against the ECU into one another. Therefore the FF/DM central parity is $6.87456 \div 2.24184 = 3.06648$. All central rates are similarly derived (see Table 5.3).

Intervention limits are calculated from these central rates. For most of the participating currencies (in fact all except the lira), the divergence limits are ± 2.25% (approximately) on either side of the central parity. For cross-rates against the lira, the intervention limits are set ± 6% from the central parities. Central banks are obliged to intervene to keep cross-rates within these limits, and there is a credit mechanism to help them do this (see below). The ECU performs two other functions.

First, it is a denominator for expressing unit of account debts and claims as between central banks. An exchange rate risk is unavoidable whenever there is a possibility of an exchange rate adjustment, but by denominating debt and claims in ECU, the EMS has introduced the concept of Community burden-sharing in respect of the exchange rate risk, in that the risk is no longer borne wholly by the debtor nor wholly by the creditor (this point is discussed below).

Secondly, it is an instrument of settlement between Community central banks. In this role the ECU is an asset, brought into existence by a procedure (described below) in which EMS members, including the UK, acquire ECUs as reserves. ECUs thus acquired are used primarily as a means of settling debts arising from official market intervention in Community currencies, with the proviso that a creditor central bank may not be obliged to accept ECUs over and above an amount equal to 50% of its claim.

Table 5.2 illustrates, using the example of sterling (not a full member of the EMS), how one calculates the ECU value of a particular currency, for any given date.

Table 5.2

The European currency unit (ECU)

	Currency amount	Sterling equivalent (pence)	Share of total value (%)
Deutschmark	0.719	18.69	31.47
French franc	1.310	15.35	25.84
Pound sterling	0.087	8.70	14.64
Italian lira	140.00	3.30	5.55
Dutch guilder	0.256	5.93	9.98
Belgian franc	3.71 } 3.85	4.96	8.35
Luxembourg franc	0.14		
Danish krone	0.219	1.58	2.66
Irish punt	0.008	0.71	1.19
Greek drachma	1.15	0.17	0.32
Sterling value of ECU (18.9 1984)	—	59.39	100.0

A grid of bilateral central rates and the agreed margins of fluctuation set the limits at which official exchange market intervention is obligatory. These rates are illustrated in Table 5.3. Thus, the Bundesbank will buy deutschmarks for French francs at FF 2.9985 per DM 1, and sells deutschmarks for French francs at 3.1363 per DM 1. In France, the Banque de France will buy francs for deutschmarks at DM .31885, per FF 1 and sells francs at DM 0.3350 per FF 1. Note that these intervention rates are calculated in such a way that when the deutschmark is weak, both central banks are intervening in the same direction. Similarly, for the other countries. This can be seen from the respective cross rates, i.e.

$$\frac{1}{2.9985} = DM\ 0.3350$$

$$\frac{1}{3.1363} = DM\ 0.31885$$

Changes in central rates are to be made by 'mutual agreement' and in accordance with a 'common procedure'. The Committee of Central Bank governors and the Monetary Committee of the Community, as well as the European Commission, are involved here. However, final decisions are taken by the ministers of the countries participating in the EMS, as happened on October 4 1981. The European Council's resolution of December 1978 states that 'there will be reciprocal consultation in the Community framework about important decisions concerning exchange rate policy between countries participating and any country not participating in the system'; hence the UK can participate in decision taking.

In addition to the grid of central rates, there is a 'divergence indicator', which serves as an early warning device that signals whether a currency diverges in its development from the average of the others. For this purpose, 'divergence' is measured by the divergence of a participating currency from its central rate in terms of the ECU, not in terms of any of the other participating currencies. The indicator flashes when the market value of a currency crosses its 'divergence threshold', expressed as a specified percentage divergence from its central value in terms of the ECU; see Table 5.4. The calculation of the ECU was illustrated in Table 5.2. Due to the wide intervention limits and to the presence of sterling and the Drachma within the ECU but not within the EMS it is necessary to adjust the ECU rate accordingly. This is the explanation for the column entitled '% change adjusted for divergence'.

The rationale behind the device of the 'threshold of divergence' is that one currency can be strong against all others and thereby exceed its threshold of divergence, without any other currency necessarily falling below its threshold. The symmetry which on the parity grid system dictates that for every sinner (i.e. a weak currency) there must be a saint (i.e. a strong currency) is broken. One country is singly to blame for divergence and the onus of adjustment is placed uniquely upon it.

Thus the alleged problem with the predecessor of the EMS, the currency snake, was that it usually placed the burden of intervention on the weakest currencies, even if the root cause of the divergence in cross-rates was that one particular currency, e.g. the Deutschmark, was strengthening against all the others. When the new rules were established for the EMS in 1979, it was felt by several countries (including the UK) that this situation should be remedied. As a result, the 'divergence indicator' against the ECU was introduced. This works as follows. Each currency has a central rate set against the ECU, and maximum deviations from this rate are also agreed. If any currency comes anywhere near these limits (within three-quarters of its maximum divergence), there is a presumption that the central bank concerned will take immediate action to hold its currency within the divergence limits. The idea is that if a single currency moves out of line with its EMS neighbours, then the presumption should be that the central bank responsible for the divergent currency should have the prime responsibility for rectifying matters. This was particularly aimed at the Bundesbank which, under the 1972–1979 'snake' arrangements, often failed to take action to prevent upward pressure developing on the Deutschmark. This forced other currencies down to their intervention limits against the Deutschmark, and resulted in deflationary measures being brought in to protect weak currencies against the strengthening Deutschmark. Under the new system, the intention is to place the burden of adjustment onto the divergent 'rogue' currency, whether it is, for example, a strong Deutschmark, or a weak lira.

Table 5.3

European monetary system: bilateral central rates and intervention limits (effective March 21, 1983).

		100 Belgian/ Luxembourg francs	100 Danish kroner	100 Deutsch mark	100 French francs	1,000 Italian lire	1 Irish pound	100 Netherlands guilders
Belgian/ Luxembourg franc	U	—	564.10	2,048.35	668.00	33.970	63.2810	1,818.0
	C	—	551.536	2,002.85	653.144	31.9922	61.8732	1,777.58
	L	—	539.30	1,958.50	638.60	30.130	60.4965	1,738.0
Danish krone	U	18.54300	—	371.40	121.11	6.159	11.4735	329.6300
	C	18.1312	—	363.141	118.423	5.80057	11.2184	322.297
	L	17.72700	—	355.06	115.78	5.463	10.9687	315.13
Deutschmark	U	5.106	28.165	—	33.350	1.696	3.160	90.770
	C	4.99288	27.5375	—	32.6107	1.59733	3.08925	88.7526
	L	—	—	—	—	—	3.021	86.780
French franc	U	15.650	86.365	313.63	—	5.2010	9.6885	278.35
	C	15.3106	84.4432	306.648	—	4.89819	9.47313	272.158
	L	14.97	82.565	299.85	—	4.6130	9.2625	266.10
Italian lira	U	3,318.9	18,305.0	66,473.0	21,677.0	—	2,053.53	58,997.0
	C	3,125.76	17,239.7	62,604.3	20,415.7	—	1,934.01	55,563.0
	L	2,943.8	16,236.0	58,960.0	19,227.0	—	1,821.45	52,329.0
Irish pound	U	1.6530	9.1168	33.1015	10.7964	0.549015	—	29.3832
	C	1.61521	8.91396	32.3703	10.5562	0.517061	—	28.7295
	L	1.5803	8.7157	31.6455	10.3214	0.486965	—	28.0904
Netherlands guilder	U	5.7535	31.7325	115.235	37.58	1.91100	3.5600	—
	C	5.62561	31.0273	112.573	36.7434	1.79976	3.48075	—
	L	5.5005	30.3375	110.1675	35.925	1.69500	3.4030	—

Source: Commission of the European Communities

Legend: U = Upper limit
         C = Bilateral central rate
         L = Lower limit

When a currency crosses its 'threshold of divergence', this results in a presumption that the authorities concerned will correct this situation by adequate measures, namely:
● diversified intervention;
● measures of domestic monetary policy (in particular interest rate changes);
● changes in central rates;
● other measures of economic policy (e.g. fiscal policy or incomes policy).

A country is not obligated to take immediate action when its divergence indicator flashes, but the early warning triggers consultations in the appropriate Community bodies – such as the Committee of Central Bank Governors, the Monetary Committee, the Economic Policy Committee, or the Council of Ministers.

Table 5.4

EMS European currency unit rates

	ECU central rates	Currency amounts against ECU February 11	% change from central rate	% change adjusted for divergence	Divergence limit %
Belgian franc	44.9008	44.6591	−0.54	+0.22	±1.5428
Danish krone	8.14104	7.95611	−2.27	−1.51	±1.6421
German d-mark	2.24184	2.22697	−0.66	+0.10	±1.1463
French franc	6.87456	6.79647	−1.14	−0.38	±1.3659
Dutch guilder	2.52595	2.52064	−0.21	+0.55	±1.5165
Irish punt	0.72569	0.715968	−1.34	−0.58	±1.6671
Italian lira	1403.49	1368.87	−2.47	−2.31	±4.0511

Changes are for ECU, therefore positive change denotes
a weak currency. Adjustment calculated by Financial Times.

Source: *Financial Times*, February 12 1985

The divergence threshold for each currency against the ECU is three-quarters of the theoretical-maximum divergency which would result from its being 2¼% below the central-parity for all other member currencies (6% for the lira). In practice, because each currency has a different weight in the ECU, this divergence indicator varies between currencies.

For example, the Deutschmark has a weight of approximately 32% in the ECU basket. So a maximum appreciation of 2¼% in the Deutschmark against all other currencies would increase the DM/ECU parity by only about 1.52% (see below). The divergence threshold is then set at three-quarters of this maximum divergence – approximately 1.146. The formula to calculate divergence limit is:

$$75.0\% \times \pm \text{Intervention band (1 minus the weighting)}$$

Applying this to the Deutschmark and Lira threshold gives:*

DM divergence threshold:

$$\frac{75}{100} \times \pm 2.25 \times \left(1 - \frac{32.10}{100} \right)$$

$$= \pm 1.146$$

Lira divergence threshold:

$$\frac{75}{100} \times \pm 6.00 \times \left(1 - \frac{10.20}{100} \right)$$

$$= \pm 4.051$$

EMS CREDIT MECHANISMS

The EMS incorporates and expands the three previous EEC credit mechanisms, the very short-term financing and the short-term monetary support (STMS), both of which are the responsibility of the central banks, and medium-term financial assistance (MTFA), which is granted by the Council.

Very short-term financing

This formed part of the mechanism for operating the old snake, and with minor improvements fulfills the same role in the new supersnake. It is not available to the UK unless and until the Government decides to join the supersnake. Very short-term credit facilities are unlimited in amount, and are granted by the participating central banks to each other in order to permit official market intervention in Community currencies. The duration of such financing has, under the EMS, been extended to 45 days from the end of the month in which it is drawn, compared with 30 days previously. The repayments period may be automatically extended for three months, subject to a ceiling equal to the debtor quota of the central bank concerned under the short-term monetary support arrangement and provided this does not result in the relevant debt remaining continuously outstanding for six consecutive months. This ceiling may be raised and the period for repayment extended with the agreement of the creditor or creditors.

---

* As the currency weights vary each day the divergence indicator can only be approximate.

Short-term monetary support

The STMS was originally established as an agreement among the central banks of Community members in February 1970. It was widened in January 1973 to cover the three countries then joining the Community (the United Kingdom, Ireland and Denmark), and was substantially enlarged in 1974. Under the EMS, it has been enlarged again (see Table 5.5), though the UK's participation will have limited practical significance for the foreign exchange market while she remains outside the supersnake. The STMS provides for credits to the central banks of Community members for the financing of temporary balance of payments deficits. Credits are granted without economic policy conditions, but they trigger subsequent consultations. The mechanism is based on a system of debtor and creditor quotas, which determine each EC central bank's borrowing entitlement and financing obligations. Where circumstances so justify, a *rallonge* mechanism enables the amount of support which a debtor country may receive to be increased over and above the quotas; likewise, a creditor *rallonge* enables a creditor country to be called upon to contribute in excess of its creditor quota. Under the rules of the expanded STMS, a debtor country may not receive more than one-half of the *rallonge*.

Until 1980, the duration of STMS credits was three months, renewable for a similar period at the request of the beneficiary central bank. The possibility of a further three-month extension has now been introduced, and the rules governing the operation of the mechanism have been adjusted to allow support to be denominated in ECUs if granted in the form of a prolongation of a debt contracted within the framework of the very short-term financing facility.

Medium-term financial assistance

The MTFA facility was originally set up by a decision of the Council of Ministers of March 22 1971. As with STMS, an enlargement took place in connection with the accession of new members to the Community in 1973. A doubling of the amounts was decided on in December 1977. Under the EMS there has been a further increase, in which the UK is participating *ab initio* (see Table 5.6). Credits may be granted to any member country in difficulties or seriously threatened with difficulties as regards its balance of payments: they are for two to five years, and will be subject to economic policy conditions to be laid down by the Council of Ministers. The MTFA has creditor ceilings, but no debtor ceilings for individual countries, except that normally no member state may draw more than 50% of the total credit ceilings. There are no *rallonges*.

The total of the short- and medium-term credit facilities just described amounts to about 25 billion ECU of effectively available credit.

Financial assistance is crucial. Without it, the weak would have little to gain from their commitment to a joint venture to stabilise exchange rates. They sacrifice part of their freedom to determine domestic economic policy in return for greater freedom to decide what their exchange rate should be. Alone, a weak currency country with limited reserves can be forced to depreciate but not to deflate. A strong currency country, however, always has the freedom to choose between appreciation or reflation. This is the basic asymmetry which assistance redresses.

Table 5.5

Short-term monetary support (m. ECUs)

	Debtor quotas		Creditor quotas	
	Old	New	Old	New
France	720	1,740	1,460	3,480
Germany	720	1,740	1,460	3,480
United Kingdom*	720	1,740	1,460	3,480
Italy	480	1,160	960	2,320
Belgium-Luxembourg	240	580	480	1,160
Netherlands	240	540	480	1,160
Denmark	108	260	216	520
Ireland	42	100	84	200
Sub-total	3,270	7,900	6,600	15,800
Rallonge	3,600	8,800	3,600	8,800
Total	6,870	16,700	10,200	24,600

* These creditor and debtor quotas for the United Kingdom will be used only after this country has become an active participant in the exchange rate mechanism; in the meantime its old quotas will remain applicable.

Table 5.6

Medium-term financial assistance (in ECUs)

	Old creditor ceilings	New creditor ceilings
France	1,200	3,105
Germany	1,200	3,105
United Kingdom	1,200	3,105
Italy	800	2,070
Belgium-Luxembourg	400	1,035
Netherlands	400	1,035
Denmark	180	465
Ireland	70	180
Total	5,450	14,100

If a weak country runs down its foreign reserves to prop up its currency, it accepts both the risk (i.e. the extra cost of rebuilding reserves if it is ultimately forced to depreciate) and the domestic deflationary consequences. If, instead, the strong country builds up its reserves by supporting the weak, it also both runs the risk (i.e. of its reserve holdings being depreciated) and accepts the domestic reflationary consequences. But when the strong lends to the weak (assuming credit is bought by deposits of the weak currency with the strong's central bank, with FECOM or the EMCF) and the proceeds are used for market intervention, the weak bears all the risks (i.e. from the need to repay foreign currency debts), while the strong accepts the principal domestic consequences (i.e. from the need to borrow at home the money it lends to the weak).

In practice, all the EC members, including the UK, have duly deposited 20% of their reserves of gold and dollars with the EMCF in return for ECUs. The deposits run for three months: the gold and foreign exchange are then repaid in their original amounts, revalued on a formula based on the recent market prices of gold and of reserve currencies, and then deposited once again in return for the appropriate amount of ECUs. This procedure was explained by M. Raymond Barre, at some length, in a session of the French National Assembly on April 24 1979, in response to anxious inquiries as to whether the gold deposited by France thereby ceased to be French property. M. Barre's statement leaves the impression that the depositing procedure is in fact little more than a book-keeping ritual. No gold physically leaves the strong-rooms of the Bank of France, which remains in charge of the gold and foreign exchange 'deposited' with the EMCF. Nevertheless, the notional deposit of gold in exchange for ECUs does serve to 'mobilise' monetary gold, in that it is more convenient to make settlements between monetary authorities by a simple transfer of ECUs than to settle in foreign exchange obtained by selling gold or borrowing against gold collateral.

THE EUROPEAN MONETARY SYSTEM: THE PRACTICE

The six years since the start of the EMS may conveniently be divided into phases which typify the constraints on the domestic monetary policies of both weak and strong EMS participants. Several economists, in particular Masera and Thygessen, have identified the several major phases and these have been updated by myself.

First phase: Dec '78 – March '79

The first phase begins with the initial agreement on the EMS in December 1978 and ends in late May 1979. The system did not begin to operate until March 1979, awaiting a compromise on the phasing out of Monetary Compensatory Amounts under the Common Agricultural Policy. During this period the external environment continued to be marked by a gradual firming of the dollar, following the measures taken by the US Administration in November 1978. The corresponding weakening of the EMS currencies initially affected mainly the Deutschmark as portfolios were readjusted in favour of dollar-denominated assets. Of the weaker currencies the Danish krone and the lira began to show strength, as the pull of their interest differentials *vis-à-vis* Germany increased in step with the spreading confidence among investors that the initial EMS central rates would be maintained.

Constraints on domestic monetary policy were felt, in this early phase, particularly by Denmark, Italy and Belgium. In the first two countries interest rates eased, although there was nothing in the domestic situation to warrant such a trend, and both countries intervened substantially to check further appreciation. In the case of Denmark, a major part of the inflow took the form of non-resident purchases of government bonds; after such sales had been stopped by administrative action, approved by the Community, the problem subsided, while in Italy a policy conflict lasted through the second phase as well. Given the resurgence of inflation and the generally strong trend in real demand, it would have been appropriate on domestic grounds for Italy to raise interest rates to match at least some of the acceleration in inflation, but to avoid further inflow this course was not followed. Although Italy had a relatively strong current account position in 1979, which might in any case have strengthened the lira, it seems likely that EMS membership aggravated the dilemma for monetary policy.

The opposite policy conflict was faced by Belgium whose relatively low interest rates prompted by domestic considerations – sluggish growth and 4% inflation – proved untenable, as the Belgian franc was driven to the floor of the band and across the threshold of divergence. Official interest rates were raised, starting in April, by four percentage points over the following six months, as the policy conflict proved more permanent. The authorities stuck to their monetary target (total domestic credit) and did not offset the drain in liquidity through the widening current deficit and net capital outflows.

In the case of Belgium it is not clear whether the start of the EMS aggravated a policy conflict which would have followed anyway from the strong preference of the Belgian authorities for a relatively ambitious exchange-rate target as part of their anti-inflation strategy. It appears more likely that the initial effect of the EMS lessened any conflict by making that target more credible than it would have been, if set unilaterally. But the tendency of the Belgian franc to remain the weakest EMS currency throughout most of the following phases as well, may indeed have added to the problem of monetary control.

Second phase: May '79–Sept '79

In the second phase lasting from the end of May to the September 1979 realignment, a conflict between domestic and external considerations was felt primarily in Germany, Belgium and Denmark. After the Bundesbank had intervened substantially in May to check the rising dollar and thereby brought the Deutschmark to the top of the band, the Deutschmark remained for some months close to its intervention points against the two weakest currencies. Between mid-June and September 23 Bundesbank net purchases of foreign exchange reached DM9bn in the EMS and 18.6bn *vis-à-vis* the dollar. Such massive interventions were hard to reconcile with the moderate target for central bank money and the decision in late June to aim for the lower part of the target range of 6–9% for the second half of the year. Increases in the discount and Lombard rates in July underlined this determination. They may have appeared more controversial to Germany's EMS partners than to Germany at the time; although they quickly pulled up short-term rates in the weaker countries, the problems of monetary control in Germany remained difficult, until Germany resolved the conflict by taking the initiative to revalue moderately in September.

This second phase resembled closely what had been anticipated at the start of the EMS: Germany pursuing a restrictive monetary policy, designed for domestic purposes, and her EMS partners trying hard, but inadequately, to offset the impact on their international reserves through competitive increases in their interest rates.

Third phase: Sept '79–Jan '80

A third phase may be identified as lasting from the September realignment until early January 1980. The realignment took the pressure off the EMS, though substantial intra-marginal interventions continued. There was less of an inflow of funds into the weaker currencies than had been observed on similar occasions during the final two years of the Snake. The dollar was unstable without any clear trend, though the announcement of tighter monetary policies in the United States in early October and greater emphasis on the part of the Federal Reserve to control the monetary aggregates brought a temporary surge in the dollar. The Bundesbank was approximately neutral in its dollar interventions during this phase as a whole; the German authorities used their greater freedom of movement to increase its discount rate in November. Although there was a further realignment in the form of the surprise unilateral devaluation of the Danish krone at the end of November, this third phase appears to have been fairly calm.

Fourth phase: Jan '80–March'80

During a fourth phase lasting from early January to the end of March 1980, by far the most significant event was the strengthening of the dollar, as US interest rates rose rapidly relative to European ones. During March, as the US prime rate shot up to nearly 20%, the dollar appreciated by 6–7% against most EMS currencies.

The German authorities tried, as in the similar phase in the late spring of 1979, to stem the appreciation of the dollar by large interventions; and the discount and Lombard rates were once more increased at the end of February. It is probable that these moves, and more specifically the policy-mix of tighter monetary policy and some fiscal relaxation, resulted from the constraint imposed by the rising dollar, and the EMS did not accentuate the policy conflict for Germany. In any case the effects of the German interventions to stem the rise in the dollar did not lead to any problems analogous to those of May–June 1979; despite them the Deutschmark weakened inside the EMS. A remarkable feature of this phase was the persistent firming of the French franc, which became the strongest EMS currency in this phase, nearly reaching its upper divergence threshold in March. There is no evidence that countries other than Germany were forced during this phase by external conditions to pursue monetary policies different from what their domestic situations indicated; when their interest rates were insufficiently high to attract spontaneous capital inflows to finance their growing current account deficits, they were able, through official borrowing abroad, to maintain their currencies comfortably within the EMS band and to increase their international reserves.

Fifth phase: April '80–July '80

Again in the fifth phase from the beginning of April to mid-July 1980 the most significant events for the working of the EMS were related to the dollar. As US interest rates fell with unprecedented speed during the spring, tensions within the EMS subsided except that the lira continued to weaken until monetary policy was tightened sharply in the summer. In view of the acceleration of inflation in Italy, there was hardly any genuine policy conflict between domestic and external considerations. Otherwise this phase was marked by a narrowing of the EMS band; the two main currencies, the Deutschmark and the French franc, moved closer to one another, while the guilder joined the French franc at the top. Changes in relative interest rates were moderate and appeared to contribute little to the explanation of exchange-market convergence. The most notable lesson of this phase was the failure of the slide in the dollar – approximately 10% *vis-à-vis* the ECU – to trigger any major upward pressure on the Deutschmark; in this respect the contrast to the second phase (from late May to the September 1979 realignment) is remarkable.

Sixth phase: July '80–Oct '81

A sixth phase started with the recovery of the dollar after US interest rates had bottomed out in July. Tensions in the EMS became highly visible in October with the French franc and the Deutschmark at or near their upper and lower intervention points respectively. Interventions both in the $/DM-market and inside the EMS are reported to have been very substantial, the former being undertaken primarily by the US rather than the German authorities. The strains in October 1980 came from outside the EMS countries as heavy flows of funds moved into the US dollar, the pound sterling, and the Japanese yen – currencies in which interest rates remained very high or, as in the US case, were rising. But the interest rate disparities within the EMS and the relative freedom of funds to move also played a role. With the exchange markets turning generally bearish over the outlook for the German mark, funds moved out of the mark and into other EMS currencies. To the extent that these funds gravitated to the currencies at the top of the EMS band – the French franc and Dutch guilder – the EMS intervention mechanisms were soon triggered.

Intervention mounted quickly, and talk began circulating of a possible widening in the intervention limits or of a temporary withdrawal of the mark from the joint float arrangement. Such approaches were openly rejected by the authorities of the respective EMS-member countries. In early November, the French took measures to ease money market conditions, making explicit their intention to reduce the selling pressures on the German mark. Meanwhile, the German Federal Bank was allowing the heavy intervention within the EMS to tighten its own money market. The market sensed the resolve of the authorities to maintain existing parities, and the tension gradually eased. Even so, the EMS joint float continued to decline against the major currencies outside the group, including the dollar, the pound sterling, the Japanese yen, and to a small degee the Swiss franc. Apart from a rise in the Danish krone, reflecting a 1980 current-account deficit for Denmark that was lower than expected, and a downward movement in the Irish punt from its temporarily high position in the band, the configuration of currencies hardly changed within the EMS.

The currencies in the group at first recovered slightly against the dollar when US interest rates were receding from their mid-December highs. But it soon became apparent that US interest rates would not drop off as sharply as some market participants had originally believed. Moreover, in early 1981 the market remained concerned about the prospects for EMS-member countries in reversing their current-account deficits and dealing with domestic policy dilemmas. As market sentiment toward the dollar became increasingly bullish, the dollar came into demand towards the middle of 1981 against the currencies in the EMS band. As before, the brunt of the immediate selling pressures fell on the German mark, and that currency touched its lower intervention limit. The Belgian franc also came under selling pressure, and both the mark and the franc required official support within the EMS.

Seventh phase: Oct '81–Feb '82

The commencement of a seventh phase can be identified with the realignment which took effect from October 5. On that date the Deutschmark and the Dutch guilder were revalued by 5.6%, the Belgian and Luxembourg franc, the Irish punt and the Danish krone were revalued by 0.1% and the French franc and Italian lira were devalued by 2.9%. These exchange rate changes are all against the ECU. The main reason for these exchange rate changes was differential inflation rates. In August 1981, for instance, consumer prices in Italy were 19.5% higher than a year before, and those in France were up by 13.6%, while in Germany the inflation rate came to 6.0% and in the Netherlands to 6.4%. Since the EMS was established (in March 1979 until August 1981) cumulative price rises amounted to 54% in Italy and 36% in France, but to only 16% in the Netherlands and 14% in Germany. Given such divergent trends in general price and cost levels under a system of basically fixed exchange rates (as mentioned earlier the rates can only move within the narrow intervention margins), the competitive position of the countries with higher inflation rates deteriorated, while the countries with relatively stable prices registered competitive advantages, but also an increase in imported inflation. The EMS realignment of October 4 was designed to rectify the accumulated price discrepancies.

Eighth phase: Feb '82–June '82

An eighth phase can be said to have started with the announcement of the realignment which took effect from February 22. On that date the Belgian franc was devalued by 8.5% against the ECU. At the same time the Danish krone was devalued by 3%, again against the ECU. This gave the Belgian franc the same devaluation against the currencies of its two main trading partners, West Germany and the Netherlands, as France and Italy secured against the same currencies from the broader realignment which took place in the seventh phase.

Ninth phase: June '82–March 1983

The June 1982 Versailles Summit was quickly followed by yet another EMS realignment. The French franc was devalued by 10% and the Italian lira was devalued by 7% both against the Deutschmark. The franc and lira devaluations were partly achieved with the help of a 4.25% revaluation of the Deutschmark and the guilder and partly by a 5.75% devaluation of the franc against all other EMS currencies except the lira which was reduced by only 2.75%.

The cross rates between the other EMS currencies – the Danish krone, the Belgian and Luxembourg francs and the Irish punt – remained unchanged.

The franc's devaluation followed an 8.5% drop against the two strongest EMS currencies eight months earlier (the Dutch guilder and the Deutschmark).

Tenth phase: March 1983–present

While there have been periodic speculative attacks on various currencies the system has suffered no further parity adjustments although the ECU weights were altered in September 1984. Cost and price level differences between member states have considerably diminished.

HAS THE EMS BEEN A SUCCESS?

Foremost among the objectives of the EMS is the achievement of a high degree of exchange rate stability as a basis for further economic integration within the EC.

The variability of EMS exchange rates appears to have declined since the system was introduced, compared wth a number of non-EMS currencies inside and outside Europe. For all EMS currencies, except the Danish krone, average variability in 1979–1981 was less than in 1974–1978.

It appears that the operations of the EMS have had a moderate effect on the exchange rate variability of the participating currencies, with this influence spreading to those European currencies outside the system that have close economic and financial ties with the participants. In contrast, the variability of nominal effective exchange rates of the US dollar, the Japanese yen and the pound sterling have risen sharply since 1979 (see Table 5.7 and Fig. 5.1).

Table 5.7
Changes in EMS exchange rates

	Dates of realignment						
	24.9.'79	*30.11.'79*	*22.3.'81*	*5.10.'81*	*22.2.'82*	*14.6.'82*	*21.3.'83*
Belgian franc							
Luxembourg franc	0	+5	0	0	−8.5	0	+1.5
Danish krone	−2.9	0	0	0	−3	0	+2.5
German mark	+2	+5	0	+5.5	0	+4.25	+5.5
French franc	0	+5	0	−3	0	−5.74	−2.5
Irish pound	0	+5	0	0	0	0	−3.5
Italian lira	0	+5	0	−3	0	−2.75	−2.5
Dutch guilder	0	+5	0	+5.5	0	+4.25	+3.5

Realignment of central rates (%) in relation to the group of currencies whose bilateral parties were not changed.

Source: European Economic Community

Fig. 5.1 Variability of Nominal Effective Exchange Rates

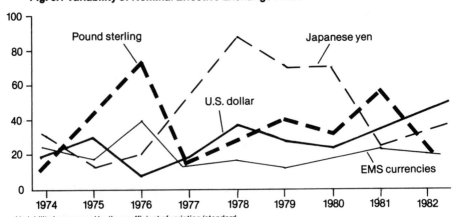

Variability is measured by the coefficient of variation (standard deviation divided by the average) multiplied by 1000, of the nominal effective exchange rate. The variability of EMS currencies is measured by the simple average of variability of nominal effective exchange rates of participants.
Data: IMF, *World Economic Outlook*, 1983.

A second criterion of the system's success is less easily satisfied however. It is not good enough to merely preserve stable exchange rates if inflation rates continue to vary between the member countries, necessitating either large or frequent currency realignments.

Until 1983 there was no sign that the inflation rates were 'converging' – indeed Europe's inflation rates moved further apart in 1980 and 1981, since the oil crisis was met in Germany and the Netherlands with a tight fiscal and monetary policy, while the French and Italian governments embarked upon reflationary policies in order to expand their way out of the worldwide recession.

However, since late 1982, and particularly since the last EMS realignment on March 21 1983, the French and Italian governments have shifted to clearly restrictive policies and their inflation rates have come down. Both Italian and French governments stated explicitly that the need to stay within the EMS was a major consideration in their new policies.

It is worth remembering that Europe's last attempt to co-ordinate exchange rate policy – the so-called Snake of 1972 – effectively fell apart within two years, when France withdrew. The very fact that the system still exists, after five of the most financially turbulent years in postwar history, shows that European governments have begun to recognise the external constraints on their macroeconomic policies – and to do so, in most cases, before the recognition was forced on them by the markets through crisis.

One little known success of the EMS has been the increased usage of the ECU. After the US dollar and the Deutschmark it has evolved into the most actively traded currency in the foreign exchange market. Pressure from the European Commission in favour of its wider use and the increasing willingness of a growing number of banks to offer ECU current and deposit accounts have aided its progress. As a result it is now possible to invoice and pay for goods and services with ECUs world wide. Some 300 banks are now involved in the ECU interbank market.

The ECU's stability in times of exchange rate volatility have encouraged its use by a number of EC based companies as an accounting unit. In addition it is now the third most important currency in the Eurobond market with total bond issues, by early 1985, of around ECU 6.5bn ($4.39bn) held by private investors.

APPENDIX

Chronological History of the Snake and the EMS

1972

April 24   Basle Agreement enters into force for narrowing of the margins of fluctuation between EC currencies: the Snake (margins of 2.25%) in the tunnel (plus or minus 2.25% against the dollar). Participants: Belgium, France, Germany, Italy, Luxembourg, the Netherlands.

May 1   The United Kingdom and Denmark join.

May 23   Norway becomes associated.

June 23   The United Kingdom withdraws.

June 27   Denmark withdraws.

Oct 10   Denmark returns.

1973
February 13 Italy withdraws.

March 19   Transition to the joint float; interventions to maintain fixed margins against the dollar ('tunnel') are discontinued.

March 19   Sweden becomes associated.

March 19   The deutschmark is revalued by 3%.

April 3   The establishment of a European Monetary Co-operation Fund is approved.

June 29   The deutschmark is revalued by 5.5%.

Sept 17   The guilder is revalued by 5%.

Nov 16   The Norwegian krone is revalued by 5%.

1974
Jan 19   France withdraws.

1975
July 10   France returns.

1976
March 15   France withdraws again.

Oct 17   Agreement of exchange rate adjustment ('Frankfurt realignment'): The Danish krone is devalued by 6%, the guilder and Belgian franc by 2% and the Norwegian and Swedish krone by 3%.

1977
April 1   The Swedish krone is devalued by 6% and the Danish and Norwegian krone are devalued by 3% each.

Aug 28   Sweden withdraws; Danish and Norwegian krone are devalued by 5% each.

1978
Feb 13   The Norwegian krone is devalued by 8%.

July 6,7   European Council in Bremen: agreement on the main lines of a European Monetary System.

Oct 17   The deutschmark is revalued by 4%, the guilder and the Belgian franc by 2%.

Dec 12   Norway announces decision to withdraw.

1979

March 12   European Council in
Paris: announcement of
the formal introduction of
the EMS on March 13
1979.

March 13   EMS comes into force.
Participants: Belgium,
Denmark, France,
Germany, Ireland,
Luxembourg, the
Netherlands (bilateral
fluctuation margins
2.25%), and Italy
(bilateral fluctuation
margins 6%).

Sep 23   Realignment of central
rates among EMS
currencies: 2%
revaluation of the
deutschmark and 3%
devaluation of the Danish
krone.

Dec 29   5% devaluation of
Danish krone.

1981

Oct 4   The deutschmark and
Dutch guilder were
revalued against the
ECU, whilst the French
franc and Italian lira were
devalued by 3%.

1982

Feb 22   The Belgian franc was
devalued by 8.5% and the
Danish krone was
devalued by 3%, both
against the ECU.

June 13   The French franc was
devalued by 10% against
the deutschmark and the
Dutch guilder. The
Italian lira was devalued
by 7% against the
deutschmark. The
French franc was
devalued by 5.7% against
all other EMS currencies
except for the lira where
the devaluation was
2.75%.

1983

March 21   The French franc was
devalued by 8% against
the deutschmark,
achieved by a 5.5% franc
devaluation and a 2.5%
deutschmark revaluation
against the ECU. The lira
followed the franc.

1984

Sept. 18   The ECU weights were
altered.

Chapter 6
How to Forecast
Exchange Rates

WHY FORECAST EXCHANGE RATES?

Some companies continue to avoid the complexities of foreign exchange, usually under the rationale of 'We're in the business of manufacturing and exporting widgets and not buying and selling foreign currencies.' Many of these companies instead often adopt a policy of hedging all or most of their exposures all the time. While such a policy may have merit under certain restrictive circumstances, most multinational companies have moved, or are moving towards, a more sophisticated approach to foreign exchange problems, in most cases involving the use of foreign exchange rate forecasts.

These forecasts can be used for strategic planning, budgeting and exposure management. These will be discussed in turn. Strategic planning is clearly undertaken within a foreign exchange environment. As part of its strategic plan a multinational will evaluate its existing overseas subsidiaries in light of the projected foreign exchange outlook. For example, in order to compensate for projected continuing exchange losses on a net asset position in a given foreign subsidiary, it may choose to adjust its pricing policies, restructure the balance sheet or even withdraw from the country. All these decisions are predicated on a foreign exchange rate forecast.

Budget foreign exchange forecasts should be incorporated into the multinational's annual operating budgets for its overseas subsidiaries. The budgets should encompass monthly projections of foreign subsidiary income and expenses, assets and liabilities, profit or loss and other financial factors. Although a multinational's foreign subsidiary performance is evaluated in local currency terms, foreign exchange gains and losses are also budgeted for the parent company, *vis-à-vis* the projected exposures for each subsidiary.

Foreign exchange exposure management enables the company to weather the turbulent foreign exchange markets. Techniques for exposure management are discussed further in chapters eight and nine.

A foreign exchange rate is the price of one currency in terms of another. Since the exchange rate is a price it is determined by supply, demand and stockbuilding. Stocking or destocking occurs when the official authorities intervene to keep exchange rates higher or lower than they would otherwise have been.

The principal factors which influence sellers of foreign currency, buyers of foreign currency, and government intervention policy now need to be enumerated.

Day to day influences on foreign exchange rates can cause the rate to move in the opposite direction to that indicated by longer term fundamentals. Consequently short term influences will initially be discussed and this in turn is followed by more longer term factors. The chapter concludes by examining exchange rate forecasting by the use of single variables viz. relative inflation rates and relative money supply growth.

SHORT-TERM INFLUENCES ON EXCHANGE RATES

Charles Coombs, former Senior Vice-President of the Federal Reserve Bank whilst responsible for US Treasury and Federal Reserve operations in the gold and foreign exchange markets, described in *The Arena of International Finance*, the foreign exchange market in the following terms:

> By its very nature, the foreign exchange market is a nervous, high risk ultra sensitive mechanism primarily geared to short-term developments. Of the tens of billions of dollars in daily transactions cleared through the market, only a fraction derive from such fundamental factors as foreign trade and long-term investment. On a day-to-day basis, the market is instead dominated by short-term capital movements in search of a quick profit or a hedge against exchange rate risks.

Coombs is arguing that movements in the trade figures and capital accounts figures determine the behaviour of a currency over a long period of time. However, operators in the markets are very sensitive to short-term psychological and technical reactions which may reverse temporarily the basic longer-term trend of exchange rates.

These short-term movements are influenced by:*

(i)   forthcoming economic news;
(ii) official and unofficial forecasts;
(iii) political new items;
(iv) technical market factors.

1. Forthcoming economic news

Because of the widespread awareness of the importance of new items about the economy upon exchange rates, many foreign exchange dealers try to forecast

---

* An excellent discussion of these is provided by J. Heywood (see bibliography).

economic news. Much economic data, such as balance of payments figures, retail price indices, key interest rate changes, money supply growth and so on are published in the news media on a definite schedule on dates known in advance; even at times of day known in advance. So dealers try to forecast what the numbers will look like when they are published at, say, 3p.m. two days hence. If, for instance, US inflation figures are expected to be worse than previously, market operators may start to buy dollars (on the expectation that interest rates and consequently the dollar will also increase). All this activity in discounting prospective economic news items and reacting to actual news items is a major contributor to day-to-day fluctuations.

2. Official and unofficial forecasts

The publication of official forecasts of the economic prospects for particular countries can also have an impact upon exchange rates. Organisations such as NIESR in the UK (National Institute for Economic and Social Research), the OECD in Paris, and the EEC Commission in Brussels publish regular economic forecasts. The existence of the forecast often generates considerable comment in the financial press, all of which serves to highlight the particular economic problems and opportunities within the various economies and so influences the climate of opinion.

In addition news of unofficial forecasts, made by the most well-known forecasting companies can also influence rates.

3. Political news items

Political news items of all types may alter the prospects for an individual currency. Such items include:

- key announcements of policy changes;
- statements by senior politicians;
- appointments and resignations;
- public opinion polls (popularity of leaders, policy priorities, voting intentions);
- elections;
- trends in international relations;
- trade agreements;
- threatened or actual war.

4. Technical market factors

These provide a different source of day-to-day fluctuations in exchange rates. One source arises from isolated large transactions going through the market which temporarily upset the market's ability to balance supply and demand.

Like ripples spreading across a pond, the impact of the original large transaction will react around the market until the full amount can be absorbed.

Similarly, some currencies are subject to regular monthly or weekly cycles due to the impact of large regular payments, typically for oil. During 1974 and 1975 there was a pronounced monthly pattern for sterling as oil companies purchased sterling for delivery on the 15th of each month to pay for oil from the Arabian Gulf. During the late 1970s and early 1980s sterling was also influenced on certain days by the need by certain oil companies to pay petroleum revenue tax (PRT).

One example of technical factors influencing exchange rates is the close link between some currencies whereby if one rises/falls against a key currency the other must rise/fall against the same currency. An example of this is the close link between the Deutschmark and the Swiss franc, whereby if the Deutschmark rises/falls against the dollar then the Swiss franc must rise/fall against the dollar. An example will make this clear. Assume that the rate between the Deutschmark and the Swiss franc maintained by the Swiss central bank is DM1 = 80 Swiss cents (this is approximately correct) and that DM1 = 80 Swiss cents = US$ 1. Now assume that the DM doubles in value against the dollar, i.e. DM1 = $2. In order for DM to be still equal to 80 Swiss cents then the Swiss franc must rise so that now DM1 = 80 Swiss cents = US$ 2, i.e the Swiss franc rises to 40 Swiss cents = US$ 1. So in this case as the Deutschmark appreciates against the dollar so does the Swiss franc.

It may be instructive to take the case where the DM halves in value so that DM is now worth only 50 US cents. Therefore it now takes 2 DM to purchase 1 US dollar. Since DM is fixed at 80 Swiss cents then 2 DM must be worth 1 Swiss franc 60 cents. In other words the Swiss franc has halved in value against the dollar.

Another technical factor is that some currencies are used as world reserve currencies. These currencies are held as a store of value as well as a medium of exchange. Participants in the foreign exchange market who hold, e.g. the dollar, as a store of value may react very nervously to expectations that in the short run the dollar is expected to fall while in the medium-term the fundamentals are in the dollar's favour. Since these arbitragists may need to convert their funds at short notice it is not surprising that fears of capital losses worry them. It is not much use to them to be told the market is overreacting.

MEDIUM/LONG-TERM FACTORS INFLUENCING EXCHANGE RATES

In the medium/long-term three factors influence exchange rates:

(i)   the balance of payments;
(ii) government economic policy;
(iii) the international monetary system.

1. The balance of payments

The need for foreign exchange transactions arises because goods, services and capital are traded across national boundaries. As discussed in Chapter 2 these three items form a constituent part of a country's balance of payments.

When a country is in current account deficit, that is, when it buys more goods and services abroad than it sells, there will be an excess supply of its currency on the exchange markets. This excess will have to be absorbed either by inflows on capital account or by central bank intervention.

The country's exchange rate will fall unless foreign investors are prepared to buy the excess currency at the prevailing rate, or the central bank is willing and able to finance the current account deficit by running down its foreign currency reserves.

The current account is worth including in the forecasting both for its direct effect on exchange rates and for its indirect effect on exchange market expectations. While a current account surplus causes some operators to buy a currency, the rate at which other operators will be willing to satisfy this demand by selling the currency in question depends, among other things, on their view of the future direction of the current account. If the surplus is expected to rise, existing holders will probably be unwilling to sell unless they are offered a higher rate (since they probably expect the exchange rate to move higher in the future). Conversely, if the surplus is expected to fall, existing holders will probably be willing to sell at the existing, or even at a lower, rate.

There are two variables which largely determine the nature of the trade accounts:

(i)   relative prices;
(ii) relative incomes.

The word 'relative' is used because the absolute level of prices or incomes in a country are meaningless unless they are compared with the levels in the countries with which the country trades. Only those prices of goods traded in each country are relevant for comparison. Changes in prices of non-traded goods, such as service industries, affect prices of traded goods only indirectly.

As incomes expand, consumption and investment also tend to expand. Given an economy with full resource utilisation this leads to price increases. The impact on the trade account depends on how the increase in demand is channelled. An increased demand completely channelled into consumption increases the amount of goods imported. On the other hand, an increased demand completely channelled into investment, particularly in the export industries, make these industries more competitive and increases exports.

A good current account forecast is no guarantee of a good exchange rate forecast. The reason is fairly obvious. Exchange rates are also influenced by capital movements. When currencies are floating freely, a current account surplus (or deficit) must be offset by a capital account deficit (or surplus). The problem facing the forecaster is that of determining how much, if at all, the exchange rate will have to move to bring forth these off-setting capital flows.

It has already been suggested that the expected trend on current account is one of the factors international money-managers consider when buying or selling a currency. However, the capital account is subject to many other influences. Direct investment overseas may be for raw materials, cheaper production costs or simply because the company wishes to increase the size of its market. Capital flows will depend on expected levels of profit and political stability. Portfolio investment will depend on expected returns and risks.

2. Government economic policy

Governments are committed to several economic objectives. These include increasing the growth rate of the economy, full employment, price stability and improving the balance of payments. The problem is that policies designed to solve one problem may have adverse effects on other problems. Three major policies are available to the government to achieve their objectives; these are: (i) monetary policy, (ii) fiscal policy, (iii) other policies such as price and income controls. All these policies affect the balance of payments and income and ultimately exert an influence on the exchange rate. Assuming a fixed exchange rate it is useful to examine the way attempts to influence one objective ultimately influence other objectives and eventually exert pressure on the exchange rate. Table 6.1 summarises the problems faced by governments, the prescription to attack the problem, its effects and ultimately the pressure on the exchange rate.

Thus in Case I the unemployment is reduced but there is a deterioration of the balance of payments and downward pressure on the exchange rate. In case II inflation falls but unemployment rises and there is upward pressure on the exchange rate. In case III the balance of payments deficit may be eliminated but unemployment rises and there is upward pressure on the exchange rate. In case IV the balance of payments surplus is reduced by the price level rises and there is downward pressure on the exchange rate.

It is necessary to emphasise what are known as the dilemma cases. If the high level of unemployment coincides with the problem of a persisting balance of payments deficit, the government must make a conscious decision as to which objective is most important. The outcome of such a decision will affect the foreign exchange market in diametrically opposite ways. Attention to the domestic problem of unemployment will tend to aggravate the problem of balance of payments deficits. Attention to the balance of payments deficits will tend to aggravate the domestic problem of unemployment.

A similar dilemma between the external position of the country and its domestic objectives is encountered when a persistent balance of payments surplus appears in conjunction with a high rate of inflation. We discussed in Chapter 2 the fact that a balance of payments surplus causes inflation by injecting more spending into the economy. The more the government combats domestic inflation, the more competitive its goods become internationally, and the larger the balance of payments surplus. The more the government attempts to control the balance of payments surplus, the larger the potential inflation rate in the domestic economy.

Table 6.1

The effect of government economic policy on the exchange rate*

Problem	Prescription to attack the problem	Effects	Effects on other objectives			Exchange rate
			Price level	Balance of payments	Full employment	
I. High unemployment	Reflation – Expansionary	Unemployment Falls	Rises	Deteriorates	—	Downward pressure
II. High inflation	Deflation – Contractionary	Inflation falls	—	Improves	Not achieved	Upward pressure
III. Balance of payments deficits	Deflation – Contractionary	Deficit falls	Falls	—	Not achieved	Upward pressure
IV. Balance of payments surplus	Reflation – Expansionary	Surplus falls	Rises	—	Achieved	Downward pressure

* It must be stressed that current economic thinking does emphasise that there may well be only short-run effects on employment of increased government spending. This has not, however, prevented some European governments from pursuing these policies.

As is evident from Table 6.1 there may be a dilemma for governments. If high unemployment exists, the solution to this (i.e. reflation) weakens the exchange rate. If at the same time high inflation exists the solution to this (i.e: deflation) strengthens the exchange rate. This dilemma can be resolved by directly changing the country's exchange rate. The combination of high unemployment and a balance of payments deficits, with the government placing equal priority on these problems, is resolved by the policy of reflation and devaluation. Similarly, if high inflation corresponds with a balance of payments surplus, the traditional policy solution indicates deflation and revaluation.

The importance of government economic policy in influencing the exchange rate can clearly be discerned. In order to forecast its impact it is necessary to understand two factors: first, the likely response of government to changing economic conditions; and secondly, the eventual effect of these policies on the foreign exchange market.

3. The international monetary system

Having examined alternative exchange rate arrangements in Chapter 4 this section examines the implications of the international monetary system on the forecasting of exchange rates.

Between 1946 and 1971 the international monetary system was one of fixed exchange rates. The monetary authorities pledged, in the form of an agreement with the IMF, to maintain exchange rates within small margins around a target rate, called the 'par value'. This 'par value' might be changed whenever a country's balance of payments moved into fundamental disequilibrium and after it became clear that various alternative policies such as internal deflation and/or controls were effectively and/or politically not feasible.

Forecasting exchange rates in this environment consisted essentially of a three-step procedure. First, from an examination of a country's balance of payments trends and other fundamentals, such as relative rates of inflation and trade flows, a measure of the pressure on a currency was derived. Secondly, changes in the level of foreign exchange reserves (including borrowing facilities) of the central bank indicated when a situation would become critical. Finally, there was the crucial step of predicting which of the rather limited policy options the economic decision-makers of a nation would resort to in the crisis, i.e. reinforced attempts at internal deflation, intervention and exchange controls, devaluation or some combination of these policies.

The success or failure of the forecasting game depends on the final step. The difficulty in this was considerably eased by the fact that those who decided on devaluations and revaluations were, unlike private transactors, not guided by profit-maximising objectives. The motives of monetary authorities comprised the full spectrum from national prestige and domestic partisan politics to fears of post-devaluation unemployment. One particularly pleasant feature about this era of exchange rate forecasting for the foreign exchange market was that the downside risk of actions taken on the basis of such forecasts was limited;

either the exchange rate moved in the generally expected direction, or the central bank managed to hold it steady. Thus the risk of making a loss was virtually zero while the possibility of making a gain was quite high.

However, since 1971 the objectives of monetary authorities in their intervention policies have become less clear making the final step very difficult to predict. The motives for intervention were listed out at the Economic Summit Meeting held in Versailles in 1982. The various objectives of intervention since 1973 were:

A. Limited objectives related to short-term market conditions:
  1. Countering disorder
    (a) Defined in terms of narrow technical considerations (e.g. size of bid-ask spreads, size of intra-day rate movements, 'thin' and nervous trading.
    (b) Countering disorder precipitated by essentially non-economic shocks.
    (c) Countering disorder of a short-term type-market psychology and 'band-wagons'. Resisting exchange rate movements that might gain a momentum of their own.
  2. Sending a signal of determination to the market, or testing the market.
  3. Attempts to hold a rate level for very short periods (e.g. to protect a psychological benchmark.)
B. Attempts to influence exchange rate levels over intermediate periods:
  1. Resisting large short-term movements or 'erratic fluctuations' or smoothing day-to-day movements above a certain absolute size.
  2. Buying time for reassessment of economic policy.
  3. 'Leaning against the wind', i.e. moderating the movements in the exchange rate.
C. Attempts to influence exchange rate levels over long periods:
  1. Resisting rate movements 'which bear no relation to the fundamentals'.
    (a) Resisting apparent 'overshooting'.
    (b) Bridging operations to enable markets to realise that the fundamentals have already changed.
  2. Attempts to give some leeway to monetary policy by lessening the impact on domestic monetary conditions of monetary conditions abroad.
  3. Resisting depreciation out of concern over its inflation consequences or resisting appreciation in order to maintain competitiveness.
  4. Attempts to defend rate-level floors or ceilings over extended periods.
  5. EMS marginal and intra-marginal intervention by the participants in the European Monetary System to keep rates within the prescribed parity bands.
D. Other objectives:
  1. Attempts to acquire foreign currencies without re-igniting downward pressures on own currency.
  2. Dampening seasonality or offsetting very large transactions.

3. Preserving the value of international holdings of assets denominated in the domestic currency in order to avoid the potential destabilising impacts of widespread shifts in asset holdings by market participants.

As we discussed on page 91 with effect from April 1 1978, the Second Amendment to the IMF's Articles of Agreement came into effect. This involves the following significant provisions. First, a member country shall avoid manipulating exchange rates in order to prevent effective balance of payments adjustments, or to gain an unfair competitive advantage over other members. Secondly, a member should intervene in the exchange market, if necessary, to counter disorderly conditions which may be characterised, *inter alia*, by disruptive short-term movements in the exchange value of its currency. Thirdly, members should take into account, in their intervention policies, the interests of other members, including those of the countries in whose currencies they intervene.

Clearly, forecasting intervention points in the post-1971 situation is a much more complicated procedure than it was in the pre-1971 situation.

The introduction of money-supply targets also had a very significant impact on the foreign exchange market. If the money supply is controlled and inflation is reduced, this strengthens the exchange rate. However, as soon as expectations build up that the actual money-supply targets will not be met, this weakens the exchange rate. Thus the central bank must always be willing to raise interest rates when faced with money-supply growth higher than the targeted range. Faced with expectations of future interest rate rises, capital inflows may be delayed. In the UK expectations of interest-rate rises reduce the demand for fixed coupon stocks, such as gilt-edged securities, and this in turn weakens the authorities' ability to control the money supply.*

It is important to draw a distinction between short-term currency forecasts and medium and long-term currency forecasts. In the short term, capital flows – precipitated by political developments, interest rate divergencies and currency expectations – are the key determinants of currency movements. They can lead to significant short-term fluctuations either side of a currency's medium and long-term trend.

FORECASTING EXCHANGE RATES BY USING ONE SINGLE VARIABLE

Forecasting exchange rates by incorporating the various items already mentioned is a cumbersome process and is also prone to error in view of the number of variables which need to be estimated. It is for this reason that some forecasters prefer to base their predictions on a single variable. Two particular variables have been singled out:

1. the rate of inflation via the concept of purchasing power parity;

---

* For a detailed examination of the way money-supply targets influence exchange rates see *The Foreign Exchange Handbook*, Brian Kettell and S. Bell (Graham and Trotman, 1983).

2. the relative money supply via the international monetary theory of the balance of payments.

1.   Purchasing Power Parity

The theory of purchasing power parity was put forward by Gustav Cassel at the end of the First World War. The purchasing power parity theory states that the exchange rate between two countries will reflect the relative buying power of the respective currencies. An example will clarify this. Assume a motorcycle costs £500 in the UK and $1,500 in the USA. If the current rate of exchange is $3 = £1, the motorcycle will cost the same in either country, and the exchange rate reflects purchasing power parity. If, however, the exchange rate moved until £1 was worth only $2, it would be cheaper for an American to buy a motorcycle in England because he could then buy it for $1,000 (ignoring transport costs). Assuming flexible prices, as the demand for motorcycles increased in the UK the price would rise and, as the demand for motocycles in the USA declined, their price would fall. With the increase in demand by Americans for UK motorcycles there would be an increase in the demand for sterling, which in turn, would raise the value of the pound and reduce the value of the dollar. This whole process would continue until exchange rates again reflected purchasing power parity.

Purchasing power parity theory is, therefore, an hypothesis about the equilibrium relationship between an exchange rate and a corresponding relative price index; it rests on the notion that the exchange rate and relative price index cannot diverge from their proportionate equilibrium relationship without setting in motion corrective forces that will act to restore equilibrium.

Two requirements are necessary to produce an exchange rate forecast under this approach. First, a base period when purchasing power parity existed between two countries, or when domestic price levels were equal when measured in a common currency, has to be established. Secondly, a run of actual and forecast inflation rates for the two countries in question must be obtained. Taking the exchange rate for the base period and adjusting it for any subsequent inflation differential allows a specific value for the exchange rate to be projected over future periods.

Purchasing power parity is, however, subject to several limitations, one of which is that changes in domestic prices need not cause a change in exchange rates because many goods are not traded internationally. Another criticism is that indirect taxes and tariffs make exchange rates deviate from purchasing power parity. Also, transport and other transactions costs, such as high information costs involved in finding the cheapest products, leave room for large purchasing power disparities. A further problem with the theory is that a country's trade balance responds slowly to the over- or under-valuation of its currency.

Considerations other than price can also affect competitiveness. There are two broad aspects of non-price competitiveness. The first is the act of selling the goods, which includes the amount of advertising undertaken, whether to use agents or subsidiaries, the frequency and length of visits by salesmen to markets and their customer contact. The second aspect concerns the product itself, e.g. its design or fashion, ease of maintenance and operation, quality (including reliability and technical specification), delivery time, and after sales service.

Proponents of the theory often leave vague, or disagree over, which ratio of price indices should be compared with the exchange rate. Such vagueness and disagreement reflects the lack of a satisfactory model of the corrective forces that might prevent the exchange rate from diverging persistently from a proportionate relationship with an appropriate ratio of price indices. Another severe drawback with the theory as a forecasting tool is that it assumes causality runs from prices to the exchange rate and not the other way round. For some commodities, e.g. copper, it is clear that movements in the exchange rate determine the domestic price and not vice versa. Thus a movement away from the theory may imply a disequilibrium price level not a disequilibrium spot rate. The monetary theory of exchange rate determination, discussed below, has the advantage that it can handle causality from money to the spot exchange rate and then to prices or, alternatively, from money to the price level and then to the spot exchange rate.

The outcome of these criticisms is that the theory is useful in indicating the long-term trend in a currency rather than in predicting exchange rates over a period as short as a year.

2.   The Monetary Theory of Exchange Rate Determination

The international monetary theory of exchange rate determination is an old idea, with Ricardo being an early exponent. The theory, which has seen a resurgence in the 1970s and 1980s can be applied to either fixed or flexible exchange rates. Suppose that the authorities in some country on fixed exchange rates increase the rate of monetary expansion, assuming that the economy is small and fully employed, individuals now find themselves with excess money balances. They will attempt to exchange them for goods and financial assets, i.e. aggregate demand will increase. Individuals in the country which has increased its rate of monetary expansion will, since the economy is fully employed, eliminate their excess money balances through the balance of payments, that is, by exchanging them for foreign goods and securities. Thus as a result of the increase in its rate of monetary expansion the country will develop a balance of payments deficit which in turn will lead to a reduction in its foreign reserves.

In the opposite situation, when the money supply, or its rate of growth, is reduced, individuals and firms find that their real balances are below the desired level. They will, therefore, attempt to accumulate money balances. that is, the country will develop a balance of payments surplus.

Thus, under a system of fixed exchange rates, national monetary authorities lose control over the rate of expansion of their nominal money supply. Their freedom is limited to the ability to choose the level of foreign exchange reserves they desire to hold. If they want to increase their holdings of reserves they must reduce the rate of monetary expansion, and vice versa if they find that their foreign exchange reserves are in excess of the desired level.

Assume, in this case, that the economy under consideration is fully employed and that its government abstains from operations in the foreign exchange market, i.e. the country in question operates a system of flexible exchange rates. Now suppose that the rate of monetary expansion increases. This leads to an increase in the amount of real cash balances that individuals and firms hold. They now hold a volume of real cash balances in excess of that which they desire. Their response is to attempt to eliminate their excess cash balances. They will, therefore, try to exchange their excess cash balances for other assets, as well as for goods and services. Thus aggregate demand in the economy will increase. Producers cannot increase their output. Responding to the increase in the demand for their goods and services, they will attempt to hire additional labour to expand their production; but if the economy is already fully employed, all they achieve is to raise wages. Thus the excess demand created by the expansion in the money supply leads to a rise of prices and wages. As prices rise the real value of cash balances held falls. Prices rise until the excess real cash balances are eliminated with individuals now holding the desired level of cash balances. If the rate of monetary expansion is maintained at its new higher level prices will continue to rise, i.e. inflation will emerge.

However, an increase in domestic price inflation will not be the only consequence of the rise in the rate of monetary expansion. When individuals and firms attempt to eliminate their excess money balances they do so partly by offering, say, sterling, in exchange for goods produced abroad and for foreign financial securities. This increase in the supply of sterling in the foreign exchange market leads to a fall in the price of sterling in terms of all other currencies, assuming that the demand for the UK currency has not correspondingly increased. If the higher rate of monetary expansion is maintained, the international value of sterling will continuously fall. Thus an increase in the rate of growth of the money supply will lead to inflation and a falling international value for the currency in a fully employed economy on flexible exchange rates.

The outcome is that, if the money supply is higher than the money demand under fixed exchange rates, reserves fall, and under flexible exchange rates the exchange rate falls until money supply equals money demand. A falling exchange rate raises domestic prices and increases the demand for cash balances. If the money supply is lower than the money demand under fixed exchange rates, reserves rise and under flexible rates the exchange rate rises. A rising exchange rate lowers domestic prices and reduces the demand for cash balances. Again the process stops when money supply equals money demand.

The encouraging aspect about this approach is the way in which it analyses exchange rate changes within the context of the overall balance of payments. The theory recognises that a country with a large current account surplus can experience downward pressure on its exchange rate when its money supply is growing too fast; and that a country with a large current account deficit can experience upward pressure on its exchange rate, when its money supply is growing too slowly. This follows because excessive or deficient growth in cash balances can be eliminated by a movement on current account or capital account, or by a combination of the two.

The monetary theory has to be used carefully in a world characterised not by full employment but by unemployment. If there are free resources, monetary expansion can stimulate output and increase employment without necessarily producing inflation. The rise in national income might adversely affect the current account as imports are encouraged but the effect is likely to be moderate. An exchange rate forecaster using the monetary theory must make an assessment, when attempting to predict the exchange rate movements, of whether a monetary expansion will raise output or prices.

In practice the situation is somewhat easier. If the economy is depressed, inflation will be moderating and the exchange rate will be reflecting this. The monetary expansion will reduce the tendency for inflation to drop even if the full impact is on output. Thus a monetary expansion produces downward pressure on the exchange rate even if the economy is depressed.

There are two major problems with the theory. First, it is necessary to obtain accurate estimates of the future demand for money and supply of money. Secondly, given the existence of a world of managed floating exchange rates it becomes necessary to estimate the extent to which a monetary imbalance is corrected by a change in the reserves or by a change in the exchange rate or by both.

TECHNICAL ANALYSIS: BLACK MAGIC OR A VALUABLE FORECASTING TECHNIQUE?

Technical and chartist analysis has only recently been applied to exchange rate forecasting though they have a long history in attempts to analyse stock market and commodity markets.

Technical analysis refers to the study of the action of the market, especially market prices, as opposed to the study of the companies, countries or goods in which the market deals. The technical analyst does not believe that fundamentals are important, but he believes that there are other influences, perhaps psychological and/or emotional, which are also important. All these factors come together in the market place primarily in only one piece of information – the price of the currency, equity or bond. Many technical analysts believe that this is the only figure that counts. Furthermore it is a claim of technical analysis that the bulk of the statistics which fundamentalists study are past history, out of date and already taken account of in the price behaviour.

The basic tool of technical analysis is price charts. Regarding the foreign exchange markets, these charts record, in one form or another, the value of the currency, probably each day and usually taking closing levels. Over long periods, certain price patterns emerge which have then normally been associated with certain subsequent price developments to the extent that the subsequent price developments are 'predictable'. This predictability is not infallible, and technicians would never claim it to be but some patterns repeat themselves with such similarity that certain following price movements are regarded as having high probabilities.

One popular mechanical formula is the filter rule which issues buy recommendations if exchange rates rise x% above their most recent trough and sell recommendations if exchange rates fall x% below their most recent peak.

Technical analysis possesses two great strengths over more fundamentalist techniques of forecasting exchange rates. First, trends as indicated by graphic analysis tend to abstract away random movements. So the exchange rate itself is already telling you what all the factors affecting exchange rates are saying. Secondly, at any one moment in time the most probable (though by no means certain) next event is a continuation along the past trend. As technicians say 'the trend is your friend' so stay with it until it changes.

The most common problems of technical analysis are mistakenly identifying patterns that are not there, failed genuine patterns, ambiguous patterns and the inability to specify time periods in which targets will be hit. In addition if the volatility of the market changes sticking to rigid filter rules will inevitably lead to poor decision making.

Chapter 7
Foreign Exchange Risk: The Problems of Definition, Measurement and Identification

THE KEY AREAS FOR DECISION MAKING

The current nature of the international monetary system has markedly increased the frequency and size of exchange rate changes. For companies with overseas operations, whether as importers/exporters or as multinationals, this has added a dimension to business decision making which could be widely ignored prior to 1971.

Irrespective of the nature of their overseas activities companies need to control the degree of foreign exchange exposure. In order to do this it is necessary to introduce an organisational framework which generates answers and action to the following key questions:

(i)   What is the exact nature of the company's foreign exchange exposure? How is it measured by accountants and by economists?
(ii)   How can this be identified?
(iii)   Given its measurement and identification how can the degree of risk be measured?
(iv)   What is the corporate attitude to this risk?
(v)   How should the company organise for foreign exchange exposure: centralisation versus decentralisation.
(vi)   The role of a currency committee.
(vii)   What policies are available to control the risk and at what costs?
(viii) Given the adoption of policies to control foreign exchange risks, what constraints have to be taken into account?

This chapter concentrates on issues (i) to (vi) while issues (vii) and (viii) are dealt with in Chapters 8 and 9. Appendices I and II at the end of this Chapter consider The UK Accounting Position and The US Accounting Position, respectively.

THE NATURE OF A COMPANY'S FOREIGN EXCHANGE EXPOSURE

Transaction and translation exposure

In defining exposure it is traditional to distinguish between transaction exposure and translation exposure. The existence of transaction exposure indicates that the value of a transaction would be affected by an exchange rate change between its initiation and completion, for example, where a US firm exports to Britain and invoices in pound sterling. The US firm is not sure how many dollars the pounds will be worth when it is paid. The amount subject to loss is the transaction exposure, and there are three ways in which it can occur:

(i)   if a currency has to be converted to make or to receive payment for goods or services
(ii) if a currency has to be coverted to repay a loan plus the interest; and
(iii) if currency conversion is needed to make dividend payments.

Figure 7.1 gives an example of where transaction exposure exists.

Fig. 7.1 An Example of where Transaction Exposure Exists

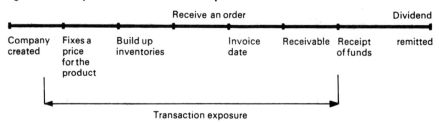

Transaction exposure

The company sets up in business and decides to export. It fixes product prices, builds up inventories, receives an order, sends an invoice, accepts credit (giving the company a receivable) and is eventually paid. During the whole time period of fixing the product price and actually receiving payment the company is subject to transaction exposure. A very important point to stress about transaction exposure is that it may involve a future cash loss to the company. In other words, it could involve a negative cash flow.

Translation exposure (sometimes called accounting exposure) arises from having assets and liabilities denominated in one or more currencies and consolidating them into a base currency. In this case, it is important to stress that no funds are actually moved and, therefore, translation exposure has no direct effect on cash flow. This is, however, only true if there are no tax effects. Figure 7.2 gives an example of where translation exposure occurs.

Transaction exposure involves current cash flows, results in realised gains and losses, may have a tax effect in that realised, and in some cases, unrealised gains and losses are taxable or allowable against tax, can affect all parts of the company, and can have important future implications for the company.

Translation exposure is an accounting concept which may affect future cash flow; it is a book value, results in unrealised gains and losses, and usually has no tax effect; it is primarily to do with the past of the company and affects principally the parent company. It is often claimed that transaction exposure affects the income statement while translation exposure affects the balance sheet. This, however, is not strictly accurate. Transaction exposure affects assets and the rules of translation exposure applied will affect profits. The parent company with receivables in a foreign currency will be affected by both translation and transaction exposure.

Fig. 7.2 Where Translation Exposure Occurs

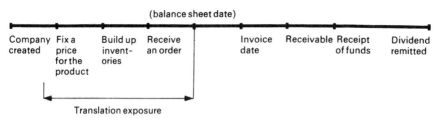

Another type of exposure is off-balance-sheet exposure. How does this arise? To take an example: a UK company bids for a contract in Sweden which has been put out to tender in which all bids are to be denominated in Swedish krone. The contract is for the supply and installation of equipment over a four-year period with payment spread over the same period. What does the UK company do when all its costs are denominated in sterling and it has no future requirement for Swedish kroner? If it bids in sterling and takes no exposure it could lose the contract for non-compliance with the currency of the contract. If it bids in Swedish kroner, what exchange rate does it use for the conversion of the sterling price, in the knowledge that there may only be a six-month forward market in Swedish kroner? In this example, if the UK company wins the contract and the Swedish kroner diminishes appreciably against sterling in the future, the UK company risks a large foreign exchange loss which is not yet incorporated into the balance sheet.

Fig. 7.3 Exchange Exposure Possibilities

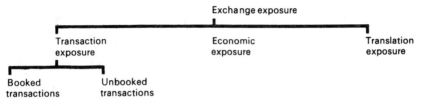

As can be seen from Fig. 7.3 a new term, economic exposure, has been introduced. Economic exposure consists of transaction exposure plus those items on the balance sheet which will actually be converted at market rates.

How does economic exposure occur? Assume the French subsidiary of a German company imports goods from Germany and sells them exclusively in France. Also, assume that the subsidiaries' annual funds flow in French francs is as follows:

SALES PROCEEDS   1000
TOTAL F.F. DISBURSEMENTS (350)

DISPOSABLE PROFIT   650
D.M. IMPORT PAYMENTS   500 (Equivalent in FF)
TAX RATE   50%

TOTAL F.F. EXPOSURE = 150 + ($\frac{1}{2}$ × 500) = 400

Economic exposure exists only for those French francs which are to be converted into Deutschmarks. In this example, economic exposure is FF 400. If the goods were obtained in France, the FF exposure position would only amount to FF 150, which is the disposable profit. There are no Deutschmark import payments but the FF 150 still has to be converted into Deutschmarks.

THE ACCOUNTING TREATMENT OF EXPOSURE

The accountant is faced with a problem when there has been a change in the exchange rate. He has to decide which exchange rate to use for translation: the old or the new rate. The core of the problem is the translation of the subsidiary's assets and liabilities as stated in its balance sheet. The profit and loss account is essentially subsidiary to the balance sheet. Once the values of a company's assets and liabilities are established, its profit is also established since its profit is, by definition, the increase in the value of the net assets of the company over the year. Thus accountants have tended to focus attention on the problem of establishing the exchange rate to be used for translating the items in the foreign subsidiary's balance sheet. Economists have approached the problem in a different way.

The problem is that there are two possible exchange rates that can be used to translate an asset or a liability; the exchange rate that was ruling at the time that the asset or liability came into existence (the 'historic rate'); or the exchange rate ruling at the date of the balance sheet (the 'closing rate').

Accountants have developed three principal different methods of translating the assets and liabilities of foreign subsidiaries. They are:

(i)   Current/non-current method (also called the working capital method).
(ii) Closing-rate method (also called the current rate method).
(iii) Monetary/non-monetary method.

Current/non-current method

This is based on the conventional accounting distinction between current items (assets or liabilities to be received or paid within one year) and long-term items. Current items are translated at the closing rate; long-term items are translated at their historical rates. The implicit argument is that only short-term items held abroad are subject to exchange-risk. Long-term items are assumed to be fixed in terms of their parent currency values, that is, until they become short-term. The accounting exposure inherent in each foreign subsidiary, as measured by this method consists, therefore, of its net current assets.

Closing-rate method

According to this method all foreign currency-denominated items are translated at the closing rate of exchange. Therefore, all foreign assets and liabilities are assumed to be equally at risk, and the accounting exposure inherent in each foreign subsidiary is simply its net equity.

Since the parent company's net equity stake in each of its foreign subsidiaries is positive (except in the unusual case of those in a loss carry-forward position) all companies using the closing-rate method are 'long' in the currency of each foreign subsidiary. In other words, in the normal case each foreign subsidiary's exposed assets exceed its exposed liabilities. Clearly, then, if the parent currency depreciates *vis-à-vis* its subsidiaries' currencies, as has been the case for most UK companies in recent years, the closing-rate method will produce persistent translation gains. Exposure Draft 21 summarises the advantages of the closing-rate method.

(i)   It deals effectively with the situation where fixed assets located overseas have been financed by foreign currency borrowings and a change in the exchange rate results in offsetting gains and losses.

(ii) The relationship existing between balances in accounts as originally prepared in a foreign currency is preserved in the translated accounts whereas this is not the case where historical rates are used for translating certain assets.

(iii) It is not necessary to maintain sterling records of fixed assets and inventories located overseas which would be required if historical rates were to be used.

(iv) It is simple to operate and the results are easily understood by users of accounts.

The arguments against the closing rate method are that it is not universally agreed that the exchange risks of holding cash or short-term investments abroad are the same as holding fixed assets; nor is a short-term debt of a subsidiary payable in the near future comparable to the long-term foreign currency debt which has been used to buy fixed plant.

Monetary/non-monetary method

Monetary items are translated at closing rates; non-monetary assets (both short-term and long-term) are translated at their historical exchange-rate. The accounting exposure inherent in each foreign subsidiary, as measured by this method, is therefore defined as its net financial assets.

The main departures from the current/non-current method are that inventory is treated as a non-exposed items and long-term debt now becomes exposed. The second difference is the most significant, since long-term debt is often the largest single component in a company's accounting exposure. This can produce very large translation (and real) losses if the parent or one of its subsidiary companies holds loans which are denominated in a currency which is appreciating *vis-à-vis* the parent currency, as was the case in the early 1970s for the USA and (to a lesser extent) for UK companies holding massive Deutschmark and Swiss franc loans.

Table 7.1 summarises the translation rules under the different accounting methods. A cross indicates whether assets and liabilities are translated at the closing or historical rates of exchange.

Table 7.1

	CLOSING RATE METHOD		CURRENT/ NON-CURRENT METHOD		MONETARY METHOD	
	Closing rate	*Hist. rate*	*Closing rate*	*Hist. rate*	*Closing rate*	*Hist. rate*
ASSETS:						
Cash/securities	+		+		+	
Receivables	+		+		+	
Inventory	+		+			+
Fixed assets	+			+		+
LIABILITIES:						
Current payables	+		+		+	
Long-term debt	+			+	+	

Source: 'An Economic Analysis of Foreign Exchange Risk', D. Walker in *Occasional Paper No. 14* (Institute of Chartered Accountants in England and Wales, March 1978).

THE ECONOMIC TREATMENT OF EXPOSURE

Having analysed the problems of exposure from the point of view of an accountant, exposure is now examined from the point of view of an economist. Accounting information is designed, among other objectives, to show the effects that currency changes have on a company in the current period. It is not designed to show the future effects currency changes may have.

Accounting records will not normally show:

(i)   the cash flow effect of a future exchange rate change;
(ii)   possibilities of price controls or high inflation in the future;
(iii)   reactions of the local labour force to wage and price changes following devaluation;
(iv)   effect of a future devaluation on the supply of loanable funds;
(v)   effect on price margins of higher future raw material costs;
(vi)   possibility of a more buoyant home market;
(vii)   greater international competitiveness in price.

Economic exposure is a means of allowing for these effects. Economic exposure is based on the possibility that the parent company's net present value of a foreign subsidiary's future cash flow will be affected by exchange rate movements.

Professor Dufey has clearly illustrated that corporate reaction to translation exposure, rather than economic exposure can be contradictory.[1] Following the expected devaluation of the French franc in 1968, the French subsidiary of a US company greatly reduced its exposed assets. Any policy to reduce exposure always involves costs. In this case, the French subsidiary reduced its cash holdings which had an adverse effect on its working capital and on its efforts to develop the company. However, the devaluation may increase the company's ability to export, thus improving the company's position.

Devaluation, therefore, can have two opposing effects. Fearing a large translation loss, the company may adopt defensive tactics, which are costly, while the possibility of increased profitability may call for greater investment. Devaluation should improve the local currency revenues resulting from a firm's export sales. The firm may either maintain its product prices in terms of foreign currency, thereby increasing its local currency receipts by the devaluation percentage, or it may lower the foreign currency price and attempt to increase its sales volume. Similarly, firms producing goods which compete with imports in the domestic market should normally see an improvement in revenues, since the devaluation adversely effects foreign competition. However, the devaluation causes a rise in the local currency cost of inputs for most firms. Those companies whose expenses include a high proportion of imported materials are hardest hit. The price of imported inputs can increase by any percentage up to the full amount of the devaluation rate, although normally it is somewhat less, the final level depending on competition.

The final effect of a devaluation on the profits received by the parent company can be computed only after the expected local currency revenue and costs have been brought into account. The effect is determined by applying the new exchange rate to the predicted net local currency profit. After translating the adjusted net local currency cash flows into dollars, the final devaluation gain or loss can be determined. The result will depend on whether the loss arising from the new rate exceeds, equals, or is less than, the change in the net local currency cash flow. It follows, therefore, that the outlook for some subsidiaries will actually improve after a devaluation, for some it will deteriorate, while for others the net changes will be close to zero.

[1]   'Corporate finance and exchange rate variations', G. Dufey, in *Financial Management* (Summer 1978).

Shapiro, like Dufey, also examined the accounting methods of measuring exchange risk.[2] He concluded by illustrating that, in contrast with accounting views, the major factors influencing a multinational firm's exchange risk include the distribution of its sales between domestic and export markets, the amount of import competition it faced domestically, and the degree of substitutability between local and imported factors of production.

The two ways of approaching the problem of the measurement of foreign exchange exposure, i.e. accounting exposure and economic exposure, are, however, linked in so much as economic exposure includes transaction exposure plus those items on the balance sheet which will actually be converted at market rates. Concentration on the two measures of exposure have resulted in two alternative systems of measuring the exposure. The two systems have been labelled the 'balance sheet approach' and the 'cash flow method'.

The 'balance sheet approach' starts by choosing a yardstick currency which, in the case of US companies' is the dollar. Current assets are then divided into 'exposed' and 'unexposed' according to whether the currency of denomination is 'softer' than the yardstick currency. Concern is only attached to imported inventories which have not been paid since only these can have a negative effect on dollar values in the event of a devaluation. Imported inventories already paid or local source inventories do not change in dollar value in the event of a devaluation. Fixed assets count entirely as unexposed because the real value of a fixed asset is the present value of the future stream of income that it will generate. Liabilities are accorded the same sort of classification analysis as current assets, again according to the effect on the payment cost of the liability as expressed in the yardstick currency. The sum of the exposed items result in an adjusted net worth measurement of exchange exposure. The deficiencies in this approach have already been enumerated (p. 143).

The cash flow approach recommended by Shapiro and Giddy[3] emphasises that gains and losses arise not from assets and liabilities themselves but rather from the cash flows that these assets and liabilities generate. Hedging should attempt to reduce the variability of cash flows by matching, whenever possible, each period's cash inflows with that period's cash outflows in a particular currency. Thus, whenever a firm has cash inflows from sales in a particular foreign currency it should seek to match those inflows by incurring contractual outflows in the same currency, either by borrowing in the same currency in which the firm has sales receipts, or by entering into a forward contract to sell the foreign currency at the time the foreign currency is received. As is explained in Chapters 8 and 9, if interest parity prevails, the additional (or lower) cost of foreign currency debt should equal the forward discount (or premium) and so the cost of either method should be the same.

Giddy, following the cash flow school, defines exchange risk as the variability of cash flows arising from currency fluctuations. These can be divided

[2]   'Exchange rate changes, inflation and the value of the multinational corporation', in *Journal of finance* (May 1975).

[3]   'Exchange risk: whose view?'. I. H. Giddy, in *Financial Management* (Summer 1977).

into contractual and non-contractual cash flows. Contractual cash flows arise from items like debts, payables and receivables. The risk here is in having excess outflows in a revalued currency or excess inflows in a devalued currency. Non-contractual cash flows are the expected revenues from sales and expected costs of purchasing inputs. Non-contractual exchange risk may occur following a devaluation with uncertainty attached to the rise in export revenues and the increase in import costs. He questions the importance of these two forms of exchange risk given the existence of two relationships. The first relationship is that between interest rate differentials and exchange rate differentials, the so-called 'Fisher effect'. The theory states that interest rates tend to reflect exchange rate expectations. If this is true, then the risk of exchange losses on contractual outflows or inflows in foreign currency may be small, since the Fisher effect also states that interest rates in 'strong' currencies tend to be low enough, and in 'weak' currencies high enough, to offset expected currency gains or losses. The second relationship is that between prices and exchange rates. According to the purchasing power parity theorem, gains or losses from exchange rates tend, over time, to be offset by differences in relative inflation rates. A firm buying inputs or with sales invoiced in a foreign currency may then find that the net effect of devaluations and revaluations diminishes in the long run.

The 'Fisher effect' leads one to predict that contractual cash flows would not, in the long run, be subject to exchange risk. The purchasing power parity theory, if valid, means that, in the long run, non-contractual cash flows would not be subject to exchange risk.

Giddy then examines the empirical evidence for these relationships for the period 1972 to 1975 for four countries, Canada, France, the UK and Italy. His results show that over three-month periods the relationships are very poor but that over a three-year period the relationships are much more robust. This leads him to conclude that: 'except where some specific bias or market imperfection can be identified, the company that is prepared to wait it out may save time and money by relying on the expectation that any exchange rate gains or losses will sooner or later be offset by interest rates and price changes'. Other studies, notably by Robert Aliber,[4] have confirmed Giddy's findings. However, the question still remains as to what to do about short-term exchange risk. In the short run, contractual cash flows may be minimised by hedging or by increasing foreign currency debt. Eliminating non-contractual cash flows is more difficult. Giddy recommends that short-term exposure can be minimised by currency diversification. This reduces risk for three reasons. First, exchange rate changes are imperfectly correlated, and frequently negatively correlated. If the pound sterling declines in value for example, the Deutschmark often increases in value when measured in some third currency such as the dollar. Secondly, business risk, defined as fluctuations in business conditions, are less than perfectly correlated between countries. Thirdly, for any given country, exchange rate changes and business conditions are less

[4] *Exchange Risk and Corporate International Finance*, R. Z. Aliber (The Macmillian Press, London 1978).

than perfectly correlated. He concludes by stressing that, in assessing exchange risk associated with cash flows in a particular currency, it is important to look not at the currency in isolation but rather at its contribution to the riskiness of the company's 'cash flow' portfolio as a whole.

IDENTIFICATION OF FOREIGN EXCHANGE EXPOSURES

The accounting definitions are, as they must be, deficient in that they are primarily concerned with what has already happened. Economic exposure, defined as the exposure resulting from the need to convert one currency into another in the future at what will be other than the present 'book' or 'planned' rates, is what is important. Economic exposure includes all transaction exposure and those items involved in translation exposure which will be converted at current exchange rates.

Transaction exposure is difficult to define quantitatively. A decision has to be be taken in deciding how many months of sales or purchases should be included in the transaction exposure position. This varies between companies. It depends on each company's pricing flexibility and how fast it can increase selling prices to offset the effect of a currency change.

Economic exposure is the measure that most accurately describes the company's foreign exchange exposure. Once defined the next problem is that of identification. In identifying foreign exchange exposures it is necessary to identify both current and future positions. A company needs to develop a reporting system which provides information as to the firm's current and projected future exposure. The first step is to ensure that each subsidiary sends into the head office, on a regular basis, its balance sheet position delineated by currency.

Table 7.2 shows how this can be done. This in turn needs to be supplemented by foreign exchange exposure forecasts and by cash flow forecasts. The company then has a broad picture of its present and future foreign exchange exposure.

Projections are essential for anticipatory exposure management. These projections need not necessarily be in detail for each item. Trends and basic changes in the most important positions frequently suffice.

In reviewing these exposure forecasts there are certain guidelines which should be followed:

(i)   review items which appear in the accounts at present, and which will not have been converted into cash by the next reporting period;
(ii) review items which appear in the accounts at present, and which can be expected to have been converted into cash by the next reporting period;
(iii) review items which do not appear in the accounts at present, but are budgeted to arise before the end of the next reporting period;
(iv) review items which do not appear in the accounts at present, but will come and go by the end of the next reporting period;

(v) review off balance sheet exposures – these include future commitments of sales and/or purchases, any leasing arrangements and forward exchange contracts.

Table 7.2

	Balance sheet (000)				

Subsidiary:

Location:

Date:

Individual currencies listed by column

	$	£	DM	FF	etc.
Assets					
Cash and short-term investments					
Accounts receivable: Third party					
Intercompany					
Short-term loans to affiliated companies					
Inventory					
Pre-paid taxes and other expenses					
Total current assets					
Long-term investments and advances					
Net property, plants and equipment					
Other assets					
Total assets					
Liabilities					
Short-term debt					
Current portion of long-term debt					
Accounts payable: Third party					
Intercompany					
Accrued expenses					
Short-term intercompany debt					
Provision for taxes, other current					
Total current liabilities					
Other liabilities					
Long-term debt					
Long-term intercompany loans					
Total liabilities					
Net worth					
Common stock					
Other equity accounts					
Retained earnings					
Total net worth					
Total liabilities and net worth					

Source: *Foreign Exchange Risk*, A. R. Prindl (John Wiley & Sons, 1976).

THE NECESSARY STEPS FOR EFFECTIVE FOREIGN EXCHANGE RISK MANAGEMENT

In order to measure the degree of exchange risk faced by the company certain steps have to be followed:

(i) Establish the total position in each currency according to both translation and economic exposure.
(ii) Undertake market analysis of the expected fluctuation range of exchange rates.
(iii) Establish the risk magnitude.
(iv) Introduce the decision format.

Once the risk magnitude is defined, the company can then decide, given the costs of hedging policies, whether to hedge or to leave the position open.

(i) Establish the total position

This has already been discussed in detail earlier in this Chapter.

(ii) Market analysis

An important step in measuring exchange risk is to identify accurately future exchange rate movements. Broadly speaking, two alternatives are open to the company. Firstly, the company can employ 'in-house' personnel. These forecast rates based on the ideas set out in Chapter 6. Alternatively, the company may use 'bought-in' exchange rate forecasts. These are supplied by the major banks and by specialist forecasting organisations. 'Bought-in' forecasts differ in the sophistication of the services they offer. Some offer point estimates while others offer target ranges of future exchange rates.

Foreign exchange rate forecasts and the forward exchange rate

However what is most important is to use forecasts which compare a forecast with the current forward rate. It is an almost impossible task to forecast exchange rates exactly. However this is not what the person dealing with a company's foreign exchange exposure needs. What he requires is a correct signal. That is to say, if the price is going to weaken or strengthen more than the current forward price implies, the forecaster should pick this up. If he does do this, the client has then received accurate guidance on the central decision he has to take – whether to cover his forward currency requirements or not – and the forecaster will have earned his fee.

This point, which is crucial to grasp in understanding the commercial value of a forcasting service, can be illustrated by an example. Suppose that a UK treasurer knows that he has to pay for a quantity of imports in US dollars in three months' time. The UK pound on day one is exchanging at $1.80, but on the 90 day forward market, it is worth only $1.75. The forecaster predicts that it will depreciate, not to $1.75, but only to $1.79, and he turns out to be right.

The treasurer, following the forecaster's advice will not have covered, but buys spot when the imports are due. He thus receives $1.79 for his pound instead of $1.75, making 4 cents on every pound.

Again, suppose the actual price when the three months was up was not $1.79, but $1.76. The treasurer will still gain by following the forecaster's advice, i.e. not covering. The gain will be less (1 cent on every pound, the difference between the forward market and three month future spot), but there will be a slight gain, and *this is* despite the fact that the forecaster in this example is actually less close to the actual outturn than the three month forward price was. The crucial fact is that the forecaster foresaw that the price was going to weaken less than the 90 day forward market view implied. In other words, the forecaster was on the 'right' side of the market. The right signal had been given, and when the right signal is given, the corporate treasurer makes (or avoids losing) money.

Forecasts of this type provide an independent means of establishing the track record of the company. 'Bought-in' services may provide certain advantages. First, they may help to provide a feel for the markets in both the short and long run. Second, they may be useful in helping the company to clarify its own thinking about many commercial decisions such as pricing and marketing policy. Thirdly, econometric services can be modified with a company's own judgment about non-econometric factors influencing exchange rates. Also a 'bought-in' service can be a way of collecting information on trade movements, interest rates, capital flows etc which can then be used for the 'in-house' forecast. Finally, 'bought-in' services can be used as scapegoats. Any multinational treasurer can use them to protect himself against often ill-informed criticism from those who do not understand the market. Thus he can claim to have taken the best advice he could obtain and, if this turned out incorrect, it is not his fault.

(iii) Establish the magnitude of the risk

The risk magnitude can be defined as:

CURRENCY POSITION × EXCHANGE RATE MOVEMENT

One means of combining differing estimates of exchange rate movements is by the use of histograms. In this way the exchange rate forecasts may be weighted by their reliability. Thus, starting with a spot rate of $1.87, the following six-month forecasts of the dollar/sterling exchange rate can be obtained (Fig. 7.4).

Assume that the foreign exchange advisors in this example were surveyed, their views can be summarised in Figure 7.4. 70% believed the rate would be between $1.80 and $1.85, 20% between $1.85 and $1.90 and 10% between $1.90 and $1.95.

Assume also that a UK company had an import payable due in six months of $500,000. Using expected values, a loss expectation may be calculated as follows:

$500,000 (70% + 2.43% + 20% × 0% − 10% × 2.94%) = $6,965 or £3,724.

Thus, given the weighted expectation of the dollar appreciation, the position should only be totally covered if the cost of doing so does not exceed $6,965.

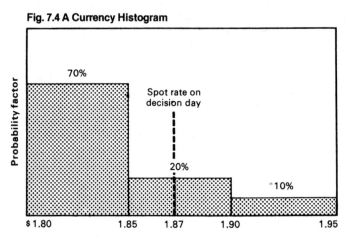

Fig. 7.4 A Currency Histogram

(iv) Introduce the decision format

Once the loss expectation has been established the company is then in a position to decide whether or not to cover. The company should then introduce a decision format, as outlined in Fig. 7.5, for its currency positions, its fluctuation factor and the expected loss or gain.

Fig. 7.5 Decision Format

	(£000)		
	CURRENCY POSITIONS (±)	FLUCTUATION FACTOR (±)	EXPECTED LOSS/GAIN (±)
U.S. Dollars			
Deutschemarks			
Japanese Yen			
French francs			
Dutch guilders			

Given this information the company can decide what policy to undertake. Whatever decision format is constructed, it should not be based on the absolute amount of gain or loss. Under such a system, one good deal could hide a multitude of bad – one lucky break conceals a consistently poor performance. It is preferable just to categorise deals as good or bad and compare totals over time. Once the decision format is intoduced the corporate hedging strategy and the organisation for esposure management should be established.

CORPORATE HEDGING STRATEGY AND ATTITUDE TOWARDS RISK

The hedging strategy depends on the corporate objectives and the attitude towards risk. This has been succinctly summarised by Prindl:[5]

'If the firm considers its primary objective to be the maximisation of sales income from home and foreign operations and is otherwise adverse to risk taking, it may well wish to cover both translation and economic risks completely. If, on the other hand, the firm sees exchange gains as an additional component of income or determines that the cost of being fully covered outweighs the potential negative effects of any exchange rate movement it may establish a currency-by-currency strategy resulting in a policy to cover certain positions fully, but to leave others either partially or completely uncovered'.

Of course the most conservative approach of all is to hedge every exposure, while the least is to hedge nothing. Except for where exposure is tiny compared to the company's overall size, both these methods are impractical and expensive. (It is said, with some justification, that the most expensive hedging policy is to cover no risks, and the second most expensive is to cover all risks.) For most companies the question is which exposure to hedge, and to what extent.

So the choice of strategy depends on company attitudes to risk. Some examples will make this clear:

● a risk paranoid manager typically concentrates on translation risk; financing is all in local currency; any exposure is fully hedged;
● a risk neutral manager concentrates on economic/transaction risks and ignores translation effects (unless he considers the financial markets to be inefficient);
● with asymmetrical risk aversion, losses loom larger than gains in the manager's eyes; interest 'costs' are preferable to exchange 'losses', above a certain trigger level, translation exposure will usually be hedged;
● the aggressive speculator uses the markets as just another business opportunity.

Most usual, in the US, is behaviour of the risk asymmetrical type.

Of the many factors involved in the hedging decision are the costs of alternative hedging policies (see Chapters 8 and 9). Other questions involve organisational implications, and the impact of disclosure rules on company results.

---

[5]   *Foreign Exchange Risk*, A.R. Prindl (John Wiley, 1976).

THE ORGANISATION OF EXPOSURE MANAGEMENT

Operational exposure management is a matter for the purchasing, production and marketing departments working in conjunction with the finance department. It focuses on the change in the value of net cash flows due to unanticipated exchange rate movements. The different departments should have different responsibilities.

The Marketing Department:	decides the degree of flexibility in terms of price and invoice currency in weaker currency markets or in deciding to switch the marketing effort to strong currency areas.
The Purchasing Department:	decides the degree of flexibility in paying in hard currencies or in switching to suppliers in weaker currency areas, i.e. using the time gap between the advantage of weaker currency purchase and the disadvantage of a higher price as a result of the corresponding inflation.
The Production Department:	decides the degree of flexibility in adding more value in weaker currency areas with a corresponding decrease in stronger currency areas, i.e. using the same parity movement/inflation, time gap.
The Finance Department:	decides the degree of flexibility in increasing the volume of stronger currency raw material inventory, in paying strong currency payables faster (at suitable trade discounts) and in collecting weaker currency receivables faster.

Centralisation versus decentaralistion

The major organisational question for a company is of deciding whether to organise the exchange exposure from the headquarters or from the subsidiary. The advantage of allowing foreign subsidiaries to manage their exposure is that local managers are frequently in the best position to judge the timing of impending exchange rate changes and/or exchange control changes. Moreover, delegating this responsibility to local managers is a stimulus to their motivation. If they can consistently perceive the benefits of their actions they are likely to become more highly motivated.

However there are strong reasons for centralising the exposure management. Indeed a centralised control is usually recommended for the following reasons:

(1) It puts the exposure management function in the hands of the officer responsible for managing the company's balance sheet – the treasurer. Exposures often have a significant effect on cash flows and liquidity, and hedging exposures always does.

(2) It ensures that there is a consistent exchange and exposure policy. Under a decentralised system, there is a danger that different departments with different objectives will follow different exposure policies, often in direct conflict with one another.

(3) Under a decentralised system there is the danger of exposures being covered twice. A centralised system also avoids the situation where one division is buying dollars while another is selling; i.e. it allows matching. Moreover, individual transactions are larger and quotes are likely to be more competitive.

(4) A dealing operation is expensive. It needs professional expertise plus an elaborate support operation. Duplication of this operation at several different points within an organisation is very wasteful. Centralisation avoids this.

Under a centralised system the individual operating units pass their exposures to the dealers thus freeing themselves from any exchange risk. It is then up to the dealing room itself to decide whether to cover or not. The operating unit records the transaction as though it was covered – i.e. at the appropriate forward rate or cost of hedging and so has a realistic exchange rate to use in its pricing policy and on which to base its operating figures. Similarly the dealing operation under this system becomes a profit centre in its own right, as it can decide not to hedge at this rate and make profits or losses. Clearly, it will be important that a conservative dealing code is in operation to prevent outright speculation. This is where the company strategy for exposure management comes in (this is discussed further in Chapter 10).

In some circumstances a compromise centralised/decentralised approach may be appropriate.

The need for a currency committee

Whether centralised or decentralised decision making is introduced the company needs to use the expertise of a currency committee. This usually consists of economists, treasurers, planners, and marketing representatives. Basically, all major areas of the business need to be incorporated. The currency committee has a two-fold role; first, to establish the currency weights needed for the histogram analysis dissussed earlier; and secondly, to educate the functional business areas as to currency developments and their likely corporate impact. The currency committee can provide guidance and consultation in the development of strategy and hedging options, bringing together knowledge and expertise outside the finance area and beyond the technical inputs, dealing with tax, accounting and legal questions. It should consider long-term hedging options which may lie outside the treasurer's authority, or which may involve conflicts of authority.

APPENDIX I

The UK accounting position

Following several exposure drafts (in particular ED 16 and ED 21), the SSAP 20 came into force from April 1983. This permits the use of both temporal and closing rate methods, although it notes that normally the closing rate should be used.

The standard says: 'the method used to translate financial statements for consolidation purposes should reflect the financial and other relationships which exist between an investing company and its foreign enterprises.

'In most cases the closing rate/net investment method . . . should be used and exchange differences accounted for on a net investment basis. However, in certain specified circumstances . . . the temporal method should be used.'

The standard goes on to specify that it recognises the parent company's interest as being in the net worth of the foreign subsidiary, not the individual assets and liabilities of that entity. It therefore opts for the closing rate method as the most appropriate one-balance sheet values of the subsidiary to be translated at balance sheet date with the rate effective on that date. The standard also allows a choice for translating the income statement of the foreign subsidiary: it allows use of either the closing rate or the average rate. 'The use of the closing rate is more likely to achieve the object of translation . . . however it can be argued that an average rate reflects more fairly the profits or losses and cash flows as they arise to the group through an accounting period. The use of either method is therefore permitted'.

However, the standard also goes on to offer a new approach to dealing with translation differences. It notes that year on year translation differences, if reported through the income statement, will distort the operating results of the entity and in any event points out that such differences do not necessarily have any connection with the trading results. It therefore requires that translation differences should be taken directly to shareholders' equity by way of an adjustment to reserves.

APPENDIX II

The US accounting position

In the US FAS 8 'Accounting for the translation of foreign currency transactions and foreign currency financial statements', was published by the FASB in October 1975. FAS 8 was based on the concept that subsidiaries are merely extensions of a single entity. Two features of FAS 8 were predominant. First, the temporal method of translation was compulsory. Secondly, foreign exchange gains and losses had to be passed through the profit and loss account as part of normal operating profit. FAS 8 was immediately subject to widespread criticism on the following grounds.

(i)   Wild fluctuations in profit figures could occur especially when reported quarterly because of the treatment of stocks and foreign borrowings.

(ii)   A weak 'home' currency gives rise to translation losses under the provisions of FAS 8. However, a relatively strong currency would lead to larger profits when expressed in terms of the dollar. Therefore, it was argued, that it is unreasonable to report a translation loss. The argument can be countered however, by suggesting that the strength of the foreign currency might adversely affect the trading position of the subsidiary by making its exports, for example, more expensive.

(iii)   As the dollar weakened US groups with substantial overseas interests found their reported income severely affected by translation losses. This generated great pressures for the abandoning of FAS 8.

(iv)   One of the main difficulties with FAS 8 arose from the fact that under the temporal method fixed assets are translated at historical rates whereas loans are translated at the closing rate. Thus if a foreign subsidiary company raises a local loan to purchase fixed assets and the overseas currency appreciates against the home currency there will be a loss on translation. This despite the fact that in foreign currency terms the value of the fixed asset and loans may be equivalent.

(v)   Because of the divergences of economic and accounting exposure companies can be induced into 'hedging' contracts in order to reduce the accounting exposure to exchange rate movements and might thereby incur real (economic) losses in order to reduce accounting exposure.

(vi)   The temporal method is based on the concept that a single enterprise is reporting and foreign operations are an extension of the activities of the parent body. Opponents of the method argue that an interest in a foreign subsidiary is one total investment which cannot be identified with individual assets and liabilities. It should, therefore, be this net investment which is exposed and not individual assets.

(vii)   One of the arguments advanced in favour of the temporal method is that the principles of historical cost account are preserved by virtue of the fact that foreign transactions stated at historical cost are translated at historical rates. However, critics of the temporal method point out that an historical cost is established in terms of the new currency of the operating unit and not in terms of the reporting currency of the holding company.

Under the weight of these criticisms, FAS 52 was introduced in December 1981. Under FAS 52 companies can choose betweeen using the closing rate method, in which case translation differences are reflected in the reserves or the temporal method in which case translation differences can turn up in the profit and loss account.

FAS 52

FASB 52 defines two new terms, 'functional currency' and 'reporting currency'. Translation itself is the process of expressing a functional currency statement in reporting currency terms.

A foreign affiliate's *functional currency* is defined as the currency of the primary economic environment in which it operates and in which it is expected to generate net cash flows. If the foreign affiliates's operations are relatively self-contained and integrated within a particular country, its functional currency will be the local currency of that country. Thus, for example, the German affiliate of a US parent doing most of its manufacturing in Germany and selling most of its output for German marks would normally use the mark as its functional currency. If the foreign affiliate's operations are a direct or integral extension of the US parent's operations the functional currency could be the US dollar. An example would be an offshore manufacturing plant that received all its raw material from the United States and resold all its output back to the United States.

The *reporting currency* is the currency in which the parent firm prepares its own financial statements. This currency is usually the home country currency.

Management must evaluate the nature and purpose of its foreign operations to decide on the appropriate functional currency. Some of the economic factors that enter into such decisions are listed in Table 7.3.

Table 7.3

Economic factors to consider in determining functional currency

| Foreign Entity's | *Functional Currency Indicators* | |
	Foreign currency	*Parent currency*
Cash flows	Primarily in the foreign currency; no direct impact on parent cash flow	Direct impact on parent cash flow; readily available for remittance to parent
Sales price	Determined by local competition; not responsive in short-run to exchange rate changes	Determined by worldwide competition or prices; responsive in short-run to exchange rate changes
Sales markets	Active local market for affiliate's products	Sales markets mostly in parent's country or denominated in parent's currency
Expenses	Primarily incurred in local currency	Primarily for components obtained from parent's country
Financing	Primarily in foreign currency, with debt service generated by foreign operations	Primarily from parent or in parent's currency, with parent funds needed for debt service
Intercompany transactions	Few intercompany transactions, with foreign entity quite independent	Many intercompany transactions, with extensive interrelationship with parent's operations

Source: *Statement of Financial Accounting Standards No. 52*, Financial Accounting Standards Board, (Stamford, Connecticut: Financial Accounting Standards Board, December 1981), derived from material on pp. 26–27.

Chapter 8
Internal Techniques For Managing Foreign Exchange Exposure

DESCRIPTION OF INTERNAL TECHNIQUES

Chapter 7 outlined the distinctions between the transaction, translation and economic exposure. In this Chapter the internal techniques (defined below) open to the firm to reduce this exposure are examined. All exposure minimisation techniques involve costs of one sort or another and, clearly, only if the benefits outweigh the costs will the technique be worthwhile. The various costs involved are outlined throughout the Chapter.

The choice of currency hedging techniques by management is determined by the type of company making the choice. A company producing goods for export in foreign currency with import payables in foreign currency is one type, a multinational company with extensive international involvement is another. Naturally, the range of techniques open to the latter is greater than to the former. This choice is also determined by the structure of the company and by corporate policy towards exchange risk which, in turn, is constrained by hedging costs, tax effects, the method of translation adopted and by various regulatory bodies.

Two distinct types of technique exist: those which internally manipulate the composition of the exposed position and which may involve reorganisation of the company structure (internal techniques), and those techniques which involve the use of external institutional services and financial markets. Appendix I contains a summary of the main hedging techniques and indicates how these should be implemented depending on whether a devaluation or a revaluation is expected. Appendix II illustrates the critical importance of using 'real' rather than 'nominal' exchange rates when making hedging decisions.

Following Prindl*, internal techniques can be broken down into:

1. Internal techniques affecting outstanding positions:
    (i) prepayment of existing third party commitments;

---

* *Foreign Exchange risk*, A.R. Prindl (John Wiley, 1976).

     (ii)   inter-company term adjustment (leads and lags);
     (iii) exposure netting.

  2. Internal techniques affecting future positions:
     (i)   price adjustments;
       (a) currency of invoicing changes;
       (b) transfer pricing through the exchange rate;
       (c) local subsidiary price increases and export price increases;
     (ii) asset/liability management;
       (a) increase of net short-term assets;
       (b) reduction of liabilities;
       (c) long-term asset/liability changes.

  3. Long-term structural changes:
     (i)   Export financing vehicle;
     (ii) Reinvoicing vehicles.

1. INTERNAL TECHNIQUES AFFECTING OUTSTANDING POSITIONS

(i) Prepayment of existing third party commitments

An importer expecting a revaluation of the exporting country's currency would be advised to pay for the goods immediately. By so doing the importer avoids the necessity, which would occur with a revaluation, of having to pay more of his own currency in the future. As this increases his need for working capital the importer will have to compare the cost of borrowing money (or its 'opportunity cost' if he already possesses finance) with the expected size of the revaluation. Similarly if a company has borrowed a strong currency which is expected to be revalued it would be advised to repay the liability as soon as possible. Again the cost of borrowing needs to be compared with the expected rise in the exchange rate.

    These policies may however be complicated by exchange control regulations. An attempt to sell one's own currency for another, stronger currency is often interpreted as speculation by the official authorities and rigorous exchange control regulations may severely limit a company's freedom to act as it wishes.

(ii) Inter-company term adjustment (leads and lags)

Forty per cent of the world's trade is estimated to be undertaken by multinational companies. This means that, even with exchange control restrictions, the scope for exposure minimisation by multinationals is much greater than for independent trading companies. Thus inter-company term adjustments, normally called 'leads' and 'lags', become feasible. 'Leads' are advance payments for imports to avoid the risk of having to pay more local currency if the supplier's currency revalues. 'Lags' involve the slowing down by exporters of foreign receipts into the local currency in the expectation that if a foreign currency appreciation occurs it can then be converted into more local currency.

Naturally leading and lagging can also be undertaken, to an extent, by independent trading companies.

A UK exporter receiving foreign currency and expecting a foreign currency devaluation should 'lead' his receipts and the same exporter expecting a revaluation should 'lag' his receipts. A UK importer paying foreign currency and anticipating a foreign currency devaluation should 'lag' his payments and the same importer anticipating a revaluation should 'lead' his payments. A non-UK importer paying in sterling and anticipating a sterling revaluation should 'lead' his payments and the same importer anticipating a sterling devaluation should 'lag' his payments. A non-UK exporter receiving sterling and anticipating a sterling revaluation should 'lag' his receipts and the same exporter anticipating a sterling devaluation should 'lead' his receipts. Table 8.1 summarises these points.

Table 8.1
A Corporate Guide to Leads and Lags

A UK exporter (receiving foreign currency):
1. expecting a foreign currency devaluation might: Lead (shorten credit)
2. expecting a foreign currency revaluation might: Lag (grant longer credit)

A UK importer (paying foreign currency):
1. expecting a foreign currency devaluation might: Lag (take even longer to pay)
2. expecting a foreign currency devaluation might: Lead (pay early)

A non UK importer (paying in sterling):
1. expecting sterling revaluation might: Lead (pay early)
2. expecting sterling devaluation might: Lag (delay payment)

A non UK exporter (receiving sterling):
1. expecting sterling revaluation might: Lag (give longer credit)
2. expecting sterling devaluation might: Lead (reduce credit)

The scope for 'leading' and 'lagging' is still influenced by exchange control requirements. The benefits for the firms concerned depend on the size and timing of the exchange rate changes and the differences in local financing costs. Thus the subsidiary which is 'leading' import payments needs to finance these at the relevant interest rate. The subsidiary which is 'lagging' export receipts will have surplus cash which could be placed in the local money market.

In order to evaluate the constraints involved in 'leading' and 'lagging', some of which have already been mentioned, the firm should set them out systematically. Table 8.2 shows how this can be done. Thus the 'leading' firm needs to know the minimum number of days exchange controls permit the 'leading', the costs of borrowing and the opportunity cost of liquidating short-term investments. The 'lagging' firm needs to know the maximum number of days

Table 8.2
Summary of Leading and Lagging Constraints

Location	Minimum Days	Total S.T. Credit Lines	Unused Credit	Cost	Short-Term Investments	Yield	Maximum Days	Prepayable Debt	Saving	Investment Availability	Yield
					LEADING					LAGGING	
US											
UK											
Italy											
Belgium											
France											
Canada											

exchange controls permit 'lagging', what the position is on pre-paying debt and the returns available on investing the 'lagged' receipts.

One development of the technique which has proved useful, where local exchange regulations prohibit lagging, is to sell the company's products to another local affiliate for local currency, which, in turn, acts as buying agent for the eventual purchaser of the good. Payment in the hard currency is thus delayed, benefiting the hard currency affiliate and mopping up excess local currency liquidity.

(iii) Exposure netting

Exposure netting involves leaving open positions in two (or more) currencies. Exposure netting is based on the assumption that the activities of the companies involved are so large and varied that all the individual 'long' and 'short' positions may approximately cancel out.

Despite moving to a period of floating rates, there are still currencies which are closely linked together. Examples of this are the EMS members, and the close link between the Deutschemark and the Austrian schilling. Thus a company with payables in Belgian francs and receivables of a similar magnitude in guilders may decide to leave these positions unhedged on the assumption that the currencies will retain fixed parity values.

2. INTERNAL TECHNIQUES AFFECTING FUTURE POSITIONS

Two types of policies are possible which affect future positions. These involve pricing policies and change in balance sheet positions. In discussing pricing policies, marketing considerations should predominate but currency issues can still be important.

(i) (a) Currency of invoicing changes

An example of an inappropriate pricing policy is given below, in Table 8.3. With receivables in a currency which devalues and payables in a currency which revalues the exporter loses £25.

Table 8.3
The Effect of Invoicing Exports in Sterling and Imports in US Dollars
Combined with a Sterling Devaluation

	Due to receive	Due to pay
Month one:	£100	$200
£1 = $2		= £100
Month two:	£100	$200
£1 = $1.60		= £125

Fall in £/$ rate causes loss of £25:

(i) *If* the firm cannot pass the higher cost of its imports commitment on in a higher price to its customers, and

(ii) *If* it has not hedged the foreign currency commitment in the forward market.

The alternative pricing policies open to companies are to invoice in:

- the home currency (we will take the example of sterling)
- the currency of the overseas buyer/seller
- a third currency
- foreign currency but link payment to a currency 'basket'

Invoice in the home currency (say sterling)

There are clear advantages to both the UK exporter and UK importer in accepting sterling as the invoice currency because the foreign exchange transaction will have to be undertaken by the overseas party and therefore:

- The UK exporter will know exactly how much he will receive in payment for his goods or services;
- The UK importer will know precisely what he will eventually have to pay for the goods he has purchased and will be able to compare the cost of imported goods accurately with similar products that may be available on the home market.

For both exporters and importers, invoices expressed in their domestic currency mean:

- That it will not be necessary for a foreign exchange transaction to be made, thus avoiding exchange risks;
- Easier accounting since existing domestic bookkeeping and administrative systems can be used.

Invoice in the currency of the overseas buyers/seller

Faced with the obvious advantages of trading in his own currency, why should the UK businessman contemplate selling or buying goods in the currency of his overseas customer or supplier?

It may well be necessary to do so in order to maintain a competitive position. The UK exporter, quoting in sterling at a time when his buyer, say in Germany, is comparing contesting bids denominated in Deutschmarks, may be at an immediate disadvantage. If the exporter switches his offer from sterling to Deutschmarks then his chances of a sale may be increased because the buyer can easily evaluate all offers on the same basis. Additionally, the buyer would not be exposed to an exchange risk since he would be paying for the goods in his own currency.

The UK importer is in a different position since he may be able to nominate the currency of the invoice. This will particularly be the case if he is in a buyer's market or if a major share of a supplier's product is purchased. In these circumstances the importer may be in a position to stipulate being invoiced in sterling. However, if he is pressed into paying in a foreign currency, he, like the UK exporter, will face a number of problems:

- An exchange risk will be incurred because the foreign currency involved has to be converted to or from sterling
- Additional bookkeeping and accounting systems will be needed
- It may be necessary to initiate some form of regular monitoring of

outstanding foreign exchange payables and receivables (known as 'exposure') which will provide management with the information to make any required decisions

Once it has been agreed that invoices are to be drawn in a foreign currency, a company's primary concern must be to ensure that planned profit margins will be protected for the time period between establishing the contract and the day payment is received or made. Use of the forward exchange market will eliminate this risk.

There are several advantages in invoicing in a foreign currency which is stronger than the local currency. Take the example of sterling and assume it is at a discount in the forward market. Firstly, the existence of the forward exchange market enables the firm to sell that currency forward which, since it will be at a premium, gives the firm either a higher sterling profit on the transaction or enables it to increase turnover by reducing the foreign selling price of the product. Secondly, the firm could finance exports in a currency with interest rates lower than sterling interest rates. Thus, if the firm had a Deutschmark receivable, it could undertake Deutschmark borrowing, which may be cheaper than sterling, without it incurring any transaction exposure. Both of these advantages enable a more competitive price in overseas market to be quoted. Pricing in a currency which is stronger than sterling and which is appreciating also means that rises in domestic costs can be absorbed without the continual need to adjust the sterling list price.

Invoice in a third currency

Contract quotations in a third currency, i.e. in a currency that is foreign to both the exporter and the importer, are particularly common when consideration is being given to the purchase of capital goods. Also, when trade is conducted with a country whose currency is regarded as 'exotic' it is usual to invoice in an internationally traded currency such as the US dollar.

In these cases, both the importer and the exporter will face the problems that are associated with invoicing in a foreign currency. Some countries' exchange control regulations, however, may preclude the use of a third currency.

Invoice in foreign exchange but link payment to a currency 'basket'

A currency 'basket' is a compilation of several currencies each with a specific 'weight' (see p. 80). As long as the 'basket' contains some currencies that are likely to appreciate and some that are likely to depreciate, the net change of the 'basket' unit against one particular currency is likely to be less than the change of any one currency against that particular currency.

For example: the *Special Drawing Right* (SDR) can be used (see Chapter 4). Suppose a UK exporter agrees to payment in Italian lire but specifices that he must receive lire worth (say) SDR 15,000. On the day of payment the exporter will receive his lire, but if that currency has depreciated sharply against sterling, but less sharply against the SDR because the latter contains some weak currencies which have also depreciated against sterling, then the exchange risk may be shared between buyer and seller depending on their own currency changes against the SDR. This is illustrated in Table 8.4.

Table 8.4

The Effect of Invoicing in an SDR-linked Currency

Rates at start of credit period	Rates at end of credit period
SDR1 = £0.625 = L.IT 1500	SDR1 = £0.55 = L.IT 1650
SDR1.6 = £1.00 = L.IT 2400	SDR1.82 = £1.00 = L.IT 3000

When the contract of sale is agreed the Italian importer accepts that he will make payment in lire worth SDR 15,000. To the UK exporter this is worth at the time SDR $15,000 \times £0.625 = £9,375$.

To the Italian importer this is worth at the time SDR $15,000 \times$ L.IT $1,500 =$ L.IT 22.5 million.

When the payment falls due the Italian importer must pay SDR $15,000 \times$ L.IT $1650 =$ L.IT 24.75 million.

To the UK exporter this is worth $\dfrac{24.75m}{3000} = £8,250$.

Summary

The Italian importer pays L.IT 2.25m more, equal to a 10% *increase in cost*. The UK exporter receives £1,125 less, equal to a 12% *reduction in receipts*.

In this way the risk has been shared between them. Of course there is no guarantee that the risk will be divided more or less equally between the parties or that they will even be divided at all!

This will depend on the degree to which both currencies fluctuate against each other and against the 'basket' unit itself.

Practical Considerations

Practical considerations may limit foreign currency invoicing. In a regular trading relationship a change in invoicing currency depends on the relative bargaining strengths of the exporter and importer and may be difficult to change. More sophisticated pricing and accounting procedures may be needed as well as expertise in managing the new system. If forward cover is not available or suitable, the company may be exposed to considerable risk due to the widespread gyrations taken by foreign exchange rates.

Companies must also remember that for some products they have no choice as to what the currency will be. For universally traded goods, e.g. oil, forest products, some raw material commodities, the United States dollar determines the world market price level.

(i) (b) Local subsidiary price increases and export price increases

The immediate effect of a devaluation is to raise import costs. Any company anticipating a local currency devaluation should, therefore, wherever possible, raise its domestic prices. This is even more important since devaluations are often followed by price freezes. Between raising its prices and the devaluation occurring, discounts may be offered to lessen the impact of the rise and to maintain competitiveness locally. However, if a new price list is printed prior to a devaluation, a price squeeze which may follow a currency's depreciation can be circumvented. Moreover, when exporting to a weak currency area price rises can offset the effect of the exchange rate change. It is essential that a company makes use of the expected movement in the 'real' exchange rate when taking hedging decisions. This is discussed further in Appendix II.

(i) (c) Transfer pricing

Another method of manipulating the exposed position is by transfer pricing. Approximately 40% of international trade is thought to be transfers between related multinational companies. Transfers within a multinational group enable tax burdens to be shifted from high tax to low tax countries as well as reducing exposure, by raising or lowering intra-group selling prices.

Transfer pricing operates by the arbitrary pricing of intra-company transfers of goods and services at a higher or lower figure than an arm's length evaluation would indicate. There is a considerable degree of subjectivity involved and consequently management's choice of a 'fair' price can lie between rather broad limits.

Transfer pricing can help to eliminate exchange losses in areas of the world where continual devaluations take place and can involve exchange gains where continual revaluations occur. Often countries with chronic inflation or balance of payments difficulties may limit capital outflows by various means. Transfer pricing may provide the only means for the investor to repatriate earnings from an economy experiencing devaluation and capital outflow controls. Intracompany transfers of goods and services to the subsidiary in question may be marked up in price; alternatively, its exports to affiliated companies may be priced as low as possible. Ideally, companies make high profits in strong currency, low tax areas and vice versa. However, even if as a result of the transfer pricing, earnings were increased in a country with a higher tax rate, this might well be more advantageous than having profits blocked, or eroded away by a continual depreciation of the local currency.

Transfer pricing does, however incur costs. It is expensive to administer and it may cause the company to run foul of the tax and customs authorities at home and overseas. Generally, transfer pricing has become more difficult as the authorities, particularly in countries prone to devaluation, have insisted on arm's length pricing.

2   (ii) Asset/liability management

Asset and liability management for foreign exchange management is directly analogous to the management of working capital. The major components of current assets are inventories of stocks, debtors or accounts receivable, prepayments, short-term investments and cash and bank balances. Typical components of current liabilities include trade creditors or payables, accrued expenses, bank overdrafts, bank loans, proposed dividends, short-term loans and tax payments due. The major items of working capital are cash, receivables, inventories, payables and short-term debts and it is upon these that working capital management tends to concentrate.

Working capital management is desirable for several reasons. First there are costs involved in holding current assets. Inventories, cash and debts are idle assets and do not generally attract interest. The cost of holding these is the interest foregone which could have been earned. If everything is equal, inventories, cash and debtors should be reduced to nil balances. However, everything is not equal. This leads to the second benefit of managing working capital, namely the cost of having inadequate working capital. A company having a low level of inventory may find that customer requirements cannot be met. This reduces potential sales and may involve a long-term loss of customers. Sales may also be lost if the company is unable to provide competitive credit terms to customers, i.e. by not allowing receivables to rise. A further problem with inadequate working capital managment is the inability to meet debts when they become due. A company may be very successful and yet may become bankrupt due to an inability to finance short-term debts.

If a subsidiary is expecting a local currency revaluation it should increase its net short-term assets. This can be achieved by building up cash, short-term investments, receivables and inventories denominated in currencies likely to revalue. Thus cash can be allowed to accumulate in the bank, receipts for receivables speeded up and possibly, payment for raw materials slowed down. A similar result could be achieved by reducing the company's liabilities, i.e. by reducing the company's payables and hard currency borrowings. If a local currency devaluation is expected the company should decrease its assets, cash, receivables and inventories, and increase its liabilities, payables and borrowings.

The basic rule in working capital management of a currency which is likely to depreciate is to reduce assets and to increase liabilities. Similarly, if a revaluation is expected, the aim should be to increase assets in that currency and reduce liabilities. However, there are costs involved in working capital management. If a company reduces its cash in anticipation of a devaluation it will need to borrow locally to finance production. In some economies this may be heavily controlled or in others, notably South America, it may be extremely expensive. Interest rates in South America of over 100% are not uncommon. Similarly, if receivables are reduced, customers, finding their trade credit greatly reduced, may refuse to undertake more business with the company.

Finally, inventory reduction, in the face of an expected devaluation, may mean a loss of customers.

The basic hedging strategies for assets and liabilities are summarised in Table 8.5.

Table 8.5
Hedging Strategies

	Assets	Liabilities
Hard currencies (unlikely to devalue)	Increase	Decrease
Soft currencies (likely to devalue)	Decrease	Increase

Long-term assets and liabilities are not so readily reducible, but the pre-payment of long-term debt is one method of reducing liabilities. Fixed assets, if their realisation is not apparent in the near future, are only exposed under the closing-rate method. Leasing of plant and equipment removes this exposure from the balance sheet, but is worthwhile only when the domestic currency is depreciating.

These actions must be undertaken in accordance with domestic exchange controls and may be limited in their implementation further by a creditor's or debtor's resistance to the variation of cash flow timing, and by the adverse tax implications which may result.

3.   LONG-TERM STRUCTURAL CHANGES – REINVOICING

Many multinational companies have altered their structure so as to improve their international currency management. Local hedging is often constrained by exchange control requirements and the actual structure of the foreign exchange market. The cost of forward cover may be prohibitively expensive or it may simply be unavailable. The most popular solution to this problem is to reinvoice.

Under reinvoicing, the subsidiaries of a manufacturing company send the goods directly to a marketing subsidiary but then invoice a separate entity – known as a reinvoicing company – in the currencies in which funds are required. The reinvoicing company would then, in turn, invoice the marketing subsidiary in the currencies received by the subsidiary thereby hedging the currency exposure. The reinvoicing company can in turn adopt appropriate exposure management.

APPENDIX I

Exposure management techniques

Anticipation of a local currency devaluation	Anticipation of a local currency revaluation
Sell local currency forward	Buy local currency forward
Reduce levels of local currency cash and marketable securities	Increase levels of local currency cash and marketable securities
Tighten credit (reduce local receivables)	Relax local currency credit terms
Delay collection of hard currency receivables	Speed up collection of soft currency receivables
Increase imports of hard currency goods	Reduce imports of soft currency goods
Borrow locally	Reduce local borrowing
Delay payment of accounts payable	Speed up payment of accounts payable
Speed up dividend and fee remittances to parent and other subsidiaries	Delay dividend and fee remittances to parent and other subsidiaries
Speed up payment of inter-subsidiary accounts payable	Delay payment of inter-subsidiary accounts payable
Delay collection of inter-subsidiary accounts receivable	Speed up collection of intersubsidiary accounts receivable
Invoice exports in foreign currency and imports in local currency	Invoice exports in local currency and imports in foreign currency

Source: 'Managing Exchange Risks in a Floating World', A.C. Shapiro and D.P. Rutenberg, in *Financial Management*, Vol 5, No. 2 Summer 1976.

APPENDIX II*

The importance of the real exchange rate for corporate decision making

The combination of large differences in inflation rates between countries and the substantial fluctuations in nominal exchange rates over the past few years presents many problems for companies heavily involved in dealing with foreign currency. The problem is particularly acute where companies are faced with long-run decisions that are influenced by the relative movements of inflation rates and exchange rates. If we take the example of a British company faced with the decision of allocating substantial resources of the development of a product for sale in the United States, then the rate of return on the investment and its location will be affected by the sterling value of the eventual sales relative to their cost. The sterling value of sales will depend upon the dollar price at which the product is sold in the US and the dollar/sterling exchange rate. If the selling price in the US follows the US average price level and the exchange rate itself moves to compensate for differences between inflation rates in the US and the UK, then the sterling value of export will move with the UK average price level. This can be seen in the hypothetical example shown in Table 8.6.

In this example we assume, for simplicity, no inflation in the United States between 1976 and 1980 and that the product sells for $200 in each case. We also assume that the UK price level doubles over the period. If the exchange rate moves exactly to offset the inflation differential then it will fall in our example from two dollars to the pound to one dollar to the pound. Expressed another way the exchange rate depreciates from 0.5 pounds per dollar to one pound per dollar, which exactly offsets the doubling of sterling prices. Under these assumptions the price of the product selling in the US for 200 dollars now converts to £200 in 1980 compared to £100 in 1976, a movement in line with UK average prices. Therefore if costs have moved in line with average inflation rates the profitability of the project remains unchanged between the two years even though sterling costs have doubled and the dollar selling price has remained unchanged.

Alternative (a) takes the case where the *currency depreciates by less than the movement* in relative inflation rates, only falling to 1.2 dollars per pound. In this case the price of the product expressed in sterling only rises to £166.7, i.e. £200/1.2 and if costs have doubled in line with UK inflation then clearly the project is now much less profitable. The second case shows the reverse situation where the exchange rate depreciates by more than the movement of relative prices and the sterling value of the price rises to £250, i.e. £200/0.8 which represents an increase considerably greater than the increase in costs.

---

*This appendix draws on London Business School Briefing Paper: 'Forecasting the Real Exchange Rate', T. Burns, P.M.W. Lobban and P. Warburton.

It follows that, in considering the profitability of different courses of action which involve exchange rate assumptions, one key ratio to focus upon is the movement of the *real exchange rate*; that is the (actual) exchange rate in dollars per pound multiplied by the ratio of the UK and US average retail price indices. In the first case in the example above the real exchange rate remained unchanged at two (1976) dollars to the pound sterling, and the profitability of the project expressed in sterling remained unchanged, (i.e. $1 × ratio of 2). In alternative (a) the real exchange rate appreciated from 2.0 to 2.4 dollars (i.e. $1.2 × ratio of 2) to the pound, and the export decreased in profitability. In the second alternative the real exchange rate depreciated to 1.6 dollars (1976) to the pound (i.e. $0.8 × ratio of 2) and profitability increased.

If the real exchange rate between two countries remains unchanged we can see that the exchange rate problem vanishes. The difficulty is that in practice, if we compare the movement of exchange rates and inflation rates the real exchange rate is not in fact constant. If the real rate of, say, sterling rises against the dollar, due to either a rise in sterling or United Kingdom prices rising faster than United States prices, the company suffers as the dollars acquired are worth less sterling. If the real rate falls, due to either a fall in sterling or UK prices rise more slowly than US prices, the company gains as the dollars acquired are worth more sterling. Therefore those taking decisions which are affected by movements in inflation rates and exchange rates must take an active view of their probable trends. As already discussed it may also be important to measure the real exchange rate.

Table 8.6

	Price of product in $	Average US price level index 1976 = 100	Exchange rate $ per £	Average UK price level index 1976 = 100	Price of product in £
1976	200	100	2	100	100
1980	200	100	1	200	200
Alternative (a) 1980	200	100	1.2	200	166.7
Alternative (b) 1980	200	100	0.8	200	250

Chapter 9
External Techniques for Managing Foreign Exchange Exposure

DESCRIPTION OF EXTERNAL TECHNIQUES

External techniques for exchange risk minimisation are those techniques which involve access to 'external markets'. The following range of techniques are open to companies with international operations:

(i)   use of forward exchange market;
(ii)   taking out a foreign currency loan (used by an exporter with weak currency receivables);
(iii)   borrowing/deposit arrangements in two currencies (used by an importer with strong currency payables);
(iv)   discount/sale of foreign currency receivables;
(v)   leasing;
(vi)   exchange risk guarantees;
(vii)   currency cocktails;
(viii) forfaiting;
(ix)   other techniques. factoring and 'lock box' systems.

As with internal techniques these alternatives involve costs and the company must ensure that the benefits outweigh the costs before committing itself to one particular technique. The final section outlines some of the internal constraints which limit a firm's ability to use either internal or external hedging techniques.

Appendix I examines the use of parallel loans, back to back loans, and currency exchange agreements.

THE FORWARD EXCHANGE MARKET

The workings of the forward exchange market were outlined in Chapter 1. The existence of the forward market enables a contract to be made, usually with the foreign exchange department of a bank, to buy or sell a stated amount of a foreign currency on a stated day in the future at a known exchange rate.

Assume, for example, that a UK company orders a machine tool from a West German manufacturer. The equipment is to be delivered in six months from the date of order, and the price is quoted in Deutschmarks. At the present time the spot rate is £1 = 4D.M. The UK company believes, however, that the value of sterling is likely to fall in relation to the Deutschmark during the coming six months. If this happens the price that the UK company will have to pay in sterling to buy the Deutschmarks they need for the machine will increase. The company can cover itself against this risk by entering into a contract now to buy the required amount of Deutschmarks needed in six months' time.

Assume that the rate quoted for six month Deutschmark is £1 = 3.75 D.M. The formula to calculate the annualised cost of cover is as follows:

$$\frac{\text{Forward rate} - \text{spot rate} \times \text{Time period} \times 100}{\text{Spot rate}}$$

$$\frac{(3.75\text{–}4.00) \times 12 \times 100}{4.00 \times 6} = 12.5\%$$

This means that if the UK company sells sterling forward to cover the exchange risk, it loses 12.5% per annum compared with selling sterling for Deutschmarks now (i.e. a spot deal). The UK company has to decide whether the expected devaluation of sterling is likely to be greater than the cost of forward cover.

Appendix II in Chapter 1 describes a more sophisticated way that companies could measure the cost of forward cover.

HOW TO APPLY FORECASTING EXPERTISE WHEN TAKING HEDGING DECISIONS

As already mentioned the forward rate provides a useful benchmark around which to judge forecasting expertise. However, the next question to ask is if the forecasting service does consistently outperform the forward market, how should one apply the expertise in taking hedging decisions. (See Table 9.1)

Table 9.1

NATURE OF FORECAST	Anticipate Devaluation		Anticipate Revaluation	
	Current Position			
	Long	Short	Long	Short
EXCHANGE RATE FORECAST LESS THAN FORWARD RATE	*Recommended Action*			
	Cover forward	Leave open	Cover forward	Leave open
	Current Position			
	Long	Short	Long	Short
EXCHANGE RATE FORECAST GREATER THAN FORWARD RATE	*Recommended Action*			
	Leave open	Cover forward	Leave open	Cover forward
EXCHANGE RATE FORECAST EQUAL TO FORWARD RATE	NEUTRAL			

FOREIGN CURRENCY LOANS – FOR EXPORTERS

If an exporter sells goods to a buyer in a country whose currency is weak and has to invoice in the currency of that country, an alternative to a forward sale would be to offset the account receivable by local borrowing in the buyer's country.

Assume that a UK exporter will receive proceeds of US$1,000,000 in eight weeks' time. In addition make the following assumptions:

● Bank lending rate for US$ for 8 weeks (56 days) = 10% p.a.
● Bank lending rate for sterling for 8 weeks = 11% p.a.
● Interest on US$ borrowings calculated on 360 day year.
● Interest on sterling borrowings calculated on 365 day year.
● the following bank buying rates have been quoted by the bank:

Spot	1.6130
1 month	1.6150
2 months	1.6170
3 months	1.6195

The exporter could now borrow sufficient dollars in anticipation of proceeds of US$1,000,000 after allowing for interest that will have to be repaid together with the loan principal. The amount borrowed is converted at the prevailing spot rate and, for the purpose of this example, the sterling so obtained is used to reduce an existing bank overdraft. The export proceeds are used to repay the foreign currency loan.

Calculations:

(i)   Exporter borrows $984,682.71
      On maturity he will repay –
      Principal   = $984,682.71

      Interest $\dfrac{984,682.71 \times 10 \times 56}{100 \times 360}$ = $\ \ 15,317.29

      Thereby matching borrowing against export proceeds $1,000,000.00

(ii) Exporter converts borrowing to sterling:
      $984,682.71 at 1.6130   = £610,466.65

(iii) Exporter uses £610,466.65 to reduce sterling overdraft for 8 weeks, and providing the overdraft interest rate does not change, saves interest of

$$\dfrac{£610,466.65 \times 11 \times 56}{100 \times 365} \qquad = £\ \ 10,302.67$$

      Total effective sterling return is therefore   £620,769.32

In this case the exporter can lock himself into a known sterling receivable, irrespective of whatever happens to be the exchange rate.

Because the currency borrowed is the same as that in which the proceeds are received, there is no exchange risk unless the buyer refuses to make payment (strictly speaking this latter case would be credit risk). Any proceeds received prior to the end of the eight week period for which the borrowing has been arranged, may be placed on interest-bearing deposit to match the loan maturity and thereby increase the overall return still further. It may be worthwhile to arrange a forward contract with the bank to cover the exchange risk on the interest that will be earned on the account. Conversely, a delay in the receipt of proceeds would necessitate asking the bank to extend the period of the loan and consideration should be given to arranging a forward contract with the bank to cover the exchange risk on the additional interest that will be charged on the loan.

A problem arises, however, if government restrictions on capital transfers make it impossible to take locally borrowed funds out of the country. This problem can be circumvented by using the euro-currency markets. It is usually possible to raise a sterling loan in the euro-sterling market instead of in the UK domestic money market. Again the proceeds can be converted into dollars and used to make a dollar loan, and the cost of the operation is the difference between the interest rate on the euro-sterling borrowed and the interest obtained when the dollars are deposited.

BORROWING AND DEPOSITING FOREIGN CURRENCY – FOR IMPORTING

In the same way that an exporter with a receivable in a weak currency can arrange to borrow the weak currency so can an importer with a payable in a strong currency place the amount due on deposit. The importer buys the strong currency, e.g. Deutschmarks, spot in exchange for his own currency, say lire, and places the Deutschmarks on deposit. Exchange control permitting, the importer then possesses the Deutschmarks and is insulated from any appreciation of the Deutschmark which takes place. Again, the relevant interest rates to calculate the cost of this transaction are the euro-rates. An importer can also prepay the liability and arrange for a cash discount.

The covering methods already described are not completely unrelated; they are linked together through the mechanism of interest rates. In theory, the cost of covering by these methods is always the same because the forward discount on one currency in terms of another is directly reflected to the interest rates between the two currencies. Thus, if the dollar is selling at a three per cent forward discount in terms of the Deutschmark, the interest rate on dollar loans will be about three per cent higher than the rate on Deutschmark loans. If there were no difference between the two interest rates, then money-markets arbitragists, realising the weakness of the dollar as shown by its forward discount, would start borrowing dollars and lending Deutschmarks. This arbitrage would quickly drive up the cost of dollar funds and drive down the cost of Deutschmark loans until the margin came into line with the forward market rates again. In the real world, however, there are three main factors which impede the working of the interest rate mechanism: government monetary and fiscal policies, central bank operations, and restrictions on convertibility and capital transfers. Moreover, there may be significant time lags in the adjustment of international interest rates. In practice these limitations are bypassed by using the euro-markets.

DISCOUNT/SALE OF FOREIGN CURRENCY RECEIVABLES

Foreign currency receivables can usually be discounted in local markets. The bank which discounts these bills will, in choosing the appropriate discount rate, combine domestic interest costs with the cost of forward cover. An additional advantage of discounting foreign currency bills is that the onus of collection falls on the bank.

LEASING

Leasing has long been used in connection with capital goods. A lease is a means by which a firm can acquire the economic use of an asset for a stated period of time. An exporter to a weak currency country may consider selling the goods outright to a leasing company which then leases them to the ultimate user. Since the exporter is paid immediately he can convert his weak currency receivables into a hard currency immediately and thus eliminate any exchange risk.

There are three principal types of lease financing. The first is sale and leaseback, in which a firm owning land, buildings or equipment sells the property and simultaneously executes an agreement to lease the property for a specified time under specific terms. Secondly, there is the service lease or operating lease, which include both financing and maintenance services, are often cancellable, and call for payments under the lease contract which may not fully recover the cost of the equipment. Thirdly, there is the financial lease which does not provide for maintenance services during the basic lease contract period.

The cost of leasing an asset must be compared with the cost of owning the same asset. Leasing may be valuable for long-term contracts where the forward markets are very thin. As can be seen from the different types of leases the administrative problems for the major parties are likely to be considerable.

EXCHANGE RISK GUARANTEES

Most governments are willing to given some type of guarantee for certain types of exchange risks. Governments, perceiving the benefits of exporting, will normally assist the exporters in many ways, including the provision of exchange risk guarantees. These guarantees are often for official overseas borrowing, for projects with very long 'lead' times where forward market cover is not available, and traditionally, for hard currency countries.

Since October 1 1976 the UK Export Credits Guarantee Department (ECGD) cover has been provided for contracts expressed in certain major foreign currencies which were supported by use of the forward exchange market or foreign borrowing. Previously, an exporter who had protected himself against exchange rate changes by use of the forward exchange market or by borrowing against the expected receipt of foreign currency could suffer additional loss in meeting these currency obligations, if he did not receive payment from overseas. This loss would not have been covered by ECGD. Under ECGD Comprehensive Guarantees, claims had been paid by the ECGD at the rate of exchange ruling at the time ECGD cover commenced. From October 1 1976 cover is related to the rate obtaining at the time the loss is incurred, if this is more favourable to the exporter. ECGD also provide for additional cover to allow for close out losses/gains when receipts are not forthcoming (likewise when a currency has been borrowed). For business on credit terms up to two years, in certain circumstances, ECGD will consider payment of up to 15% more than it would otherwise have paid on a valid claim, provided an exporter has suffered extra loss as defined above.

For business on credit terms of greater than 2 years, ECGD provide Buyer Credit Guarantees. Under this system a UK bank makes finance available to the overseas buyer with an ECGD guarantee. The overseas buyer can then pay the UK exporter immediately. In this case the exporter has eliminated his currency risk.

A scheme to assist exporters tendering for major capital goods contracts to be financed in foreign currency was introduced in 1977 by ECGD, which covers them against exchange rate movements in the period between tendering and the award of the contract.

Before this scheme was introduced, when exporters had to quote the price for their contracts in foreign currency, they had to judge at the time of tender the equivalent of the currency concerned in sterling that they ultimately hoped to receive. If at that stage they had sought cover in the forward exchange market but did not then win the contract, they would have faced a risk of loss in closing out their forward contracts if sterling had meanwhile depreciated against the forward contract rate. Or if they did not cover forward ECGD will indemnify the insured contractor against cost over-runs, which are judged by ECGD to be unavoidable and irrecoverable, incurred for reasons outside the insured's control in connection with nominated sub-contracts. The causes of loss covered are:

(i) default by a nominated sub-contractor which necessitates termination of his sub-contract and completion of his work by a replacement sub-contractor at a total cost exceeding the original sub-contract price provided for in the tender price;

(ii) unavoidable additional cost incurred by the main contractor and attributable to a nominated sub-contractor but not recoverable from him by reason of limitations imposed in his sub-contract, other than that arising from an event occurring in the buyer's country and outside the control of the main and sub-contractors.

The amount of ECGD's cover will be 80% of the admissible losses with a maximum liability of 20% of the total UK value of the project contract.

A prerequisite of the issue of this facility is basic credit insurance cover with ECGD, which should be sought from ECGD as early as possible in the negotiations.

In Germany the export credit agency, HERMES, provides special policies for transfer and conversion risks for single or recurring sales. Cover is provided for exchange risks of more than three per cent. The scheme applies to contracts exceeding two years in duration. While HERMES bears the risk it also takes any profits which may arise, but it only covers major currencies.

In Holland, the Netherlands Credit Insurance Company Limited commenced insuring exchange risks in October 1973. Cover is eligible to any exporter from the Netherlands and is confined to contracts with maturities exceeding a period of two years which are denominated in currencies that are internationally marketable.

In France, the COFACE scheme provides for: (i) guarantees which cover the loss suffered by the exporter in the event of a reduction in the rate of the foreign currency in which an export contract is expressed; and (ii) guarantees which cover the loss incurred as a result of a rise in the exchange rate of the country in which the contract for the purchase of supplies or foreign loans necessary for the execution of the export contract is drawn up.

In the USA, the Export-Import Bank (Eximbank), created in 1934, is an independent agency of the executive. It provides billions of dollars of credit to help foreigners import US goods. The credits are often in the form of insurance or a guarantee. For a fee Eximbank guarantees the payment of a receivable which the exporter has sold to a local bank, where the receivable is from a foreign customer. The guarantee covers all political risk and portions of normal business risk. The Eximbank also guarantees the direct loan by a US bank to a foreign purchaser of US goods. This guarantee is often used for capital equipment.

CURRENCY COCKTAILS

Currency cocktails are practical means of diffusing the effect of exchange rate fluctuations on international trade and investment. In addition they are used by various supra-national bodies, such as the EEC.

There are two main categories of currency units: first the official units of account including, particularly, the Special Drawing Right (SDR) and the European Currency Unit. (See Chaps. 4 and 5).

In order that the SDR can be easily used for indexation purposes its value is initially expressed in terms of one currency and the US dollar is used for this purpose. The value is calculated by converting the currency components of the basket to dollars and the example in Table 9.2 shows the method of calculation. Once the SDR/US dollar exchange rate has been determined the rate for any other currency can be calculated using the market rate for the currency in terms of the US dollar.

Table 9.2
Valuation of the SDR as at March 10 1982 (in US dollars)

	Currency units in the basket	Market spot rate currency per $	$ value of components	Currency weighting
US dollar	0.54	1.00	0.5400	47.85%
Deutschmark	0.46	2.3655	0.1945	17.23%
Sterling	0.071	1.8115*	0.1286	11.40%
Yen	34.0	237.40	0.1432	12.69%
French franc	0.74	6.0570	0.1222	10.83%
Total*			1.1285	100.00%

Source: IMF
Value of SDR in terms of US $ is $1.1285
Value of SDR in terms of Sterling is £0.6230 (computed from $/SDR and $/£ rates shown above)

* $ per £
* Total may differ from sum of components due to rounding

The value of the ECU is calculated in much the same way as the value of the SDR, and is equal to the sum of fixed amounts of the 10 component currencies.

Each of the 10 currencies which go to make up the unit has a weight based on the country's relative trading importance in the community and is reviewed every five years. Details of the basket composition are shown in Table 5.1 in Chapter 5.

The value of one ECU is expressed in US dollars using a method of calculation similar to the SDR valuation as illustrated in Table 9.2. Once the US dollar/ECU rate has been determined, the ECU value of any other currency can be derived through the dollar rate for that currency.

There could certainly be benefits for importers and exporters in using currency cocktails to reduce exchange rate risks. This is particularly true for longer term contracts or in the less universally used currencies where exchange cover is not easy to obtain.

An investor linking his deposits to the SDR or ECU receives considerable protection from the turbulence that has characterised the foreign exchange market in recent years. He is, in effect, hedging against fluctuations in exchange rates by depositing his funds in the spread of currencies contained in the baskets.

Linking deposits to the SDR or ECU enables an investor to hedge his foreign exchange exposure in one deal, thus saving the time and administration costs of undertaking several deals to split a deposit into a number of currencies.

FORFAITING

Fortaiting means the business of bankers (or forfaiters) discounting, without recourse to the holder, a series of trade drafts or promissory notes with a final maturity of up to seven years. The 'without recourse' clause means that the endorser of a promissory note has the legal right to absolve himself of liability. This is not the case in many countries with a bill of exchange where the drawer is always legally open to recourse regardless of any declaration to the contrary.

The sources of forfaitable obligations are varied. The most important are countries where the traditional export credit system is inadequate, restrictive or uncompetitive. The UK and France, for example, are not high on the list, due to the generosity and all-embracing nature of their respective export credit institutions, ECGD and COFACE. However, Switzerland and West Germany, and more recently the USA and Italy, are countries where exporters require the assistance of private (i.e. non-governmental) financial institutions. In some cases, where governmental export credit programmes require the exporter to carry a sizeable recourse risk on his books, or require unreasonable conditions for documentation or difficult payment terms, exporters turn to forfaiting as a viable alternative. This is due particularly to the non-bureaucratic nature of forfaiting.

The cost of forfaiting, i.e. the discount rate, is based upon a number of factors. The most important of these is, naturally, the refinancing cost to the forfaiting company, normally the euromarket rate for similar credit periods for the currency used in the transaction. To this basic cost is added a premium to cover the commercial, currency, economic and political risks. The commercial risk concerns the possibility that commitments may not be honoured by the obligor or guarantor. The cost charged for the currency risk being accepted by the forfaiter is reflected in the euromarket cost of covering medium-term and thus in the eurocurrency deposit rate. Economic risks arise when government intervention prevents or hinders payment of a debt. Political risks cover the non-financial difficulties which can occur, such as change of government, wars, blockades, boycotts and strikes which must be taken into account when fixing a margin for risk.

Forfaiting is normally possible for export debts with a longer period to maturity than one can obtain when factoring.

OTHER TECHNIQUES

Two other less important techniques for managing exposure are factoring and 'lock box' systems.

Factoring

The role of a factor is to buy debts incurred by business in the normal conduct of trade. For a UK based company there are two methods of international factoring:

(i) Factoring without recourse: the UK factor uses correspondent factors to guarantee debts and for collection. This method is restricted to exports to countries in which there is a chain member, i.e. mainly, most Western European countries and North America.

(ii) Factoring with recourse: the exporter relies on an ECGD policy. The factor uses a chain member where possible and otherwise uses its own resources for collection. The factor is protected by an assignment of ECGD policy and a factoring endorsement.

The covering of exchange risk is not normally a part of the factoring service; the factor normally credits the value of debts purchased provisionally and adjusts the actual value on the basis of the amount collected in sterling. It is possible for the factor to arrange forward cover.

Apart from obtaining forward cover exchange risk protection can be arranged in two ways:

(i) Early payment might be arranged with correspondent factors against warranties issued by a UK factor on behalf of the exporter.

(ii) Subsidiary or associated companies might be set up in an importer's country through which export sales are effected. An importer may obtain factoring services locally and remit the proceeds promptly on arrival of goods.

Thus the benefit of international factoring is that, if the currency of a receivable is likely to weaken, one can obtain the equivalent amount denominated in a stronger currency.

'Lock Box' system

This system is very similar to the use of hold accounts. If a currency is expected to weaken, a basic principal of currency management is to hasten the receipts of weak currencies and then to convert them quickly into a stronger currency. One means of accelerating the flow of funds is a lock box system the purpose of which is to eliminate the time between the receipt of remittances by a company and their deposit in a bank.

A company rents a local post-office box and authorises its banks in the countries concerned to pick up remittances in the box. Customers are given instructions to mail their remittances to the lock box. The bank picks up the mail sent several times a day and deposits the cheques in the company's account.

The main advantage of a lock box system is that cheques are deposited at banks sooner and, therefore, become collected balances earlier than if they were processed by the company prior to deposit. In other words, the 'lag' between the time cheques are received by the company and the time they are actually deposited at the bank is eliminated. The higher the average amount deposited and the greater the probability of a devaluation, the greater are the benefits. Similarly, if only a small average remittance is involved and the lower the probability of a devaluation, the smaller are the benefits. The principal disadvantage of a lock box arrangement is the high cost.

CONSTRAINTS ON FINANCIAL OPTIMISATION

Theoretically, the net financial benefits from systems which optimise exchange risk minimisation, whereby the aims of the subsidiaries are deliberately subordinated to those of the multinational enterprise as a whole, may be quite substantial. In actual fact, however, the opportunites for profit-maximising international financial management are seriously constrained by internal factors and, even more, by governmental exchange restrictions.

Any system designed to reduce internal constraints may have undesirable effects on the efficiency of the enterprise. Centralisation of financial management and exchange management implies that some powers of decision are taken at higher echelons, where a global view can be taken by sophisticated financial experts. Centralised financial management also subordinates the interests of the subsidiary to those of the multinational enterprise as a whole. The danger of this is that local managers are likely to resent intrusion on their prerogatives and become demotivated. Acceptance of the erosion of their decision powers calls, therefore, for adequate information and motivation.

Reshuffling of the internal payments flows through given techniques, in order to achieve systems optimisation, may distort the profit performances of subsidiaries. This occurs, for example, when transfer prices are used to obtain, say, a tax saving. Such manipulations cause discomfort in the local management teams, unless parallel, unbiased data are used to assess the real performance of a subsidiary. In addition, the rechannelling or recalibrating of financial flows, as when the 'leading' or 'lagging' gambit is practised, can affect the liquidity position of the subsidiaries involved and may necessitate expensive replenishment of working capital.

There are however inherent limits to the degree in which higher echelons (at the parent company, or at regional headquarters) can supplant local managers on routine financial decisions in the subsidiaries.

All in all, the internal impediments and costs involved in centralised financial optimisation are less serious obstacles to multinational enterprises than the panopoly of exchange controls that governments impose. These regulations mainly attempt to thwart the adverse impact of short-term capital flows, i.e. the practices most likely to have a speculative impact on the reserve position and on the exchange rate level of the currencies concerned. The tools of exchange controls appear in almost infinite variety, as the IMF's Annual Reports on Exchange Restrictions witness.

Multinational enterprises cannot, it appears, operate in an unhampered fashion. Their freedom to effectuate short-term capital flows, either in covering an open position (e.g. borrowing to offset a long position in a weak currency) or for speculative purposes (e.g. borrowing in a weak currency for conversion in to a stronger one) is frequently severely circumscribed. One particular tool of exchange management, however, cannot easily be controlled by the monetary authorities. The central bank can prescribe a maximum length of time for payment terms (and, subsidiarily, impose the conversion of the foreign currency proceeds into domestic currency), i.e. control 'leading' and 'lagging', but too harsh prescriptions would stifle the freedom which international trade needs in the realm of credit terms. Besides, time-limits to the credit terms may be imposed on commercial transactions, but would be inappropriate with respect to some important non-commercial money flows, such as dividend remittances, which can also be modulated on the basis of exchange considerations through 'leading' and 'lagging'.

Chapter 10

How Companies can make best use of their banks in Undertaking Foreign Exchange Transactions

BANK RELATIONSHIPS

A large section of banking products are concerned with corporate foreign exchange transactions, and they are increasingly seen as a growth area so far as bank relationships are concerned:

- exchange controls, spot and forward;
- date option contracts;
- put and call option contracts;
- currency swaps;
- currency hold and deposit accounts;
- currency loans;
- currency remittances;
- international letters of credit and collections;
- international cash management services.

It is therefore important in relationship terms, to get the best out of the bank. The customers can reasonably expect the following qualities from that banker:

(1) *Competitive pricing* — It is not always reasonable to ask for the best price on the market, but a good customer will expect his bank, if it is seriously interested in providing that product, to be amongst the pack leaders in price terms.

He should bear in mind that credit–related products (e.g. loans) may vary in price according to perceived credit risk and that hungry banks may use 'loss–leader' tactics to acquire his business, but he should not be satisfied with prices which are below the market norm.

(2) *Efficiency and service* — Banking is a service industry, and the customer, in transactions as important as those involving foreign currency, and particularly overseas customers and suppliers, should expect as near to perfection as possible. With human beings involved, the very occasional error

can creep in, but customers should obviously question any banking relationship, should this become too frequent.

(3) Good account management — Increasingly customers are becoming more sophisticated in currency management, and do not, as so often in the past, rely exclusively on bankers for guidance and advice in currency matters. Nevertheless, each bank will probably have an individual designated to look after a corporate customer's transactions (the 'account manager') and the customer can hope for the following virtues:

- understanding the treasury role, and particularly the customer's foreign exchange requirements;
- understanding the bank's range of foreign exchange products;
- imagination, creativity and flexibility in shaping the bank's products on the customer's behalf;
- quick negotiation and successful completion of promised transactions;
- good 'after–sales service', with adequate contact, and availablility to deal with problems.

For his part, the customer should realise that he, too, must set professional standards to get the best out of his banker:

(1) Being as good as his word — It is a great asset for a banker to be able to say, externally or internally, that a given customer has always been as good as his word. It is unacceptable to renege on transactions which are normally transacted orally such as the majority of foreign exchange contracts, and in fact the law of contract will apply in most cases. There may be shades of grey in other relevant dealings, but the customer should be sure he is as straight–forward as he can be. If not, he will damage his prospects for further business with that bank, and perhaps with the financial community as a whole.

(2) Stick to written agreements, unless otherwise negotiated — This follows from the above.

(3) Be fair about discretionary business — A great deal of foreign exchange related banking business contracts, letters of credit, collections, etc., is profitable to a bank, and desirable to acquire, but is very much in the gift of the customer. It is in the latter's interest, provided the banks are competitive (see above) to make sure that he uses such discretionary business to 'oil' other aspects of his relationship with major bankers, in order to obtain the finest prices and keenest service.

(4) Spread the custom but not too widely — A degree of competition for an important supplier of goods and services must be helpful. However, too diluted a relationship (i.e. too many banks) will reduce the quality of service and interest in the account.

All in all, the banker–customer relationship is 'people' – based, and thus is built on the following,

(1) Trust — Each side should feel confident in the other, and there should have been no let downs.

(2) A successful track record — Nothing breeds closer relationships than a number of successfully concluded transactions.

(3) Experience — Rome was not built in a day, and neither are bank

relationships. Each needs to get used to the other.

(4) *Personalities* — It is important that the actual people 'get on', in an atmosphere of professionalism, mutual respect and courtesy. In this context, politeness, good humour, lack of arrogance and a friendly attitude will all play their part.

NEGOTIATOR TECHNIQUES

The techniques of foreign exchange dealing are specifically dealt with below, but there are a number of suggestions to be made for the negotiator of other foreign exchange products, such as loans or swaps.

1. Choose a limited number of banks

If it is appropriate for relationships or other reasons to negotiate with more than one bank, a limited number of banks who are eager to provide the required product should be contacted personally, and invited to quote. Round robin letters are often offensive, and the opportunity should be used to draw in those banks who are close, in relationship terms, to the business. If the company only has one bank, consideration should be given to increasing the number as suggested above.

2. Get 'Par for the Course' in pricing terms

It is possible through keeping close to the market or contacting other corporate financial officers, to get a good feel for market rates for any given product. This level of pricing should be indicated to those banks who are invited to quote, and will prevent waste of time on both customer and bank's part, if the latter cannot compete at that level.

3. Be specific about the product required

In soliciting quotes, the bank should be in no doubt as to exactly what the customer wants. If the product is complex (i.e. a currency 'hold' account for which interest rate, transaction charge, cheque collection terms are requested), each section should be separately priced. Each bank should also be asked for a written quote for the product, plus any further suggestions, duly priced, it may have.

4. Always try to use a 'single tender' approach

This is the most equitable way of conducting such a multibank negotiation, and means basically that, once a written quote is produced, the customer will regard it as the bank's last and final bid. Thus one bank cannot be played off against another, and the negotiation can be swiftly completed after receipt of quotes.

The customer is then at liberty to choose one or more alternatives that suit him, after any necessary clarification. This he may do on a combination of relationship and pricing considerations, as well as an assessment of the quality of service provide. He has the benefit of a range of options, based specifically on his requirements.

FOREIGN EXCHANGE DEALING

It is clear that at the hub of a business' transactional foreign exchange management is the foreign exchange dealing function, usually from the corporate treasury department directly with the bank.

The first feature of this relationship is that whatever the terms of the foreign exchange contract, the bank will consider itself at risk. This is because implicit in the contract is the simultaneous exchange of currencies, but because this is done during the course of a business day, but not necessarily simultaneously, the customer may default on delivering the agreed currency, after the bank has already transacted its side of the bargain. Many banks were caught exactly this way when the Herstatt Bank was closed after dealing hours in Germany, but before the US market had closed, so that dealers expecting US dollars from Herstatt in return for European payments made earlier in the day did not receive them.

As a result of this perceived risk, a bank will always draw up a 'line' or limit for the total outstanding value of foreign exchange contracts with an individual customer. The latter should make sure that such a line is in place before commencing dealing, but has a right to expect it to be approved relatively quickly.

This line may reduce the availability of credit in other forms from that bank, and the customer should be sure he understands properly the extent of that reduction.

Line established, the following are some suggestions for corporate foreign exchange dealing activities with a bank:

(1) Establish a dealing relationship with more than one bank. This minimises the effect on overall bank credit lines of dealing lines, and enables companies to go to the most competitive source for quotes. It is a moot point as to whether this is cost (or bank – relationship) – effective when the foreign exchange turnover is very low, or the amounts of individual transactions are small. Under these circumstances, a second bank for occasional quotes to make sure that the primary bank is giving tolerably competitive rates, may be enough.

(2) Always solicit a quote from more than bank (if you are using more than one), and let the relevant banks know you are doing so. In this way the best rates are obtained.

(3) Try to do foreign exchange business with banks with whom you have an established relationship. Banks regard foreign exchange as a profit centre, and it will therefore benefit the overall relationship if they know that they will, subject to competitiveness, get a certain volume each year. For the same

reason, banks willing to break into a prospect's banking picture may use cheap foreign exchange quotes as a bait. Such opportunities should be viewed in the light of the overall benefit of such a new banking relationship, bearing in mind that the foreign exchange ones are possibly going to get less sharp as that relationship is established.

(4) Prepare carefully before soliciting a quote, and make sure you have all the appropriate details in front of you:

    (i)   Currency amount
    (ii) Buying or selling?
    (iii) 'Spot' or forward
    (iv) If forward, delivery date
    (v) Settlement instructions (if known)
    (vi) The approximate rate which you expect to get.

Be precise about each detail (particularly whether 'buying' or 'selling') when you are talking to the bank, and when the quote comes back make sure that you know whether you should be considering the higher or the lower number quoted (banks usually quote both buying and selling rate).

(5) Make sure that the delivery date is a day on which banks are open in both the countries of the currency concerned.

(6) Make sure, if you are dealing in other than a major currency, that you have checked whether special exchange controls or other regulatory restrictons apply. Many smaller currencies have very tightly controlled forward markets, where they exist at all.

(7) Be careful, if you are asking for a quote for a very substantial amount, or in a very thin market, that by asking several banks you will not automatically shift the market rate against you, since your intervention may look like a much greater volume of supply or demand that it actually is. Under these circumstances, you may prefer to confine the quote to one bank, or perhaps, not to indicate whether you are buying or selling.

(8) Always, when comparing quotes, work in the cost of the transaction. Banks will often charge a fee for each contract, usually a variant on the theme of £1 per £1,000 with a £25 maximum, but the fee structure will vary. If, as recommended below, you deal directly with a bank's dealing room, make sure that you do not get an additional charge for 'branch handling'. Accordingly, such fees should be included to compare like with like. Note that certain banks will charge telex costs for remittances made as a result of the contract. These, too, should be considered additional costs.

(9) Always deal directly with the relevant bank's dealing room unless the currency amounts concerned are very small. Some banks, particularly those with a branch network, where the main account relationship is handled away from the office containing the dealing room (which tends to be a major, if not the central branch) will try to make customers deal through the relevant branch. This is cumbersome and wastes time, and is usually proposed because it helps the bank's internal administration, e.g. recording the exchange transactions outstanding against the internal line.

(10) Expect a quick response from a bank. A bank should be able to give a firm

spot or forward quote up to one year ahead on most major currencies within 60 seconds. Bear in mind that delays may lose the competitiveness of the other quotes sought. Options, lesser currencies, and forward contracts beyond one year may take longer however.

(11) Obtain quotes only from banks found to be competitive in the relevant currency or type of transaction. Over time, with experience, some banks will emerge as being more competitive in some currencies than in others. You can then make a 'panel' of 2–5 banks for each such currency, and select the appropriate bank from those panels, when the time comes. Equally, only a limited number of banks will make a market in options. It is important to identify the appropriate banks in each case and restrict business to them.

(12) Make sure that currency payments made by banks as a result of deals are done on the basis of 'same day' value in the receiving country. Today's inter–bank remittance systems are sophisticated enough for most currency payments to be available to the recipient on the day that the payer puts the relevant banks in funds. Dealing with that bank should be conditional, as far as possible, on 'same day' arrangements.

(13) Always confirm a transaction, once it is agreed verbally, twice – once by repeating it back at the time of dealing to the bank dealer slowly and precisely, and once by written confirmation sent that day with exactly those instructions set out in 4 above. Confirmation should also contain payment instructions, indicating where precisely payment is to be made; if not immediately available, these should be communicated as soon as possible afterwards. The bank should do likewise, and bank confirmations should be checked against your own. This is an important control point, and avoids potentially embarrassing misunderstandings and defalcation on either side.

(14) Make sure that, in respect of receipts from third parties in currency transactions, the bank, number and location of the bank account to which the payment is to be made is clearly communicated to the payer, both on invoices and in any written communication.

COPING WITH UNCERTAIN DATES OF PAYMENT OR RECEIPT OF CURRENCY

A practical problem faced by all corporate dealers is the uncertainty as to exact date of payment or receipt of funds. Overseas importers rarely pay exporters on the date anticipated when the contract was struck, and which would have formed the basis for any hedge taken out. Likewise overseas exporters do not always ship and invoice on the date originally envisaged. As a consequence a forward contract taken out as a hedge to meet payment or receipt may mature before or after the relevant payment or receipt is made.

There are three practical solutions to this problem:

(1) A further forward contract may be taken out either when a revised receipt or payment date can be identified, or when actual payment or receipt is made, or when the first contract matures, whichever is earlier. This has the disadvantages that it does not finally fix the rate for the transaction when the

hedge is taken out, and that even the maturity date of the revised forward contract may not coincide with the actual payment date.

(2) The initial forward contract taken out as a hedge may be written with a date option. This means that the maturity date is not fixed, but may fall within a range of days, the period of the date option. This is a flexible alternative, but tends to be more expensive since banks habitually calculate the rate of such date option contracts on the basis of the most favourable rates to them with regard to the option period – which is, of course, the most costly rate to the customer.

(3) The company makes use of a currency account in the currency of payment or receipt which bears interest on credit balances and pays interest on debit balances. If the payment or receipt anticipates the forward contract hedge, the currency account (also known as a 'hold' account in the UK) is used to make the payment or to receive the receipt. When the contract ultimately matures, the balances on the currency account is restored. Likewise, if the delivery date of the contract precedes payment on receipt, the currency account is again used, until the payment or receipt restores the balance. This has the advantage of maintaining the rate implicit in the original contract, subject to interest rate differentials between the foreign and local currencies, but of course it requires sufficient volume in given currencies to justify specific accounts denominated in them.

Certain practical operating procedures in respect of currency accounts are worth noting:

(1) An integral condition of such an account should be interest on both debit and credit balances. The banks would normally want a differential between them, but it should not be greater than, say, 1% pa. Transaction charges on the account should be avoided, particularly if the interest differential is wide. This minimises the effective cost of the arrangement.

(2) Third parties generating payments into the currency account should be told of the bank, its number and location, and where it is maintained.

(3) Some such receipts will come in the form of cheques drawn in the relevant currency. It is usually possible for most major currencies to negotiate a standard period from paying in of, say, up to a week, after which all such cheques would be given good value, rather than wait in each case for them to be collected, which may take several weeks, or having them negotiated (i.e. purchased immediately by the bank with recourse) which may be costly.

(4) For this reason, as well as volume of that currency transacted, it may be best to choose a bank whose home base is in the country of the currency.

(5) It is worth insisting that a cheque book be available for payments from the account. Paying by cheque is convenient, particularly for small amounts, and has the additional bonus that some time may elapse before a given cheque is presented against that account, due to slow collection procedures on the part of the payee and its bankers.

Finally, a currency account may be used for 'matching'; that is to say, using it to take all the receipts in a given currency, and to make all the payments, disposing of any surplusses or deficits as they build up, and at the same time considering that the inflows and outflows are hedging each other. Clearly this can only be achieved where there is a certain volume of receipts and payments in that currency.

From the purely transaction point of view this may save money since it removes the requirement for the intermediation of a bank, which always makes a 'turn' on exchange transactions.

It does also enable one stream of currency receipts to be offset against another, and thus to provide a form of hedge. A major error is, however, to regard such a hedge as a *perfect* hedge, for although the currency and amount may be comparable, the *timing* is not. In other words, although individual payments and receipts may result in simultaneous disbursements and arrival of funds, the exposures which gave rise to such individual receipts and payments were almost certainly created at different times. Had a hedge in the form of a forward contract been taken out at creation in both cases, the implicit rates in those contracts would have been different. So 'matching' provides a partial hedge, but because it is not perfect there may be opportunity costs which would have been avoided were individual payments and receipts considered separately for hedging. Where, however, the exposures relating to individual payments and receipts are created simultaneously, as with international merchanting where buying and selling often occur at the same time, matching is both cost effective and a perfect hedge.

ADVICE

Advice is available from a number of sources for fees, or without payment, basically for the following areas:

strategic currency forecasts;
tactical currency forecasts;
international cash management.

In each case, the customer should beware of accepting advice as it stands as the basis of his decision making. Rather he should use it to develop and strengthen his own opinions, and use the latter to make decisions or recommendations. It is a good discipline in any event when contemplating external advice, to ask first whether it is really necessary. This will in the long run save fees, and strengthen the quality and confidence of internal management. International cash management is not covered by this book but taking the other two in turn:

1. Strategic currency forecasts

These usually take the form of econometric forecasts of future trends in currency exchange markets, based principally on projected spot rates, although they may also predict money market rates. They vary from fairly general forecasts to be found in professional financial periodicals, to very sophisticated and detailed econometric models produced by independent forecasting units, often attached to academic institutions, and charging substantial fees. In the middle are the bank forecasting services which are usually available free to their customers, but may occasionally attract a fee. The purpose of each forecast in a corporate context would be to help get a strategic framework for a hedge, no hedge, or partial hedge decision for any foreign currency position.

It is comparatively easy to read and assimilate the 'free' material which automatically comes to the foreign exchange manager's desk, and he will, with skill, experience and judgement learn to form his own opinions from it.

The payment of more than a nominal fee for such a service requires more careful thought; the track record and pedigree of the institution require investigation. It is easy, perhaps to ask for a number of references, and then to be satisfied, by conversations with the references, that the service is of sufficient quality for the enquirer's purposes. Above all, it is important, at the end of the day, to remember that no forecast in the world can get it right all the time. Indeed some highly sophisticated forecasters boast that they get it right no more than 55% of the time. Cynics would say that even that would be doing exceedingly well.

Remember, in finance, as in business, there is no substitute for your own judgement.

2. Tactical currency forecasts

Practically speaking, these come from two sources: bank dealing rooms and technical analysis (or 'chartistry'). The latter have developed a technique, born out of the study of free market behaviour over many years, for matching the pattern seen in the day by day performance of a given indicator, in this case purchasing currency, against such historic patterns; and from thence predicting what the next market move might be in the comparatively short–term. Chartists have their loyal supporters, and, if their own publicity is to be believed, are quite accurate over short periods. Their services are usually fee based, and a small outlay for a trial period may be justified, where the company indulges in 'tactical' dealing.

Tactical dealing is the process by which, having made a decision to effect a foreign exchange contract as part of a currency management scheme, the exact timing of the contract itself is left to the dealer; it could be done in a matter of minutes, hours, or even days, based on the dealer's judgement. It is unlikely, however, to be more than a week.

Of equal importance where a dealer has this leeway is dealing room advice. Bank foreign exchange dealers are close to the market, and must, if they are to be successful, have their own insights into the way in which it will perform in the near future. Several favoured bank dealers, with whom close relationships have been formed, can provide excellent tactical dealing advice.

Again, though, they will never accept responsibility for the decision. That will always lie squarely on the company's side.

CONTROL

Corporate commodity dealers and bank currency dealers have, in celebrated circumstances, lost money for their employers in injudicious dealing, at first undetected. The risks in foreign exchange management exist, and the physical amounts involved can be enormous. A wise company keeps an eye on control, and attempts to block as many loopholes as possible.

Here is a simple check list:

(i)   An operating manual for the treasury departments should be created, indicating specific responsibilities, and levels of authority.

(ii)   All personnel should be thoroughly vetted before being hired.

(iii)   All telephoned transactions should be immediately recorded in a sequentially numbered dealing pad from which bank confirmation should be prepared and signed, with full documentation attached, on a same day basis.

(iv)   Authorised signatories should not be connected with the initiators of, or people effecting, a given transaction.

(v)   Where appropriate, all telephones likely to be used for dealing, should be continuously tape recorded.

(vi)   All banks should be requested for confirmation of transactions, and these should be checked against those internally generated.

(vii)   All transactions and transaction/dealing sheets should be checked regularly, and the position checked, if necessary daily.

(viii) Currency hold account balances should be regularly, if necessary daily, reconciled with the appropriate cash book.

(ix)   Where large volumes are concerned, computerisation should be considered, in order to provide instant access to records of individual transactions and currency positions, for control purposes.

(x)   A 'treasury auditor' outside the department, perhaps part of an overall internal audit function should be nominated, for routine auditing and occasional spot checks, made without warning.

Back room controls are every bit as important in risk insurance terms as the currency transactions which they monitor.

CHAPTER 11
Six Golden Rules for Operating in The Foreign Exchange Market

The list of individuals, firms and banks who have found to their cost that the foreign exchange element cannot be ignored is long – Sir Freddie Laker, Herstatt Bank, Lloyds Bank Lugano, Franklin National Bank, etc. Yet a turbulent life in the foreign exchange market is not inevitable, and provided some simple rules are followed, stability and profit can be achieved.

GOLDEN RULE NUMBER 1

Foreign exchange rate move movements are a risk of doing business abroad which management should attempt to minimise (or preferably turn into a profit). Accordingly management of foreign exchange exposures cannot be undertaken on a part-time basis. Continuous monitoring, preferably with a currency committee, is essential.

GOLDEN RULE NUMBER 2

Accept that speculation in the foreign exchange market is highly risky. So do not expect nor attempt to make huge speculative profits unless you are prepared to make equally large losses. Unless you have good reason to do otherwise, exposure to currency fluctuations should be avoided. Hedging and currency matching of assets and liabilities should be routine practice.

GOLDEN RULE NUMBER 3

Unless you are a 'super' risk averter do not hedge 100% of your exposures. This will result in you exchanging a financial risk for a commercial risk. Between 1981 and 1984 a company selling in the US which had consistently hedged dollar receipts would have lost much of the benefits of the dollar's strength. Another company, not hedging, could have gained a strong competitive edge by using the currency appreciation to cut prices.

GOLDEN RULE NUMBER 4

Do not rely on a single source of currency advice. Expert analysis of exchange rate movements can be extremely valuable but totally reliable exchange rate forecasts have not been discovered – and almost certainly never will be. Several studies have shown the advantage of using more than one set of forecasting expertise.

GOLDEN RULE NUMBER 5

A regular and up-to-date flow of information is essential for smooth operations. News that is more than a few hours old is 'old hat' in the foreign exchange market.

GOLDEN RULE NUMBER 6

Be aware of the role played by governments and monetary authorities. The foreign exchange market continually changes the emphasis it places upon the balance of payments, inflation rates, interest rates and the money supply. Be aware of these changes and how government policy affects them. Avoid using an obsolete framework of analysis.

Additional Reading

Foreign Exchange Today, R. Coninx (Woodhead Faulkner, 1982).
Foreign Exchange and the Corporate Treasurer, J. Heywood (A. and C. Black, 1978).
A Guide for using the Foreign Exchange Market, T. Walker (J. Wiley and Sons, 1981).
The International Money Game, R. Aliber (Macmillan, 1983).
International Finance Handbook, 2 volumes, A. H. George and I. H. Giddy (J. Wiley, 1983).
Exchange Rate Determination, A. O. Krueger (Cambridge University Press, 1983).
Money Hard and Soft, B. Brown (Macmillan, 1978).
The Dollar-Mark Axis, B. Brown (Macmillan, 1979).
Foreign Exchange Handbook, S. Bell and B. Kettell (Graham and Trotman, 1983).
International Finance, M. Levi (McGraw-Hill, 1983).
Multinational Financial Management, A. C. Shapiro (Allyn and Bacon, 1982).
Finance of International Business, B. Kettell (Graham and Trotman, 1980).
Foreign Exchange Risk, A. R. Prindl (J. Wiley, 1976).
Foreign Exchange Markets, H. Riehl and R. M. Rodriguez (McGraw-Hill, 1977).
Foreign Exchange Markets in the United States, R. M. Kubarych (Federal Reserve Bank of New York, 1978).
The Arena of International Finance, C. A. Coombs (J. Wiley, 1976).
The International Monetary System 1945-1976, R. Solomon (Harper and Row, 1977).
The Euro-Dollar System, P. Einzig and B. S. Quinn (Macmillan, 1977).
The Dilemmas of the Dollar, C. F. Bergsten (New York University Press, 1975).
The International Debt Game, B. Kettell and G. Magnus (Graham and Trotman, 1985).

INDEX